FRAGMENTS OF THE FEMININE SUBLIME
in
Friedrich Schlegel and James Joyce

SUNY Series on the Sublime
Rob Wilson, Editor

Fragments of the Feminine Sublime
in
Friedrich Schlegel and James Joyce

Ginette Verstraete

State University of New York Press

Published by
State University of New York Press, Albany

Printed in the United States of America

For information, address State University of New York
Press, State University Plaza, Albany, N.Y., 12246

Production by E. Moore
Marketing by Dana E. Yanulavich

Library of Congress Cataloging-in-Publication Data

Verstraete, Ginette, 1961–
Fragments of the feminine sublime in Friedrich Schlegel and James Joyce / Ginette Verstraete.
p. cm. — (SUNY series on the sublime)
Includes bibliographical references (p.) and index.
ISBN 0-7914-3627-6 (hardcover : alk. paper). — ISBN 0-7914-3628-4 (pbk. : alk. paper)
1. Joyce, James, 1882-1941—Aesthetics. 2. Schlegel, Friedrich von, 1772-1829—Aesthetics. 3. English fiction—Irish authors--German influences. 4. Fiction—History and criticism—Theory, etc. 5. Femininity in literature. 6. Aesthetics, German—18th century. 7. Sublime, The, in literature. 8. Modernism (Literature)—Ireland. 9. Romanticism—Germany. I. Title. II . Series.
PR6019.09Z932 1998
823'.912—DC21 97-14377
CIP

10 9 8 7 6 5 4 3 2 1

To my mother and father

Contents

Preface

This book lifts Joyce out of the theoretical context with which he is normally associated—Vico, Hegel, Aquinas, Derrida, Lacan, Cixous—less in an attempt to be original than in order to reconsider what has by now become a commonplace, especially, and not without irony, among those who are against theory: that there is a work of art and that there is theory, and that the (lack of) meaning of the former is decided by the latter insofar as the artist's work is seen as a paradigm of what the theorist thinks art should be. It is time to question this empowerment of theory yet again by highlighting once more its radical limits and restore to art its incalculability. I hope this dialogue between Schlegel and Joyce generates some new, unanticipated ideas in the age-old debate on literature and theory, and on the role of Joyce's oeuvre in it. Let the straightforwardness of my argument be a sign of vulnerability and hence openness to the irreducible tensions not only between but also within these two authors.

I am much indebted to my teachers at the State University of New York at Buffalo: Henry Sussman, Carol Jacobs, and Rodolphe Gasché. They were my first models and critical readers at the time I was completing this project as a dissertation. In the mean time, however, I have revised this work, and several people have added further comments on its various drafts, for which my thanks: Joris Duytschaever, Geert Lernout, Wim Staat, and the anonymous readers of SUNY Press. Thanks also to Ton Brouwers and the editors at

SUNY Press for reading the manuscript with great editorial care. I have also benefited from stimulating discussions with several members of the Joyce community whom I met at various gatherings both in Europe and the States. I could not possibly begin to name them all, but I want to remember one man in particular: the late Gus Martin, who was the first to introduce me to the joys of Joyce during my master's studies at University College Dublin.

In these times of severe budget cuts in the educational field on both sides of the Atlantic, let me emphasize the importance of several years of funding which I received first from the Belgian (Flemish) and Irish Ministries of Education for study at University College Dublin, and then from the State University of New York at Buffalo and the Commission for Educational Exchange between the U.S.A., Belgium, and Luxembourg (Fulbright) for my doctoral degree. I thank them for providing me with the material basis of this intellectual enterprise.

My colleagues at the Faculty of Arts and Culture of the University Maastricht provided the incentive to "penetrate more watchfully into sublime and noble places," such that poets, art critics, philosophers, and social scientists alike could enter a complex argument that, in its interdisciplinary as well as cultural scope, should also reflect some of their own influence on me.

To my friends and family, who were my most sympathetic critics, I owe the greatest debt. And although this book cannot settle the accounts, may they find much of their patience in it.

Acknowledgments

I would like to acknowledge University of Minnesota Press for permission to quote from *Friedrich Schlegel's* Lucinde *and the Fragments*. Trans. Peter Firchow. Copyright 1971 by The University of Minnesota. Published by The University of Minnesota Press; and from *Philosophical Fragments*. Trans. Peter Firchow. Copyright 1991 by The University of Minnesota. Published by The University of Minnesota Press.

I also acknowledge permission to reprint from Friedrich Schlegel. *Dialogue on Poetry and Literary Aphorisms*. Trans. Ernst Behler and Roman Struc. University Park: The Pennsylvania State University Press, 1968. Pages 86, 99, 100, 101, 102, 103, 104, 112. Copyright 1968 by The Pennsylvania State University. Reproduced by permission of the publisher.

I further thank Ferdinand Schöningh Press for permission to quote from *Kritische Friedrich-Schlegel-Ausgabe*, volume 1, edited by Ernst Behler (1979); volume 2, edited by Hans Eichner (1967); volume 5, edited by Hans Eichner (1962); volume 8, edited by Ernst Behler and Ursula Struc-Oppenberg (1975); volume 11, edited by Ernst Behler (1958). All published at München: Ferdinand Schöningh; Zürich: Thomas, 1958-.

Chapter 1 appeared in an earlier version as part of "Friedrich Schlegel's Practice of Literary Theory" in *The Germanic Review* 69.1 (1994): 28-35. Reprinted with permission of The Helen Dwight

Reid Educational Foundation. Published by Heldref Publications, 1319 18th Street, N.W., Washington D.C. 20036-1802. Copyright 1994.

All quotations from James Joyce with the permission of the Estate of James Joyce.

Introduction

Fragments of Philosophy in Joyce's Criticism

Shortly after beginning work on *Finnegans Wake*, Joyce sent a letter to his benefactress, Harriet Shaw Weaver, in which he explains the difficulty he encounters in writing it:

> Today I send you the rough sheets with a plan of the verse and a forgotten page of H.C.E. But please don't read them yet—in fact, they are illegible. On Saturday I shall send the typed copy and the fair copy. I am glad to get rid of them as they gave me a lot of trouble . . . The construction is quite different from *Ulysses* where at least the ports of call were known beforehand . . . The answer, I suppose, is that given by Paddy Dignam's apparition: metempsychosis. Or perhaps the theory of history so well set forth (after Hegel and Giambattista Vico) by the four eminent annalists [Matthew, Mark, Luke, and John] who are even now treading the typepress in sorrow will explain part of my meaning. I work as much as I can because *these are not fragments but active elements and when they are more and a little older they will begin to fuse of themselves.*[1]

Joyce labored for another sixteen years, until the "monster," as he sometimes called it, was finally born in 1939. This struggle of one of the greatest minds of the twentieth century was with his incapacity to shape the flow of his thoughts into something as substantial as a "fragment." The veritable flood of notebooks, manuscripts, and drafts that have inundated Western libraries (Dublin, London, Buffalo, Boston, Texas, Miami) is only one result of the fluidity of Joyce's genius. Fifty years of outpourings from a productive Joyce industry—with more than ten thousand "elements" of criticism but no end in sight—constitute another. It seems that the history of *Finnegans Wake,* which is ultimately the history of its criticism, has confirmed Joyce's complaint that the book's form is not to be stopped but starts fusing in and of itself. Indeed, *Finnegans Wake* criticism is one of the most flourishing industries in the academic world, revitalizing itself even before it reaches a single point of agreement, let alone of completion. Promising years still lie ahead, but, it seems, not without a growing need to re-assess what has been achieved so far. For the self-generative fusion has gone far beyond any (wo)man's intellectual power of absorption, which explains why of late the Joyce industry has started to produce its own bibliographical and metacritical surveys in an abortive attempt to bind what Joyce himself had left un-bound.[2]

How, then, are we to understand Joyce's "fusing elements"—both of his text and of his critics, for the two, as we will see, are inseparable—and how are they different from the fragment?[3] This, in turn, raises the questions: what is a fragment? *Is* it at all? And what does it have to do with criticism? The answers we owe to the German romantic philosopher Friedrich Schlegel (1772–1829), undoubtedly the most important theorist of the fragment. But before turning to a discussion of Schlegel's concept of the fragment, and in order to respond to some of my most critical readers, first this: to claim that Joyce read Schlegel would be as preposterous as saying that he did not—not simply because it is impossible to ascertain which books escaped Joyce's voracious reading, but also because Joyce was undoubtedly influenced by many works that he may never have read but that were, nevertheless, passed on to him through his reading of other works. In this context, one is reminded of Joyce's admiration for James Clarence Mangan, the great Irish romantic poet famous for his parodic translations of, among others, the German romantics.[4] And there are other paths meandering between Schlegel and Joyce, via Schelling, Hoffmann, Baudelaire, and Mallarmé, to name only a few. More important, at least for our purposes, are the veiled references in Joyce's *Critical Writings* to Bernard Bosanquet's *History of Aesthetic,*[5] a dialectical survey of aesthetic thought from the pre-Socratics to Walter Pater, including a special (although minor) section on Friedrich Schlegel. Jacques Aubert has demonstrated the extent to which the work of the neo-Hegelian English philosopher might have functioned as a useful source at a time when the young Joyce was trying to formulate an aesthetic theory of his own.[6] It would be useless to repeat Aubert's argument that Joyce may have relied on Bosanquet's study in his search for a dialectical—Hegelian—synthesis between Aristotelianism and Thomism. That Joyce's interest in Hegel's historical aesthetics (also witnessed by the letter cited above) was fed by the neo-Hegelian debate on the British isles at the end of the nineteenth century, and that Bosanquet played a crucial role in this debate, Aubert could not have argued more conclusively. But what this focus on Hegel necessarily hides from our view, and what I think is crucial for a better understanding of Joyce's later writings, is the inconclusive nature of Joyce's aesthetics. A totalized, Hegelian perspective hides not simply the fissures in Joyce's critical writings—gaps in which is heard the voice of another philosopher, as I shall argue shortly—but much more significantly, it neglects the degree to which Joyce's arbitrary theories and artistic enterprises do not let themselves be described in terms of objective truth, moral laws, or the absolute reality of the idea. As a true Lacanian, Aubert, of course, is sensitive to the insurmountable divisions within Joyce's thinking and even makes of this inner conflict the central theme of his work. Joyce, for him, is a neo-Hegelian only to the extent that the ultimate idea transcending all opposites functions as a personalized "temperament," an individual experience that in its connection with the real, "verges on pantheism." Having recognized Hegelian dialectics as the conflict within an individual(ized) mind, Aubert can then go on to locate Joyce's protean displacements of Hegel's system in a variety of manners, the reconstruction of which would lead us much too far. Suffice it to say that Aubert is working toward a psychological, indeed Lacanian, reformulation of Joyce's famous (neo-Hegelian?) definition of the epiphany as "a sudden spiritual manifestation, whether in the vulgarity of speech or of gesture or in a memorable phase of the mind itself."[7] From this perspective, Joyce's art is seen to emerge, and dissolve, in "a lightning flash of individuality" (the words are Hegel's), which, according to Aubert, becomes nothing less than the unity of the most abstract idea with the most concrete presentation—the material letter—in a Lacanian concatenation, even conflict, of signifiers in which nothing is affirmed but the irruption of the other.[8]

Joyce's "personal," indeed arbitrary, application of Hegel's model and his predilection for an aesthetics rooted in "real experiences" lead the young artist (still according to Aubert) to search for his literary ideal in terms of a Hegelian synthesis between "Drama and Life," which Joyce redefines as "the symbolic presentment of our widely related nature":

> By drama I understand the interplay of passions to portray truth; drama is strife, evolution, movement in whatever way unfolded; it exists, before it takes form, independently; it is conditioned but not controlled by its scene. It might be said fantastically that as soon as men and women began life in the world there was above them and about them, a spirit, of which they were dimly conscious, which they would have had sojourn in their midst in deeper intimacy and for whose truth they became seekers in after times, longing to lay hands upon it . . . At times it would seem that the spirit had taken up his abode in this or that form—but on a sudden he is misused, he is gone and the abode is left idle . . . However subdued the tone of passions may be, however ordered the action or commonplace the diction, if a play or a work of music or a picture presents the everlasting hopes, desires and hates of us, or deals with a *symbolic presentment of our widely related nature,* albeit a phase of that nature, then it is drama. I shall not speak here of its many forms. In every form that was not fit for it, it made an outburst, as when the first sculptor separated the feet.[9]

Aubert may have a point in associating Joyce's preference for drama with Hegel's definition of that genre as the highest (for Hegel, romantic) form of poetry—but what about Joyce's search for a "symbolic" presentation of human nature? Surely this combination of symbolism and drama can hardly be called Hegelian, as Aubert also recognizes, considering that in his *Aesthetics* the speculative philosopher concentrates all his energy on the construction of a logical and historical system in which the symbolic functions as the lowest form of artistic expression and the romantic (ultimately, the dramatic) as the highest form. As is well known, Hegel discovers the symbol among the art forms of the East (the Persians, Indians, and Egyptians), forms he regards as preartistic modes of expression, because in them the emergent—indeterminate—idea is still struggling to find a concrete form. Characterized by a disjunction between the natural and the ideal, the latter exteriorizes itself in a negative fashion: by exaggerating the natural shapes, doing violence to them, exploding them into grotesque and chaotic forms, nature is endowed with an abstract content. In this fashion, symbolic art is characterized by what Hegel, in imitation of Kant, calls "sublimity":

> Hence, in view of the unsuitability of the two elements to each other, the relation of the Idea to objective reality becomes a *negative* one, for the former, as in its nature inward, is unsatisfied with such an externality, and as being its inner universal substance persists in exaltation or *Sublimity* beyond and above all this inadequate abundance of shapes.[10]

As the first phase in the substantiation of the spirit through art, the symbolic is characterized by a negative "sublime" moment in which the spirit remains exterior to the natural form that is to give it an outward shape. Not until the classical art of the Greeks does the spirit find a concrete form adequate to itself: the human body. However, the harmonious unity between mind and body, the divine and the human, here constituted is—despite its artistic perfection—still sensuous and, hence, incapable of fully expressing the intellectual being that the spirit in its very inwardness is. It is only in romantic art, the third and final phase, that the spirit is united with itself in infinite subjectivity, that is, in an inward subjective *knowledge* of the latent unity achieved in classical art. This elevation into self-conscious knowledge produces a radical difference between man and his natural surroundings, thereby enabling the human subject to come into its own (become real). Art is now almost freed from its sensuous existence and addresses itself to the inward mind in a succession of forms: as painting, music, and finally poetry (epical, lyrical, and dramatic poetry). In the final stage of romantic art, the materiality of the word transpires in the face of the eternal spirit: art reaches its end and becomes philosophy.

If we consider Hegel's classical art as the phase in which the spirit finds a fixed—harmonious—form in which to express itself, then both the symbolic and the romantic can be regarded as the art forms in which the sensuous completion of the classics (epitomized by Greek sculpture) is negated, depleted, put into motion. (This explains Joyce's reference to the "dramatic" moment in which the sculptor first separated the feet of his statue.) Hegel's symbolic and romantic art forms are modes of anti-classical art, differing, however, in degree of self-consciousness or universality. Thus to say, as Joyce does, that ideal drama is "symbolic" (the symbolic presentation of human nature) is to attribute to the symbolic a universality that in Hegel's philosophy it does not have. Alternatively, it implies equating the lowest (negative) symbolic with the highest (negative and positive) romantic form of art, thereby abolishing the Hegelian third term. If Joyce's idea of "symbolic" presentation in his theory on drama extends the symbol to include the whole realm of art and reality—as I think it does, considering that "drama and life" to him are coexistent—then we are dealing not so much with a Hegelian concept as, precisely, with an early German romantic one. Bosanquet has this to say about the symbol:

> The addition of the symbolic art-form [in Hegel's philosophy] as a pre-classical stage is a reflex, materially, of the interest excited by the Schlegels and other Romanticists in Oriental poetry and antiquities, and thus the parallel drawn by Hegel between the Symbolic and the Romantic tendency corresponds to the fact that the same anti-classical contrast and rebellion brought the data of both into notice. The technical term Symbolic appears to be a special application of the idea of symbol or allegory, the former being extended to the whole of art by Solger, and the latter by Fr. v. Schlegel.[11]

Leaving aside the problematic comparison that Bosanquet, in imitation of Hegel, sets up between Solger and Schlegel—I am thinking of the manner in which the latter abolished the opposition between symbol and allegory that the former, in true Goethean fashion, wanted to preserve—I would argue that Joyce's view on symbolic-dramatic art is much closer to the early German romantics than to Hegel. Whereas the latter reduces the symbolic to a particular phase in the history of art, the former conceive of it in terms of a universal principle that allows them to *artistically* unite the different genres and forms of art (and philosophy). To put this more provocatively, one could say that Hegel objects to Schlegel's definition of the (universal) symbol because it attributes to one, arbitrary art form the unifying function that Hegel believes to be the task of his speculative philosophy. Limiting the scope of the symbol to the lowest period in the history of art, while reducing the function of art to one phase in the phenomenology of consciousness, Hegel constructs a teleological system in which the symbol cannot but pave the way for its transcendence into the philosophical word—a word that, far from being an abstract, riddling symbol, logically displays before us the superiority of the philosopher's mind. In contrast to Schlegel's "subjective" (the word is Hegel's) preference for the artistic symbol stands Hegel's objective, philosophical insight into the symbol's true (i.e., radically limited) meaning. In short, in Hegel's system, art and philosophy—inseparable in Schlegel's concept of the symbol—are to be kept separate enough if the philosopher is to achieve a superior view on what exactly the universal is. Whatever Schlegel understands by the word *symbol,* he definitely does not fully know what he is thinking. Not yet a self-conscious philosopher in Hegel's sense, his ideas are still vague—like those in the Orient—and too wrapped up in semblance or irony.

Schlegel's contention that all art is symbolic needs to be read in conjunction with his theory on irony. His is a movement away from Hegel's hierarchical order, in which the Orient ranks far below the West, while the artist is to be subsumed by the philosopher. Instead Schlegel is developing concepts that will allow him to question absolute divisions between periods, genres, and cultures, while at the same time never losing sight of the problematic, ironic status of the unity thereby produced. This self-critical approach to art and philosophy—through which he insists that neither can ever be perfected—I believe to be much more fruitful in a discussion of Joyce than Hegel's scientific system, in which art finds its perfection in philosophy. More particularly, I propose to regard (what Aubert calls) Joyce's "personal" appropriation of Hegel's dialectics as a mode of practicing theory with an irony that brings him much closer to Friedrich Schlegel than to Friedrich Hegel. A brief discussion of the Schlegel-Hegel controversy over the status of irony will clarify what I mean.[12]

In his *Lectures on the Philosophy of Right,* Hegel makes the following disparaging remark about Schlegel's controversial novel *Lucinde*:

> It has been suggested that the solemnity with which a marriage is contracted is superfluous; the fact that it is not a contract was already mentioned; according to some, the ceremony is superfluous, a mere formality which might be discarded, for love is the substance of marriage, it has even been suggested that love would thus diminish in value. This theme was put forward by Mr. Fried. v. *Schlegel* and a follower of his [Schleiermacher], the former in *Lucinde,* the latter in

> the Anonymous Letters: Surrender to sensual impulse is here represented as necessary to prove the freedom and inwardness of love; this is plain sophistry, an argument not unknown to seducers, to require and obtain the desired surrender, thus rating this higher than when the surrender of the body is only a consequence of the relationship.[13]

That Schlegel in his work, as in his life, dares to question the value of matrimony—*Lucinde* was believed to be a reflection of Schlegel's love affair with a divorcee, Dorothea Veit, whom he did not marry until 1804—is unacceptable to a man for whom the citizen's subordination to the state is the ultimate precondition for the establishment of an ethical order. Although Hegel's critique of *Lucinde* reflects the public view on marriage in early-nineteenth-century Germany, it leaves no doubt that his stance vis-à-vis Schlegel's (fictional) love-life expresses a much broader disagreement between the two philosophers—one that concerns the very difference between early German romanticism and Hegelianism that we are interested in.

By the time Hegel is writing his defense of legally contracted matrimony, he has already repeatedly accused Schlegel of intellectual frivolity, arbitrariness, and lack of objectivity. The prime targets of Hegel's impatience are Schlegel's "ironic" view of philosophy and, closely related, his refusal of systematicity. Schlegel's concept and practice of irony, which we will deal with at greater length during our discussion of the fragment, Hegel considers to be nothing more than the "Spitze der sich als das Letzte erfassenden Subjektivität."[14] In the introduction to his *Aesthetics*, he sharpens his attack as follows: having identified Schlegel's ironic enterprise as the application to art of Fichte's absolute self-positing "I," Hegel then goes on to describe his irony as the unwillingness to take seriously anything except himself:

> And then this skill in living an ironical artist life apprehends itself as a *God-like geniality*, for which every possible thing is a mere dead creature, to which the free creator, knowing himself to be wholly unattached, feels in no way bound, seeing that he can annihilate as well as create it . . . The proximate form of this negativity which displays itself as irony is, then, on the one hand the futility of all that is matter of fact, or moral and of substantive import in itself; the nothingness of all that is objective, and that has essential and actual value.[15]

Hegel here repudiates Schlegelian irony because it rejects the absolute synthesis between subject and object that alone (in Hegel's view) can guarantee the stability and substance of the subject's existence. Although Schlegel's concept of irony, as we will see, is developed in an attempt to bridge the gap between the subject and the object that Kant left vertiginously open—although, in other words, Schlegel, not unlike Hegel, develops a philosophy that is to found the possibility of knowing the Kantian *Ding an sich*—Schlegel never believes that this knowledge is anything more than a fiction that the subject constructs for itself in order to be able to live with the chaos around itself. Man's ideas about the world do not find their origin in the objectification of a totalizing spirit, as Hegel believes, but in an unmediated, empirically based intuition that gains "truth" only insofar as it knows itself to be impermanent. While Hegel rejects this kind of negative knowledge as a merely abstract *Sophisterei* on the part of a self-indulgent subject, Schlegel considers it the only justifiable approach to the conflicting exigencies of daily existence. Thus, confronted with the chaos of the outside world, Schlegel develops a philosophy that finds its roots not in the reflective powers of an all-encompassing mind, but in the creative powers of an incomplete and infinitely divided subject. The absolute certainties that Hegel develops in the systematicity of his dialectical philosophy, Schlegel declines as a self-deceptive work of fiction. Whereas Hegel unites subject and object in a third term—*objective spirit*—and reduces the particularities of life to the manifestation of this all-embracing (plural) totality, Schlegel relativizes the existence of the mediator as unreal and, instead, affirms the creative powers of a subject that never simply "is" precisely because its condition for existence—the unification with the object—is contradictory.

We will have ample opportunity to further elaborate on Schlegel's philosophy of irony. For now, let me conclude this Schlegel-Hegel debate by saying that in the former's "lightning flash of *Witz*" is felt less the absolute reality than the irreality of a (contradictory) subject. What Schlegel's "epiphany" reveals is not the superiority of an abstract (for unreal) "I," as Hegel negatively claims, but a direct intuition of human finitude. Whatever insight is gained, the subject immediately laughs away in irony. Whatever system the philosopher builds up is creatively destroyed in the realization that no totality can ever grasp the infinite fullness of (the subject's) life. Human knowledge of the Kantian *Ding an sich* takes place in this constant motion between creation and destruction.

His is what he later calls a *Philosophie des Lebens*, grounded not in conceptual labor but in the irrationality of living experience (in physical love, as *Lucinde* illustrates). Schlegel's mature counterattack on Hegel (and Fichte) could not be more clear about this:

> In the latest period of German philosophy, productive paths of investigation have been explored here and there . . . but on the whole, a pure and abstract mode of thinking that is totally divorced from life is still considered to be the only proper method of philosophy, and is indeed altogether identified with philosophy. This so-called pure and abstract thinking admits no presupposition, is founded on no presupposition, and indeed has no foundation whatever except [that which it creates] itself . . . these exercises in dialectics might very well lead to a fruitful result, if only to a negative one: to the result that the truth and genuine knowledge cannot be reached, should not be sought, and will not be found in this way, and that all this preparatory dialectic exercise in its entirety is nothing more than a mere exercise, that at most can serve but as a first step and an introduction to another manner of fruitful thought, which is in closer touch with life.[16]

It is in the light of this—what I would call—ironic "realism," characterized by what is often superficially described as a romantic return to nature, that we can understand first of all the attraction of Spinoza's pantheism for the early Schlegel and, secondly, his symbolic view of art as well as of nature. Symbolism, rather than referring to a particular (pre-romantic) form of art as it did with Hegel, is the universal mode of expression for an indeterminate, mobile mind. Philosophers and artists alike are to rely on symbols if they want to convey to their audience the ineffable intuition of the living spirit. The meaning of Schlegel's symbol lies in the "absolute difference" (to use Hegel's words) between content and form that it installs in the intuition of a nonexistent truth. Hence, it is the task of the philosopher to write self-consciously like an artist, in the full awareness that one can never univocally say what one means. Schlegel's symbol, therefore, is as indeterminate as it is suggestive, so that we might well say—with Bosanquet—that it dissolves the distinction between Hegel's symbolic and romantic phase. The result is that for Schlegel the history of art stages a bipolar opposition between the classical and the romantic, the unity of which is to take place in the modern dramatic work. Actually, to be more precise, Schlegel conceives of a future synthesis between classical poetry (i.e., natural, objective, beautiful, as in Sophocles) and modern poetry (i.e., artificial, subjective, interesting, as in Shakespeare) to be achieved in the romantic period, the beginnings of which he recognizes in Goethe's work.[17] But since the terms *romantic* and *modern* are closely interwined in Schlegel's thinking, I will, for the time being, gloss over the difference and provisionally relate Schlegel's terms to Joyce's own terminology.

About this age-old *Querelle des anciens et des modernes* Joyce says the following in his essay on Mangan:

> It is many a day since the dispute of the classical and romantic schools began in the quiet city of the arts, so that criticism, which has wrongly decided that the classical temper is the romantic temper grown older, has been driven to recognize these as constant states of mind. Though the dispute has been often ungentle (to say no more) and has seemed to some a dispute about names and with time has become a confused battle, each school advancing to the borders of the other and busy with internal strife, the classical school fighting the materialism which attends it, and the romantic school to preserve coherence, yet as this unrest is the condition of all achievement, it is so far good, and presses slowly towards a deeper insight which will make the schools at one.[18]

The deeper insight that will bring the classical and romantic schools together is the one that, by seeing the inner contradictions in both, is able to relate their particular achievements to an all-encompassing, universal strife between subject and object, spirituality and materiality. This unrest that "is the condition of all achievement" is what Joyce points at when he recognizes in Mangan's excessive, romantic fantasies the struggle with a life which Novalis had already described as "a malady of the spirit." Precisely at those moments in which Mangan's imaginative creations seem totally subjective, "History encloses him so straitly that even his fiery [romantic] moments do not set him free from it."[19] It is these contradictory moments of insight that enable us to see that artistic freedom—the goal of every romantic worthy of that name—is restrained by a larger historical order as limiting as the materiality of the classics.

Joyce here comes close to Schlegel's attempt to demarcate the classical from the romantic as two constant states of mind, while relating them in a historical, rather than simply teleological, continuum: at the same time that the romantics universalize the (sensuous) classical school, they oppose it, thereby limiting it to the there and then of the historical epoch in which it came about. Romanticism thus stands for the knowledge of Greek unity as essentially past, or lost to the here and now of its own achievements.

In the opening paragraphs of his essay on Mangan, Joyce is making a similar dialectical move: by recognizing the fantastic, anti-realistic stance of the romantics as inherent in their temperament rather than as something objectively given (say, due to reality itself), Joyce literally situates their universalist claims. He limits the fantasies that they regard as unlimited. Thus, the dangers of romantic art lie not so much in its high-blown fantasies as in its tendency to take as universally true, even natural, what is merely a subjective and historically determined figment of the imagination: "A song by Shakespeare or Verlaine, which seems so free and living and as remote from any conscious purpose as rain that falls in a garden or the lights of evening, is discovered to be the rhythmic speech of an emotion otherwise incommunicable, at least so fitly."[20] The rain may fall endlessly and free from whatever plans we have made, the human mind and its interests are not unlimited, even if (especially when) that is what we believe. By thus taking the romantics for the specific subjects that they are, Joyce is paving the way for a different kind of art: one that has as its starting point the conflict not only between mind and nature but also between past and present. By the end of his essay it is clear that he has found the antidote to romanticism in Ibsen's symbolic realism.

At the same time that Joyce harks back to Schlegel's interpretation of the fight between the two schools—more about that in chapter 6—he echoes his ironic definition of art as the synthesis of creation and destruction. Art is the product of "the imagination which he [Mangan] called, I think, the mother of things, whose dream are we, who imageth us to herself, and to ourselves, and imageth herself in us—the power before whose breath the mind in creation is (to use Shelley's image) as a fading coal."[21] The power of the imagination lies in the uncompromising severity with which it reveals the so-called inward—subjective—experiences of consciousness and memory to be based on mediation, call it the artifice of poetry. The truth revealed by the imagination is an ironic one, in that it unmasks the order of the subject to belong to the realm of mere appearances. While on the one hand offering the "mind in creation" an imaginary means of escape from the exigencies of life, it also on the other hand deprives it of its authenticity and confronts it with impermanence, historicity, even death. Shelley's imagination is to the artist what Schlegel's irony is to the philosopher, an ambiguous figure of mediation explicitly feminine. Let me explain.

The Feminine Sublime

The imagination as the "mother of all things," who kills as she gives life to her sons' creations, adds an important gendered dimension to Joyce's reflections on romanticism. The lightning flash through which the spiritual manifests itself in the natural—from an art-historical perspective we can add: through which the romantic unites with the classical—turns out to be the literal stroke of lightning with which the maternal ghost ruins the representations that the filial subject has come to inhabit. In one stroke, the dark core of Mangan's life—Novalis's malady of the spirit—returns in the guise of a castrating woman:

> In the final view the figure which he [Mangan] worships is seen to be an abject queen upon whom, because of the bloody crimes that she has done and of those as bloody that were done to her, madness is come and death is coming, but who will not believe that she is near to die and remembers only the rumour of voices challenging her sacred gardens and her fair, tall flowers that have become the food of boars. Novalis said of love that it is the Amen of the universe, and Mangan can tell of the beauty of hate; and pure hate is as excellent as pure love.[22]

Contrary to the neutrality that the artist's search for the synthesis between the subject and the object might seem to suggest, this passage makes clear that for Joyce the dialectics of art are grounded in the empirical contingencies of a whole tradition of feelings of love and hate. However, reprojecting this finitude of romantic art onto a dying maternal object allows the artist to pose as free from his own historicity and to universalize a theory about the imagination (as the horrifying mother of all things) that is valid only for himself (for a traditionally sexist self). Thus it is that, in the midst of death, the creative subject recuperates its transcendental stature.

What I find to be the crucial element in Joyce's early reflections on Mangan's romantic imagination is his need to read his artistic achievements against the background of his personal life—we learn, for instance, about Mangan's unhappy love life—as well as his historical inheritance. To the extent that Joyce believes that Mangan's "fiery moments" of fantasy do not set him free from history, he can identify his poems as bearing the marks of their individual and collective creators—progenitors that, in turn, are marked by nationality (Irish), culture (the West), and gender (overtly masculine). By thus rephrasing the tension between romanticism and classicism in terms of a conflict between universalism and historicism, the private and the public, Joyce is unwittingly moving toward a critique of artistic freedom and the power relations that tend to go with it. His invocation of Ibsen's *When We Dead Awaken* over and against "the sterile and treacherous order" of artistic tradition suggests that much.

Two years before writing his essay on Mangan, Joyce completes an article on Ibsen's *When We Dead Awaken*, a play about the tragic conflict between a sculptor, Rubek, and his female model, Irene. In it, he tries to delineate the contours of a new aesthetic form that will avoid the traps of the falsely innocent indifference of romantics such as Mangan and Shelley to their own vocabulary. As in Mangan's poetry, death is the central topic of Ibsen's play, and again it is associated with a woman threatening to destroy the artist's creation. What is different, however, is the self-consciousness with which this drama plays out the sexual stereotypes that have governed Western art for many years. As I will discuss in chapter 7, if Ibsen's ghostly "mother of all things" comes back to haunt Rubek, it is not to sadistically confront him with art's "bitter mysteries," as Stephen Dedalus still calls it, but to claim her rightful share in the work to which *she* was violently subjugated. Ibsen's final play offers a remarkably feminist critique of the Western view on art and representation. It seizes on the demonization of the act of creation to show us the price paid *by women* for man's nostalgia for the whole. Here the male artist's desire to unite art and reality by means of an accomplished masterpiece proves to be totally indifferent to the reality of the female model. Whereas the terror that Shelley and Mangan confront in their escape from the world ultimately constitutes a deliverance to the unconscious forces (of history or psychology) *that they themselves have generated*, Irene's horror consists in the fact that Rubek's definition as well as execution of art has left her literally out of the picture, with little else besides an experience of exclusion and even death. Thus confronting us with the difference that gender makes in the production and reception of art, Ibsen's heroine challenges our Western ideas of autonomous self-conception and invites us to break through the boundaries with which we have fixed the narrow circle of the patriarchal self.

In these early reflections on the gendered aspects of art, Joyce is rethinking the eighteenth-century concept of the sublime in a way that reminds me of Schlegel's critical redefinition of that term. Indeed, it will be my argument in this book that Schlegel's aesthetic theory of the fragment is based on a rejection of Kant's sublime as the negative marker of totality. Without going into details just yet, let me simply summarize my point by saying that for Kant the subject's feelings of the sublime are triggered by the violence done to the imagination: confronted by an immeasurable object of nature, the subject is made aware of its incapacity to comprehend what it perceives and hence is filled with feelings of terror. What is at stake is the manifestation of an insurmountable disjunction between the natural and the spiritual, incorporated (sublimated), however, as the victory of reason over the sensuous imagination. For the fact that our senses feel overpowered by the grandeur of nature is, according to Kant, an indication of the a priori unity of the (rational) self without which this feeling of conflict with the outside world would not have been possible in the first place. Threats from the outside become the occasion for feelings of joy at being able to think (our own) totality. As Thomas Weiskel has argued, Kant's sublime offers the rational subject an occasion for recognizing its supersensible totality as its ultimate vocation: "Hence the sublime is apocalyptic in the strict sense that it reveals final things, and the defeat of the sensible imagination accomplishes subjectively the end of the natural order."[23]

In the romantic sublime, by contrast, the negative synthesis of senses and reason is "naturalized" as immanent to the imagination. To the extent that the romantics believe reason to exist only by virtue of its sensuous presentation by the imagination, their sublime feelings of transcendence are indicative less of the disruptive intervention by an external reason than of the self-aggrandizement, even complacency, of an imagination that subsumes all otherness. However, at the same time that this "egotistical sublime," according to Weiskel, reduces otherness to a mere fiction, it "strips fictions of their ontological significance—their power, as symbol or epiphany, to crash through the phenomenal and articulate essence of eternity."[24] Confronted with this fictionality, Wordsworth and, as we have seen, Mangan and Shelley lose their faith in their poems and themselves, and disillusionment sets in. In this manner, the romantic sublime triggers its own counterforce, namely, desublimation. The poet may well be nourishing a self-aggrandizing ego; at one point he is bound to take his unlimited powers as signs of his own incompletion. As Hegel also noted in his discussion of symbolic art, the positive (Weiskel's "egotistical") sublime sooner or later yields the true, negative sublime, in which reality and fiction are irrevocably at odds.

Hegel, of course, regards the negative sublime as dated: it belongs to a primitive past, when the spirit first emerged in a natural form that was totally opposed to it. By thus applying to history what was for Kant an ahistorical category, Hegel at once limits and extends the realm of the sublime: rather than either an absolute natural or spiritual phenomenon (as it still was for Kant, who thought it was a moral feeling triggered by nature), it becomes the dynamic synthesis of both. *Das Erhabene,* dissolving as *Aufhebung,* is incorporated as the negative driving force behind the course of history (the spiritualization of nature). Hence, it is universal history that for Hegel is the carrier of infinity: of that which takes art beyond itself to what only philosophy can name.

If Friedrich Schlegel interrogates the status of Kant's sublime, it is not to repeat what Hegel did: to fully realize (and thus bring to an end) what the *Third Critique* postulated as a philosophical hypothesis. By contrast, Schlegel emphasizes the fictive and art-historical nature of this category. This brings him close to romantics like Wordsworth and Shelley, but he also differs from them in a crucial way. While their awareness of the fictiveness of their ideal—the process of desublimation—fills them with melancholy and fear (toward woman as the figure of finitude), Schlegel self-consciously mobilizes this *Sehnsucht* as the departure for an ironical and historical view of the subject's productivity. I will argue that by rethinking the sublime as the most comprehensive presentation of the aesthetic idea at a particular time, and for Schlegel this means an intuition of the infinite perfectibility of art, the German philosopher strips the sublime of its absolute negativity and relates it to its positive counterpart. *An integrative part of the infinity of beauty,* the sublime is the result not of a violent conflict between the imagination and reason but of an inner conflict within the idea of beauty—as the synthesis of the real and the ideal—itself. Rather than an insurmountable division between subject and object,

Schlegel's sublime signals the incomplete—fictive—union of the two. The paradoxical synthesis thus generated protects beauty from being too easily closed off by bourgeois philistines or disinterested philosophers. If the sublime takes beauty beyond itself, it also opens it up to itself, in its otherness, in what is at once a disruption and an extension of its illusory nature. Because of this essential interest in art, I would regard Schlegel's sublime to belong not so much to philosophy as to the domain of literary (or art) criticism. In modern terms, we could call his a "textual" sublime designating the otherness of the artist's medium.[25]

There are several ways in which Schlegel fictionalizes the sublime, thereby stripping it of its grandeur: he reduces the feelings of terror that it generates to a theory of ugliness (*Häßlichkeit*); he ironizes the superiority of the subject; in still another way Schlegel reformulates the "natural" quality of beauty as the sublime autonomy of art vis-à-vis the outside world, that is, as anti-mimesis; in a similar vein, he resorts to the mechanism of decontextualization, which is a mode of dissociating words and images from their "natural" surroundings—a process which, in turn, installs a (symbolic) gap between form and content. Thus, by de-idealizing the sublime Schlegel restricts its potential chaos and prevents it from deteriorating into that kind of formlessness about which one can only speculate. Assimilating what for Kant had to remain unspoken, Schlegel engages in a process of textualization that greatly dissolves the privileged status of sublimity and, not unlike Longinus,[26] reduces it to a rhetorical category.

If, as Andreas Huyssen has argued, Friedrich Schlegel develops his aesthetics of the fragment out of the subversion of the negative sublime, it is because he regards it as "a sign of the falseness of bourgeois accommodation to absolutist culture."[27] Whatever else the negative sublime stands for, it is a reminder of the absolute that since the Enlightenment (and up to Lyotard) has kept us in the grip of terrorizing power relations.

It will be my argument that Schlegel's ironic reduction of the Kantian ideal to its fictive proportions cannot be dissociated from his feminist critique of the eighteenth-century bourgeois concept of art.[28] By extending the borders of classical beauty—that is, by making it infinitely perfectible—in such a way that it incorporates bourgeois (modern) ugliness, Schlegel develops a self-reflexive mode of representation centered around the gap between the beautiful life that Greek women had in art (Sophocles) and reality, on the one hand, and the ugliness of their subjugated eighteenth-century counterparts, on the other. At the heart of the (sublime) crisis of beauty, Schlegel articulates an incisive criticism of the way real women have been kept in the home, far removed from art, politics, philosophy—public life, in short. Hence the title of this book: in what I consider to be "fragments" of the (traditional) sublime, Schlegel explodes the old concepts of sublimity as well as beauty, while raising questions as to how the two have for centuries been framed. Who is considered the (sublime) subject, who the (beautiful) object? Who can freely create while the other merely inspires? Whose presence substitutes for whose absence? In short, who has traditionally been endowed with the sublime power to demarcate (discriminate) the boundaries between subject and object, and to subjugate the rest of the world in doing so. The sublime as the eighteenth-century concept denoting the conflict between universal and sensuous (situated) knowledge is the realm par excellence to generate a counterdiscourse to man's self-aggrandizing recuperation of that strife. The "feminine sublime" emerges when man's self-legitimating concept of sublimity is thought through and applied to the people and things that were left massively unthought. Having incorporated its own margins, Schlegel's sublime paves the way for a radical debunking of the subject-object dichotomy and, hence, of the category of the sublime *tout court*.

In the chapters to follow, I will trace this process of de-idealization of the sublime in the writings of Friedrich Schlegel and James Joyce, and consider it in the context of their sexual politics. Starting with a general discussion of Schlegel's theory of the fragment (chapter 1), and his reformulation of the Kantian sublime (chapter 2), the book then goes on to trace the art-historical definition of that term: Schlegel's argument that the crisis of beauty first emerged in Greek comedy will be read in the light of his search for a romantic—ironic—novel that combines the objectivity of the Greeks with the subjectivity of the moderns. I will explain how this integration of the (sublime) strife between the ancients and the moderns at the heart of his *Roman*, serves to open up the closed format of the eighteenth-century novel, such that—not unlike Aristophanes's works—it accommodates and reconsiders the conflict between sublime male artist and beautiful female model.

My fourth chapter on Schlegel continues this debate on gender and genre through a detailed analysis of the opening fragments of Schlegel's novel *Lucinde*. Here, I will illustrate, theory is put into practice. The epistolary dialogue between Julius and his beloved, Lucinde, becomes the occasion for a far-reaching rhetorical experiment with such concepts as beauty and sublimity, of course, but also subjectivity, objectivity, femininity, masculinity, literature, and criticism. Julius's uncontainable self-aggrandizement leads to the subversion of all carefully constructed distinctions: his pathos turns into bathos. In this ironic movement of decentralization, the man's sublimely empowered self dissipates in the spatial, and unstable, construction of the novel. It is Schlegel's way of restraining the universalizing tendency of the romantic imagination to the here and now of its fictive instantiation in front of a female reader whose absence puts into doubt the meaning-making capacity of the signifier. Ironically, the nonpresentability of Julius's ideas is the outcome not of their grandeur but of Lucinde's absence outlining the very redundance of the man's writings. The importance of this novel lies in the way it self-consciously addresses women's exclusion from art as the basis on which men have, for centuries, built their artistic achievements. In the process, an alternative mode of creation is generated that subverts this stereotypical male artist versus female model/reader framework.

The second part of my book argues that the sublime as the site of non-transcendence, or excess, is an appropriate concept with which to begin to describe Joyce's struggle to find an adequate expression for the stream of his thoughts. Already in his earliest writings, he points out the need for a different approach to the sublime:

> [O]ften when a person gets embarked on a topic which in its vastness almost completely swallows up his efforts, the subject dwarfs the writer; or when a logician has to treat of great subjects, with a view to deriving a fixed theory, he abandons the primal idea and digresses into elaborate disquisitions, on the more inviting portions of his argument. Again in works of fancy, a too prolific imagination literally flys [*sic*] away with the author, and lands him in regions of loveliness unutterable, which his faculties scarcely grasp, which dazzles his senses, and defies speech, and thus his compositions are beautiful indeed, but beautiful with the cloudiness and dream-beauty of a visionary. Such a thing as this often affects poets of high, fanciful temper, as Shelley, rendering their poetry vague and misty. When however the gift—great and wonderful—of a poetic sense, in sight and speech and feeling, has been subdued by vigilance and care and has been prevented from running to

> extremes, the true and superior spirit, penetrates more watchfully into sublime and noble places, treading them with greater fear and greater wonder and greater reverence . . .[29]

It is against Shelley's post-Kantian definition of the sublime as the mind's confrontation with an idea too grand to be expressed that the young critic defends the need for a better grasp on what precisely our sense of limitation entails. If not contained within a manageable form, the idea of the sublime will dwarf us and eventually destroy itself. Joyce's solution lies in a shift from a (conceptual) subject-centered to a more (sensual) object-centered approach to order. Joyce believes not in a violent subjugation from above but in the principle of the "miller's wheel which although it restrains the stream yet allows it to proceed on its own way."[30] What exactly this transition from the vertical axis of romanticism to the horizontal flux of realism means in relation to Joyce's particularization of the human spirit will be the main focus of the second part of my book.

Chapter 6, "Joyce's Drama and the Conflicts of Realism," analyzes the author's early writings with respect to his fascination with Ibsen's symbolic realism and the consequences of this dramatic model for the concept of the sublime, on the one hand, and for Stephen Dedalus's view of art, on the other. I show that the young Joyce's interest in Ibsen is motivated by a search for an affective definition of reality: reality as the strife of temperaments. This conflict between passions constituting our relation to, and our definition of, the real, is the driving force of Ibsen's plays, not only as a theme to be *represented* but, more importantly, as the form in which his controversial drama is *presented* to the audience. Confronting the public with the falseness of its tastes and feelings, Ibsen's realistic drama represents the social reality of the audience at the same time that its emotive impact (of attraction and repulsion) immediately modifies it. Thus constrained to the here and now of the performance, the sublime manifests itself in the affective address (presentation) to the audience, which stages an effect (a reality) in excess of what is represented.

Having considered Joyce's investment in Ibsen's symbolic realism in the light of the latter's critique of his social surroundings, we can further develop the political implications of Joyce's pragmatist-rhetorical approach to the sublime: his reformulation of the opposition between subject and object, but also between art and reality, in the performative utterance (drama talking about a reality that is being produced, and immediately modified, in the utterance or performance itself) is based on a revolt against the idea that women's procreative bodies (the object) are the instruments of so-called intelligent men (the subject). I therefore turn to *Exiles* and regard the conflict between subject(ivity) and object(ivity), as well as between symbolism and realism, in the context of Richard's and Robert's struggle over Bertha's body. I argue that Bertha functions as the medium that turns the two men's words into flesh but that this vehicle of transposition does not guarantee them the masculine superiority aspired to. Instead it opens up a conflict between the two opponents—as well as between dramatist and medium—that neither can contain.

Chapter 8 reads Joyce's realism in conjunction with his youthful reflections on Greek comedy, which I confront with Nietzsche's theory on Dionysian art, only to stake out the differences between the two: Joyce's interest in real life is based on a concept of the sublime (if we can still call it that) as a feeling of dreary sameness—the boredom of the eternal return as it goes on and on and on. This reduction of the feeling of the sublime to its daily occurrence will be, in turn, the basis for our theory on laughter as the affect of expenditure.

Upon viewing this all but heroic excess of life in the perspective of Joyce's portrayal of the secreting body, I analyze the "Oxen of the Sun" episode in *Ulysses* to give this expulsion a more concrete, gendered form. Indeed, chapter 9 continues to reflect on what I have called the "feminine sublime" as the counterdiscourse to man's self-empowering cultural narrative. Central to the discussion is again the plight of a maternal figure: Mina Purefoy's delayed pregnancy. Man's consciousness of superiority over nature now takes the form of a far-reaching subjugation of the female pregnant body to science (medicine) and technology. Horne's Maternity Hospital is the site of a fierce struggle for power between the male fetus and the child-bearing mother, but also between male doctors (students) and female midwives. If the traditional sublime is about the violent but self-assuring linkage between the world and the self, the outside and the inside, then this chapter is about a mother's liminal experience of having to expel a content that she does not control. The sublime "influx of power" she is allowed to feel is that of man's technology invading her womb in order to secure his own origins. The result, however, is less certain than the medical students might have wished. For what if man is born not from nature but from a scientific and discursive construction? Instead of being a place of origins, childbirth engenders a gap and endless layers of text with which to frame it. What started as man's reproductive dream deteriorates into a carnivalesque nightmare, Kristeva's "semiotic" order.

The book ends with a return to the sublime as the presentation of conflict beyond comprehension. *Finnegans Wake* pursues this to the very end. All that the book writes out, I will claim, are the limits at which the reader is hesitantly, for sensually, situated. It is this expenditure of theory—what in the letter at the opening of this chapter is described as the incapacity to know "the ports of call . . . beforehand"—that turns the writing (and reading) of the *Wake* into a monstrous enterprise. For having left behind the restrictions of a theoretical ideal (including that of the sublime), Joyce is faced with a freedom of creativity for which he has no other measures than the ones the text is developing in its concretization. Ironically, then, his sense of freedom has left him with unlimited restraint—unlimited for immeasurable by anything but the work in progress. This inseparability of freedom and limitation is the plight of the "modern" subject who, since Schlegel, took it upon itself to write out the as yet unthought. What is different now is Joyce's dissolution of this absence through excessive presence. Wanting to take it all in, Joyce has written it all out. Not limited by anything but its own material, the text overflows with substance: excess, litter, wasteland, the writer's tea-stained signatures.

Schlegel's provisional and Joyce's terminal rewriting of the sublime serve as critical weapons in the hands of two writers, who see it as their task to confront bourgeois society with the hypocrisies characterizing its aesthetic tastes. More particularly, they set out to develop a counternarrative that breaks the surface of art in order to point out the ugliness of its material conditions. Transgressing the traditional borders of beauty, the two artists go *beyond* limits only to detect what lies *underneath*: the hierarchical conflict of passions epitomized by man's beautifying gaze. Incorporating what has self-assuringly been left out of man's field of vision, Schlegel and Joyce reformulate the dynamics of the sublime such that it becomes a critical tool with which to question the material basis of what men call "beauty." The "feminine sublime" is what we get to see when beauty is unmasked as man's way of concealing as well as appropriating the female body. This self-critical stance of art, in which beauty extends its borders to incorporate what lies outside—or underneath—greatly contributes toward the aesthetic dissolution of both the beautiful and its traditional other, the sublime.

In its political scope, this book about the "feminine sublime" further develops the critical revisions of Enlightenment and romantic thinking begun by such feminist critics as Irigaray, Cixous, Kristeva (to whom I will return in chapter 9), and, more pertinently, Patricia Yaeger and Anne Mellor. Of course, the stakes of my enterprise are much more limited in that I have opted for a close analysis of only two writers. Furthermore, my study of the sublime differs from the splendid work begun by critics like Yaeger and Mellor in that it focuses on the feminist critique by two male authors. Hence the term *feminine* rather than Yaeger's "female" sublime. (*Feminine* is to *female* what *gender* is to *sex*: it applies to the social and cultural divisions accompanying the biological-sexual differences.) What is more important, however, is that I have elaborated the category of the feminine sublime much beyond Yaeger's definition of that term, according to which the "feminine" in the sense of "pre-oedipal" sublime (a subcategory of the "female" sublime) arises when the desires for the mother, repressed in the "oedipal" sublime (the self-assuring conflict with the father), break into consciousness: "it engenders a zone where self-empowerment and intersubjective bliss entertain one another in an atmosphere free of paranoia."[31] An instance of this world of pleasure Yaeger finds in Elizabeth Bishop's poem "The Moose," about the visit of an otherworldly creature to a busload of people who, rather than feeling threatened, engage in a pleasant, communal response, the heterogeneity of which reveals each subject's moment of "self-structuring" to be double. Accordingly, there emerges a harmony between those people and the strange "moose" at the same time that each individual proves to have his or her own conception of the creature. This subtle movement between identity and difference, the unity of beauty and the conflict of the sublime, Yaeger identifies as "an intersubjective dialectic of grandeur in which the poet refuses to annex what is alien, but revels, for a brief poetic moment, in a preoedipal longing for otherness and ecstasy."[32] This "feminine," twentieth-century version of the sublime closely parallels Mellor's "domesticated," nineteenth-century counterpart. What Yaeger finds in Bishop, Mellor recognizes in Lady Morgan's *The Wild Irish Girl*: a sublime experience of intimacy, "an experience inspired not solely by the grandeurs of nature but also by the rituals of a human community, here the religious practices of Irish Catholic vespers . . ."[33]

While both critics' search for an experience of transgression that does not necessarily entail a violent loss—and recuperation—

of self partly prefigures my own interest in Schlegel's celebration of love, and Joyce's exploration of human nature, I find such single-mindedly "social" domestication of conflict disturbing and false. Unless one keeps in mind the specificity of the group-spirit evoked, one falls into the traps of a Hegelian, falsely neutral world-spirit that, when viewed in its (German) context, is in fact as empowering as Kant's ego-tripping. Thus, Yaeger's bunch of individualists seems to me quite American, while Mellor's Catholics could not be more Irish. Having thus identified the social group, we can recuperate a more complex ideological investment in the writers' social redefinitions of the sublime. Uncannily enough, Yaeger's "intersubjective dialectic of grandeur" feeds into the American sublime—into the dream that America alone is liberal enough not to want to incorporate the other. Or it may, alternatively, be a reminder of what Rob Wilson has described as "a way of doing battle . . . with the hegemonic British tradition."[34] What Yaeger believes to be an act of freedom on the part of a self-conscious female writer can, on another level, be made into an ideological instrument of national consensus.

As for Mellor's analysis of Lady Morgan's interest in peace and community, surely the critic must be aware of the fact that *The Wild Irish Girl* was written by a conservative romantic and determined Whig who preferred to see Ireland in the light of a peaceful union with Britain at a time when the United Irishmen were waging a bloody—but justified—battle for independence. Morgan's celebration of Irish femininity as inspiring "dignity and natural grace" becomes grotesque when compared to the human degradation that the Irish Catholics—men and women alike—suffered in reality. From this perspective, Mellor's feminine sublime instigated "by the rituals of a human community, here the religious practices of Irish Catholic vespers," becomes an epitome of the kind of artistic hypocrisy that Joyce rejects. For what else is heard in this tale of Catholic consensus but a tradition of religious imperialism by a church that uses this feeling of communion as the lie with which to "domesticate" the Irish women, and Ireland's nation as a whole.

In order for the domesticated, intimate sublime not to become a new mode of complacency, one must remain attentive to the exigencies of the context—the inevitable conflicts so to speak. Only by incorporating *within* the redefinition of the sublime the very power relations *against* which these authors are conceiving something new can one avoid the risk of invoking, in Lee Edelman's words, "a universalized pre-oedipal 'sublime of nearness' that is characteristically female."[35] Admittedly, Yaeger is trying to avoid this risk by deciphering different kinds of female sublimity: besides the "pre-oedipal" she also recognizes the "failed," "sovereign," and "violent" sublime. But the fact that she calls the first "the most striking revision"—and hence, implicitly, the only "feminine"—clearly indicates her need to move away from "the old-fashioned [read: European] sublime of domination." That this break cannot be enacted without generating a new conflict and a substantive influx of power over the other becomes clear when concretizing Bishop's liberal sublime against the background of a vast American democracy—a cultural ideology itself not always tolerant toward the female subject.

The sublime as the cracked mirror refusing to reflect unifying narratives about beauty, selfhood, or love takes us beyond the surface of art and reveals its economy of representation to be based on the oppression of women, on the one hand, and on the concealment (domestication) of that conflict as universal and hence objective, on the other. Here the disinterested stance toward art—echoed by the Joycean artist paring his fingernails—is contradicted as man's hegemony over his surroundings. To achieve this self-critical stance, both Schlegel and Joyce resort to drama as the genre from which to launch a new mode of writing that takes the conflict between life and art as the source for an unceasing ironization of art. More about drama later.

Within the context of Joyce studies, and besides the obvious influence of Aubert's work on my own philosophical approach to Joyce's early writings, I find the sociopolitical aspects of my project to have certain affinities with Margot Norris's book *Joyce's Web: The Social Unraveling of Modernism*, which too is trying to recuperate the political force of ugliness in Joyce's aesthetics.[36] Where we part company, however, is firstly in Norris's bifurcated view on modern art as either transhistorical, autonomous, and bourgeois (the traditional view on Joyce), or self-critical, political, and socially belabored (the neo-Marxist perspective). Associating the former strand with the "romantic plot of the heroic artist saving art's power to transcend its degradations in the modern world,"[37] the latter with the political engagement of the historical avant-garde, Norris's procedure consists in identifying Joyce himself as the avant-gardist critic of the modernist aestheticism that he is using. Countering the myth of the Joycean aesthete (propagated by, among others, T. S. Eliot and Richard Ellmann) with that of the socialist writer, Norris—as she herself claims—wavers between the ahistorical approach of her early deconstructive reading and the historicist corrective she claims to have found in Peter Bürger's Marxist *Theory of the Avant-Garde.* That one need not be(come) a Marxist in order to recuperate the political impact of experimentalist-formalist art I hope to illustrate in my own study, which in fact construes a theory of the romantic autonomous work as it self-consciously stages its own (institutional) border, the otherness or irreality of bourgeois art. When Norris argues that in Joyce's texts "art lies about itself [leaves out the historical conditions] in order to tell the truth about its lying,"[38] she is repeating the very romantic aestheticism that she purports to be criticizing: what we are dealing with is a self-referential gesture on the part of the text that at once betrays its own incompletion, that is, its being rooted in a larger structure of (auto-)production (called "labor" by Marxists). Why Norris favors such a heavily determined political concept as socialism in order to describe what can alternatively be seen as the inherently self-critical—unraveling—mechanism of aestheticism itself is never adequately explained (invoking Ellmann's apolitical biography as the rhetorical straw man confirms, more than questions, its canonizing effect). Still, one cannot but praise the breathtaking subtlety and immense learning with which she goes on to situate Joyce's artistic accomplishment within an ever-widening textual, sociopolitical web.

My second point of criticism concerns the way Norris all too easily defines Joyce's technique as "desublimation," a misnomer attributable to her rather facile interpretation of the sublime as beautiful and sublimation as idealization or purification: "Instead of epiphanizing and sublimating the ugly modern world, I will describe Joyce's strategy in reverse, as desublimation of aesthetic convention by restoring to art and poetry the social truth of those occluded by art, the female figures whose labor negates art but underlies it in the most personal way."[39] Although Norris does repeatedly refer to Bürger's theory as well as to Adorno's definition of ugliness as a necessary part of beauty, she never fully explicates precisely how in her view beauty and ugliness are related and how one moves from a *formal* category such as ugliness (as opposed to beauty) to a *social* issue such as a woman's labor in the house. Unless one resorts to the (romantic) sublime as the site where this impossible transition between form and content, the ideal and the particular, is enacted, one cannot adequately explain the politics of Joyce's concern for the ugly or the complexities of "desublimation" (according to Weiskel, an essential part of romantic sublimation).

How a feminist approach to the sublime can help us to better understand the "stifled back answers" articulated in Joyce's taste for ugliness—and comedy—will be the focus of my study. In the process, other crucial issues will be raised: what is the connection between genre and gender? How does the philosopher's theoretical view differ from the artist's beautifying gaze? What do irony and symbolism have to do with the oft-cited "irruption of the real"? How modern is a romantic like Schlegel, how romantic is Joyce, and what role does the sublime play in the transition between the two? To what extent does Joyce's definition of life as drama entail a critique of the myths that nineteenth-century society reproduces about (women's) reality?

These and other questions will have to be answered in due course. What requires further attention now is Schlegel's view on the sublime, which I have argued to be a much more pertinent model for understanding Joyce's heterogeneous aesthetics than is Hegel's totalizing system.[40] This, however, does not mean that I shall try to "fix" the problems we have encountered so far by identifying Joyce as a belated neo-Schlegelian. Our approach will have to go beyond a mere tracing of influences for three reasons. First, it is all but certain that Joyce felt stimulated by Bosanquet's *History of Aesthetic* to go out and read the several German and English editions of Schlegel's work that were available at the time.[41] Second, one can situate Joyce within a philosophical context only as long as one keeps in mind that the man was a writer, not a philosopher—although I would call him a "critic" in Schlegel's sense of the term: somebody who reads texts with an eye for the particular and with an interest in the contradictions rather than the unified whole. In fact, it is this tension between the particular and the general that for Schlegel makes up the difference between literature and philosophy—a conflict that every literary critic involved in the business of interpreting texts should make her own. The third reason for reading Joyce as much against as with Schlegel is the fact that if the parallels between the two can be said to make anything clear at all, it is that both were too self-conscious to let some other thinker determine the truth of what they were doing, too ironic also to set store by one conclusive theory.

ONE

Friedrich Schlegel's Theory of the Fragment

In his *Gespräch über die Poesie, Fragmente,* and *Ideen,*[1] Friedrich Schlegel addresses the question as to how to make concrete a philosophical idea, or how to reconcile the intelligible and the sensible. It is an impossible synthesis of *Geist* (spirit) and *Buchstabe* (letter) that Schlegel sees fulfilled—and lost—in Greek nature poetry as this was characterized by an organic-instinctive vitality that was at once an imitation and a perfection of nature's self-subsistence. In contrast, the romantic (post-classical) era, still according to Schlegel, is inflicted with a radical split between mind and matter. It is a division through which poetry (Schlegel's general term for literature) has lost its perfection, but through which it has gained a progressive nature. For having lapsed into a duality—one through which the work of art is suspended between ideality and reality, or content and form—it is now the purpose of the work of art to overcome that split in a third realm: the synthesis of the artist's idea and the concrete work of art. In this moment the organic unity of Greek nature poetry will be restored on a spiritual level, as the self-presentation of the artistic idea. However, since this involves a unification of two opposites—of spirit and nature—the ideal can never be achieved as such, and thus renders poetry's progression infinite. No sooner is the idea concretized by the singular work than both lie fragmented and, in their imperfection, require further completion. The fragment is, in this way, the moment when the idea and the concrete work unite in an act of annihilation, in an instant of self-destruction that reduces the work to a seed—or sketch—awaiting fulfillment in the future. To the extent that Schlegel's fragmentary work thus exists in its dissolution, its future completion—its ideality—is guaranteed. Such is the nature of the fragment: forever incomplete (only a part) and hence caught in an unceasing progress through which the idea as ideality, that is, as future fulfillment, is presented—although only in a fragmentary way.[2] The idea is concretized insofar as it is never completed and renders its self-presentation infinite. The idea *is*, then, the process of production in which nothing ever simply *is*, but in which the work is suspended in continuous self-irony.[3]

In his justly famous *Athenäum Fragment* 116, Schlegel describes this self-production of the idea (or subject) as the infinite self-completion of romantic literature:

> Die romantische Poesie ist eine progressive Universalpoesie. Ihre Bestimmung ist nicht bloß, alle getrennte Gattungen der Poesie wieder zu vereinigen, und die Poesie mit der Philosophie und Rhetorik in Berührung zu setzen. Sie will, und soll auch Poesie und Prosa, Genialität und Kritik, Kunstpoesie und Naturpoesie bald mischen, bald verschmelzen, die Poesie lebendig und gesellig, und das Leben und die Gesellschaft poetisch machen, den Witz poetisieren, und die Formen der Kunst mit gediegnem Bildungsstoff jeder Art anfüllen und sättigen, und durch die Schwingungen des Humors beseelen. Sie umfaßt alles, was nur poetisch ist, vom größten wieder mehre Systeme in sich enthaltenden Systeme der Kunst, bis zu dem Seufzer, dem Kuß, den das dichtende Kind aushaucht in kunstlosen Gesang. Sie kann sich so in das Dargestellte verlieren, daß man glauben möchte, poetische Individuen jeder Art zu charakterisieren, sei ihr Eins und Alles; und doch gibt es noch keine Form, die so dazu gemacht wäre, den Geist des Autors vollständig auszudrücken: so daß manche Künstler, die nur auch einen Roman schreiben wollten, von ungefähr sich selbst dargestellt haben. Nur sie kann gleich dem Epos ein Spiegel der ganzen umgebenden Welt, ein Bild des Zeitalters werden. Und doch kann auch sie am meisten zwischen dem Dargestellten und dem Darstellenden, frei von allem realen und idealen Interesse auf den Flügeln der poetischen Reflexion in der Mitte schweben, diese Reflexion immer wieder potenzieren und wie in einer endlosen Reihe von Spiegeln vervielfachen. Sie ist der höchsten und der allseitigsten Bil-

dung fähig; nicht bloß von innen heraus, sondern auch von außen hinein . . . Die romantische Poesie ist unter den Künsten was der Witz der Philosophie, und die Gesellschaft, Umgang, Freundschaft und Liebe im Leben ist. Andre Dichtarten sind fertig, und können nun vollständig zergliedert werden. Die romantische Dichtart ist noch im Werden; ja das ist ihr eigentliches Wesen, daß sie ewig nur werden, nie vollendet sein kann. Sie kann durch keine Theorie erschöpft werden, und nur eine divinatorische Kritik dürfte es wagen, ihr Ideal charakterisieren zu wollen. Sie allein ist unendlich, wie sie allein frei ist, und das als ihr erstes Gesetz anerkennt, daß die Willkür des Dichters kein Gesetz über sich leide. Die romantische Dichtart ist die einzige, die mehr als Art, und gleichsam die Dichtkunst selbst ist: denn in einem gewissen Sinn ist oder soll alle Poesie romantisch sein.[4]

[Romantic poetry is a progressive, universal poetry. Its aim isn't merely to reunite all the separate species of poetry and put poetry in touch with philosophy and rhetoric. It tries to and should mix and fuse poetry and prose, inspiration and criticism, the poetry of art and the poetry of nature; and make poetry lively and sociable, and life and society poetical; poeticize wit and fill and saturate the forms of art with every kind of good, solid matter for instruction, and animate them with the pulsations of humor. It embraces everything that is purely poetic, from the greatest systems of art, containing within themselves still further systems, to the sigh, the kiss that the poetizing child breathes forth in artless song. It can so lose itself in what it describes that one might believe it exists only to characterize poetical individuals of all sorts; and yet there still is no form so fit for expressing the entire spirit of an author: so that many artists who started out to write only a novel ended up by providing us with a portrait of themselves. It alone can become, like the epic, a mirror of the whole circumambient world, an image of the age. And it can also—more than any other form—hover at the midpoint between the portrayed and the portayer, free of all real and ideal self-interest, on the wings of poetic reflection, and can raise that reflection again and again to a higher power, can multiply it in an endless succession of mirrors. It is capable of the highest and most variegated refinement, not only from within outwards, but also from without inwards . . . Romantic poetry is

> in the arts what wit is in philosophy, and what society and sociability, friendship and love are in life. Other kinds of poetry are finished and are now capable of being fully analyzed. The romantic kind of poetry is still in the state of becoming; that, in fact, is its real essence: that it should forever be becoming and never be perfected. It can be exhausted by no theory and only a divinatory criticism would dare try to characterize its ideal. It alone is infinite, just as it alone is free; and it recognizes as its first commandment that the will of the poet can tolerate no law above itself. The romantic kind of poetry is the only one that is more than a kind, that is, as it were, poetry itself: for in a certain sense all poetry is or should be romantic.[5]]

If, for Schlegel, romantic poetry first of all aims at the fusion not only of different genres—of poetry and philosophy, poetry and prose, artistic inspiration and criticism—but also of art and life, or art and nature, it is because romantic poetry is universal and progressive. It is a plural universality that Schlegel describes as poetry's "state of becoming" dictated by no other law than the absolute freedom of the artist's will. This implies that poetry's ideality is to be situated in the creative freedom of its producer, or in the autonomy of his (the masculine is intended) imaginative production. In the free play and self-determination of the artistic imagination lie enclosed a multiplicity of genres and, more precisely, the impossible coexistence of two opposites, of philosophy and literature—one which involves the self-concretization of the artist's spirit in the incompletion (the state of becoming) of the letter.

This peculiar confusion of letter and spirit—or of the work and its artist—in the former's progressive character Schlegel further defines as the moment in which art loses "itself in what it describes" (in the portrayed) to such an extent that the representation takes on a life of its own (it assumes the shape of a "poetical individual"), and in this manner becomes indicative of the *Willkür* (the capricious wings of reflective freedom) inherent in poetic inspiration (the portrayer). Thus, although the romantic synthesis of the artist and what he has brought forth is constituted by the former's incapacity to control (or complete) the latter, it is exactly in this independence of the work that the artist confirms his creation as an act of absolute freedom. More specifically, forever a project in need of completion, the artist's (self-)creation promises fulfillment in the future and, through this temporal self-transcendence, gains the freedom to embrace "everything that is purely poetic," from the most complex of the artist's systems to the artless songs of a child. Encompassing all other novels and genres in its uncontainable growth, the romantic work thus manifests itself as the literary genre par excellence, the genre of literature in general.[6]

Now the question arises: does Schlegel's preference for the term *Romantisch* have anything to do with his appreciation of the *Roman*? Following Eichner's discussion of this extremely complex matter,[7] I would argue that it does, but only if we consider the term *Roman* in its widest sense: not simply as the modern genre that arose in the eighteenth century but as the postclassical art form that first emerged during the Middle Ages in the writings of Boccaccio and Dante and, later on, in Ariosto, Cervantes, and even Shakespeare. The word *Roman* in the eighteenth century refers to the romance, according to Schlegel's *Gespräch über die Poesie*, "written in the age of chivalry, love and fairy tales." When the philosopher declares the novel to be the romantic poetry of his age, he interprets this genre broadly enough to incorporate prose as well as poetry, romance as well as realism, fantasy as well as sentiment: a form varied enough to combine all traditional—classical—genres either in one work (as he would accomplish in *Lucinde*) or in a series of subcategories such as the sentimental novel, the historical novel, the gothic novel, the realist novel. Flexible in form but also in content, the romantic novel is the genre of all genres, the minimal fragment incorporating the whole of literature, and indeed the idea of production itself: "Alle P[oesie] soll Prosa, und alle Prosa soll P[oesie] sein. Alle Prosa soll romantisch sein.- Alle Geisteswerke sollen romantisiren, dem Roman sich möglichst approximiren"[8] [All p(oetry) should be prose, and all prose should be p(oetry). All prose should be romantic.- All spiritual works should romanticize, approximate the novel as closely as possible (my translation)]. Hence, Schlegel's *poetische Roman* is both more and less than the novel in its traditional sense: "The romantic kind of poetry is the only one that is more than a kind, that is, as it were, poetry itself: for in a certain sense all poetry is or should be romantic." *Romantic*, as should be clear by now, refers to the ideality of the *Roman*, which, being both a work of art and the idea or genre of art, is as much present as it is absent, as much singular as it is plural. This duplicity, for Schlegel, makes for a self-contained novel concerned with "the joining or separating of the ideal and the real" as this characterizes fragments and projects:

> Das Wesentliche ist die Fähigkeit, Gegenstände unmittelbar zugleich zu idealisieren, und zu realisieren, zu ergänzen, und teilweise in sich auszuführen. Da nun transzendental eben das ist, was auf die Verbindung oder Trennung des Idealen und des Realen Bezug hat; so könnte man wohl sagen, der Sinn für Fragmente und Projekte sei der transzendentale Bestandteil des historischen Geistes.[9]
>
> [What is essential is to be able to idealize and realize objects immediately and simultaneously: to complete them and in part carry them out within oneself. Since transcendental is precisely whatever relates to the joining or separating of the ideal and the real, one might very well say that the feeling for fragments and projects is the transcendental element of the historical spirit.[10]]

What is crucial in Schlegel's conception of art is its deliberate fragmentariness, for it is through this incompletion that the ideal presents itself in the real. Insofar as romantic literature is a fragment, the philosophical idea of literature is present in the work itself. The fragment *as fragments* (for in its synthetic nature the fragment is plural) is what unites the work and the philosophy of the work, or in the words of the passage quoted above: it makes of poetry a transcendental poetry. And given that—as *AF* 116 has it—"only a divinatory criticism would dare try to characterize" the romantic poetic ideal, then the fragment Schlegel has in mind—the fragment as synthesis of the concrete and the ideal—might well be regarded as a mixture of transcendental or "divinatory" *poetry as well as criticism*. After all, does not Schlegel explicitly state that romantic poetry "should mix and fuse . . . inspiration and criticism?" It is this interdependence of literature and its critique, or of practice and theory, that we need to explore in more detail.

Schlegel's criticism, or what he occasionally refers to as "theory," is the moment in which the opposition between the universal and the singular, between the spirit and the letter, dissolves and their synthesis takes place. The synthesizing view of plurality thus presented is one that undoes not only the opposition between but also the individuality of the two opposites, who, in their mutual destruction, reaffirm their polarization on a higher synthetic level.[11] Schlegel's concept of criticism as this self-generative process of dissolution and re-combination, of destruction and production, of unity and separation is constitutive of the artist's spirit positing itself on an increasingly concrete level without ever fully realizing itself. At times, Schlegel speaks of criticism as a "pure sensible seeing," a "self-intuiting idea" that the artist has, but that can never be known as such. At other moments, he defines it as *intellektuelle (or intellektuale) Anschauung,* which designates the immediate self-apperception of human consciousness or, more radically, the capacity of the mind to create itself in its reflection.[12] However, since intellectual intuition thus involves the mind's mode of being as pure reflection or as an imaginative projection of non-being, since it is in the process of thinking that the artist's idea presents itself, the synthesis at which it aims—the coincidence of consciousness (subject) with itself (object)—necessarily belongs to the future. The idea is, in other words, still to be created—theory is praxis—and its truth or content is that which needs to be known. That explains why Schlegel compares intellectual intuition to Kant's moral or categorical imperative: "Die intellektuale Anschauung ist der kategorische Imperativ der Theorie"[13] [An intellectual intuition is the categorical imperative of any theory[14]]. The self-constitution of consciousness in intellectual intuition asserts itself as a project or a tendency that ought to be fulfilled, while theory is not simply an "understanding" of truth (a self-understanding by the mind) but rather the subject's immanent consciousness of its necessity to create truth—a call for self-realization that in its immediacy already determines the direction in which this will be realized. (From here it is only a small leap into a moral or religious imperative, that is, faith, which Schlegel will radically perform in his conversion to Catholicism in 1808: "Der Verstand, sagt der Verfasser der Reden über die Religion [Schleiermacher], weiß nur vom Universum; die Fantasie herrsche, so habt ihr einen Gott. Ganz recht, die Fantasie ist das Organ des Menschen für die Gottheit"[15] [The mind, says the author of the *Talks on Religion* (Schleiermacher), can understand only the universe. Let imagination take over and you will have a God. Quite right: for the imagination is man's faculty for perceiving divinity[16]].

Thus it is that in Schlegel's philosophy artistic self-creation becomes a mode of balancing between *Geist* and *Buchstabe.* Here theory and praxis are one in an act or fact of the imagination that progresses (as praxis or artistic production) in a permanent reflection (as theory or criticism) upon itself. Consequently, Schlegel's *Einbildungskraft* as this artistic synthesis of the sensible and the intelligible, of art and criticism, exists as moments of suspension. What it makes present is its own nonbeing (its being a mere reflection), so that one can say that the presentation is such that it insists on something very different from what has been created (we are reminded of Schlegel's use of the symbol). For in its self-annihilation the creation is never what it is. In fact, it never simply is, and hence—here is the point—one needs to speak of the work of art in terms of appearance. It belongs, indeed, to the essence of artistic presentation that it dissolves in its self-positing, so that its reality (the work of art) is always preliminary (*vorlaufig*, a *Tendenz*) and never more than a simulacrum. That Schlegel's work of art approximates or mimicks what it presents but never coincides with it implies that, in the same breath, Schlegel's art is and insists that it is not. For romantic art is only in this self-negating revelation of its appearance. Only by critically referring to itself as unreal does the work affirm its "true" nature: that it is mere *Schein* or *Einbildung*. Criticism is just this power of artistic production to offer a vision of truth—a very ironic truth which Schlegel calls *Witz*—in a continual confrontation with its own *Darstellung*. Or as the *Gespräch über die Poesie* puts it: the theory of the novel is itself a novel "der jeden ewigen Ton der Fantasie fantastisch wiedergäbe, und das chaos der Ritterwelt noch einmal verwirrte"[17] [which would reflect imaginatively every eternal tone of the imagination and would again confound the chaos of the world of the knights[18]].

This moment of critical self-destruction within art is what Schlegel occasionally defines as the sublime. Although the sublime in Schlegel's theory does not hold the special status that it does in Kant—or at least not in the post-Lyotardian, present-day Kant—it is important enough, and indeed recurs often enough, to merit careful consideration. A brief recapitulation of Kant's reflections on the sublime will serve as a model against which to read Schlegel's personal revision of the concept.

TWO

A History of the Sublime

As is well known, Kant's *Critique of Judgment* is based on the distinction between the aesthetic feelings of the beautiful and those of the sublime. Whereas the experience of beauty is associated with the experience of form and harmony within the subject, the sublime is connected with what is formless. In the aesthetic judgment of beauty, there is a free accord between imagination and understanding based on the objective form of nature. One finds an object of nature (its form) beautiful when a contingent accord takes place between the purposelessness of nature and the free harmony between the faculties. In the judgment of beauty, the imagination—instigated by the purposive freedom of nature—freely produces indeterminate forms that, although not yet bound by the laws of the understanding (concepts), are limited by the subject's assumption of common sense: the idea that our feelings of beauty are universal. The assumption of the communicability of such a thing as beauty is what freely brings imagination into harmony with understanding.

In the feelings of the sublime, by contrast, the imagination is faced with what is formless in nature and, confronted with its own limits, goes beyond itself, thereby bringing about an accord with reason. In the face of overwhelming depths, immeasurable heights, and violent thunderstorms, Kant says, the mind is overpowered with a sense of its own inability to grasp the totality of the scene in one moment of perception, in one form. We are made aware of our incapacity to gather, let alone understand, the magnitude and the power of what we see. This defeat of the imagination (the faculty responsible for synthesizing the manifold impressions into one image) fills us with feelings of pain and fear. At the same time, however, we realize that although nature appears to us as threatening, there remains a comfortable distance between ourselves and the immense object. The secure position we occupy in front of such a vastness or even destructiveness fills us with confidence, with a sense of our own superiority, and hence with feelings of delight. What was first perceived as the threatening grandeur of nature now becomes a sign of the infinity of human reason. In other words, the sublime is a feeling with a double face: upon contemplating what exceeds the human imagination we are filled with fear; at the same time this sense of limitation awakens us to the awareness that there is a force inside us that does not let itself be subdued by nature. This is the force of moral reason, filling us with moral joy.

The Kantian sublime concerns the conflict between man and nature insofar as this takes place inside the subject, namely, between the faculties of reason and imagination. In the defeat of the imagination reason forms its ideas of totality and infinity. It is clear that Kant's theory of the sublime is based on that profound dualism that Schlegel aimed to overcome: here the natural, physical self is threatened by an immense object, only to evoke an awareness of the unfathomable depth of the supersensible, the moral, and eternal within the self. The feeling of the sublime in the end affirms—in true Kantian spirit—the victory of reason over the senses.

Kant's *Third Critique* takes it upon itself to think the realm of the aesthetic as the site where nature and freedom paradoxically unite. Ironically, the sublime as the feeling in which this synthesis directly takes place (in the feelings of beauty it occurs by way of the forms of nature) is also the place where the imagination yields its freedom to the moral laws of reason. How aesthetic can this moral feeling of freedom be? Doesn't Kant, in the end, sacrifice his aesthetic feelings for the sake of an ethical idea? It is not in his analysis of the sublime but in his definition of genius that the philosopher seems to find a more aesthetic harmony between nature and spirit.[1] Genius, defined as the innate disposition of the mind through which nature gives art its synthetic rules, is the capacity to recreate nature in such a way that its distortions become expressive of the aesthetic idea. The latter seems to be the sensuous counterpart to the idea of reason: whereas the ideas of reason defy sensuous presentation (as in the sublime), the aesthetic idea involves a sensuous presentation that gives the mind too much to think: now it is the understanding (and even reason?) that is made to face its limits. In the latter case, the freedom of the imagination is no longer bound by the assumption of common sense (as in the beautiful), nor by a rigid moral law (as in the sublime), but by the laws of creativity itself. It is this recuperation of transgression as intrinsic to the subject's productivity (Genius) itself, that will become the romantic way of conceiving a more positive sublime.

It is undoubtedly because Schlegel, in contrast to Kant, never developed a clear-cut view on the relation between the beautiful and the sublime that Schlegel critics have been particularly silent on the matter. In fact, as Dietrich Mathy—one of the few critics to give this subject some serious thought—has convincingly argued,[2] in Schlegel's aesthetic philosophy, the sublime and the beautiful are qualitatively indifferent. In contrast to Kant, for whom the negative sublime exists in an opposition to the beautiful, Schlegel views it as a negative phase immanent in the self-transcendence of the beautiful. The clearest statement on this matter comes from *AF* 108: "Schön ist, was zugleich reizend und erhaben ist"[3] [Beautiful is what is at once charming and sublime[4]].

Both negative and positive, the sublime in Schlegel's *Über das Studium der griechischen Poesie* is identified as *erhabne Schönheit,* filling the audience with complete joy, and *erhabne Häßlichkeit,* producing effects of despair, pain, and indignation. Hence, also, Schlegel's insistence that the intensity of sublime ugliness depends on the degree of anticipated beauty that it negates: "Die notwendige Bedingung des Häßlichen ist eine *getäuschte* Erwartung, ein erregtes und dann beleidigtes Verlangen"[5] [The necessary condition of ugliness is a *deceived* expectation, an aroused and then offended longing (my translation, my emphasis)]. When a few lines later Schlegel calls sublime ugliness a deception (*Täuschung*), its disharmony a mere *Schein,* he means nothing less than the fact that to the extent that disorder can only be perceived in relation to the unity that it disrupts, ugliness as such does not exist. In contrast to Kant, for whom the sublime is a negative sensation of the (idea of the) absolutely great, Schlegel emphasizes that there is no negativity without a positive force to produce it. Furthermore, the latter insists, the absolute is by no means a universal concept beyond which nothing can be conceived. Rather than being an absolute maximum, the sublime points up the necessary incompletion (perfectibility) of such an idea. Schlegel calls it a relative maximum, the highest point of beauty one can reach at a particular moment in time. This idea of the sublime as the perfectibility or incompletion of beauty explains why, in fact, Schlegel prefers talking about it in terms of ugliness: *das Häßliche* is the sublime conceived as the negative *of beauty*. Bosanquet hints at the importance of Schlegel in this respect and identifies the German philosopher as the first to make mention of a "theory of ugliness" that seems at first not simply reducible to a theory of the beautiful but, in the end, turns out to be co-ordinate to it.[6]

The passage Bosanquet has in mind comes from *Über das Studium der griechischen Poesie*, section 5, in which Schlegel defends the seeming incoherence and lack of taste in Greek tragedy and comedy (Aristophanes) against the narrow conception of aesthetic beauty of his contemporaries. In opposition to the prudish view of eighteenth-century art criticism, and in order to understand Greek literature on its own terms, Schlegel extends the concept of the beautiful to include the sublime. Against the beautiful in its limited sense—concerned with the limited unity of a limited multiplicity—he posits the idea of the sublime appearance of infinite fullness and harmony, characterized by endless lack (*Mangel*) and disharmony. Now what else is this chaos that Schlegel recognizes in Greek drama if not the dissolution of classical beauty at the very peak of antiquity? Or, to use Schlegel's own oppositional terms: what is the sublime ugliness of Greek drama if not the self-transgression of "objective" (natural) unity into a "subjective" (artificial) particularity. Rather than negatively presenting a (Greek) universal ideal, the sublime in Schlegel is historicized (it presents a historical ideal) and made relative to the subjective disposition of the person experiencing it, "denn es gibt für jede individuelle Empfänglichkeit eine bestimmte Gränze des Ekels, der Pein, der Verzweiflung, jenseits welcher die Besonnenheit aufhören würde"[7] [since every individual receptiveness has a certain limit of repulsion, of pain, of despair, where level-headedness would come to an end (my translation)]. With this emphasis on the receptive powers (*Empfänglichkeit*) of the subject, Schlegel disconnects the operation of the sublime from the productive powers of the Greek artist to relate it to the presence of a perhaps more prudish audience. Equally, the disharmony that was first recognized as part of *objective nature* poetry now becomes relative to the *human nature* receiving it. By thus contextualizing the production of Greek art, the romantic philosopher accomplishes two things: he draws out the historical limits of what the Greeks achieved and he assigns to the category of the sublime the task of designating these borders of the classical, natural ideal of beauty, while heralding the arrival of its other—modern literature. In fact, one could go as far as saying that the sublime here points to the presence of the "modern" receiver—let's call him Schlegel for the time being—at the end of the natural cycles of birth and death along which Greek poetry evolves.[8] With this move from artist to reader—from text to context—as well as from the classics to the romantics, we have historicized the sublime, which now is made to present the sensuous perfection of the Greeks as radiant with a more than universal power, namely, a historical one.

As a conditioned maximum, Schlegel's sublime is different from the Kantian experience of a transcendental conflict between the faculties of reason and imagination. For Schlegel, the sublime is inherent in art, which is not, as for Kant, an imitation of the purposelessness of nature—a universal ideal which the Greeks finalized—but an incomplete creation by a subject limited by its very interests in nature. This subjective appropriation of natural beauty implies a fragmentation of its ideal. What is important is that the conflict between the subjective and the objective thus generated cannot be interpreted simply as the negative manifestation of an unattainable idea but also as a positive, individual—and I will argue, self-critical—appropriation of that ideal. Whereas in Kant the feelings of the sublime result from the blockage or self-violation of the imagination in the face of the laws of reason (freedom) *exterior to it*, Schlegel's sublime denotes the excessive freedom *of* the imagination transgressing its own lawfulness and harmony to a point of perversion or self-parody. In the words of Bosanquet: "The positive negation will be, so we should say, in some degree a confusion—a parody or perversion of the type of beauty to which it is correlative."[9]

One of those moments in which beauty perverts itself, thereby signalling the historicity of its achievement, is the birth of Greek comedy. In his essay "Epochen der Dichtkunst" Schlegel embeds the arrival of Attic comedy in the development of Greek poetry: from its origins in the Homeric epic and its ironic counterpart—the iambic poetry of the Ionians—via the lyric, and Sophocles's harmonious tragedy, to its fulfillment in Aristophanes:

> Stoff und Urbilder fanden die Stifter der tragischen Kunst im Epos, und wie dieses aus sich selbst die Parodie entwickelte, so spielten dieselben Meister, welche die Tragödie erfanden, in Erfindung satyrischer Dramen. Zugleich mit der Plastik entstand die neue Gattung, ihr ähnlich in der Kraft der Bildung

> und im Gesetz des Gliederbaus. Aus der Verbindung der Parodie mit den alten Jamben und als Gegensatz der Tragödie entsprang die Komödie, voll der höchsten Mimik die nur in Worten möglich ist. Wie dort Handlungen und Begebenheiten, Eigentümlichkeit und Leidenschaft, aus der gegebnen Sage zu einem schönen System harmonisch geordnet und gebildet wurden, so ward hier eine verschwenderische Fülle von Erfindung als Rhapsodie kühn hingeworfen, mit tiefem Verstand im scheinbaren Unzusammenhang. Beide Arten des attischen Drama griffen aufs wirksamste ins Leben ein, durch ihre Beziehung auf das Ideal der beiden großen Formen, in denen das höchste und einzige Leben, das Leben des Menschen unter Menschen erscheint.[10]

> [The founders of the art of tragedy found their material and their prototypes in the epic. Just as the epic developed parody within itself, so did the same masters who invented tragedy delight in the invention of satyrical plays. Simultaneously with sculpture, there originated a new genre similar to it in the power of form and the laws of structure. From the union of parody and the old iambic poetry there arose, in contrast to tragedy, comedy, which abounds in the highest kind of mimicry that is possible only in words. Whereas in tragedy actions and events, characteristic features, and passion were harmoniously ordered and formed out of a given legend into a beautiful system; here, a lavish abundance of ingenuity was boldly cast as a rhapsody, with deep understanding in seeming incoherence. Both kinds of Attic drama intruded most effectively into life through their relationship to the ideal of both great forms, in which the highest and only life appears, the life of man among men.[11]]

What is so unique about Greek comedy, what makes it sublime in the sense that the *Studium* essay attributed to it, is the seeming incoherence, the abundance of ingenuity, and the excess of mimicry (play of masks) with which the highest form of life—that of man among men—is dramatized. Where tragedy brings "drama and life" (the words are Joyce's) together in a harmonious fashion, comedy portrays human relationships with a taste for the inadequacy of content and form, reality and fantasy, life and art, text and context. Closely related to this intimation of conflict between the artificial (the masks) and the real (everyday life) is the rise of comedy out of the primordial antithesis between the natural, Homeric epic and its artificial, iambic counterpart. Schlegel's history of Greek literature is such that its "natural" development could be said to generate its own (artificial) self-parody, which runs from the iambic poem, via the choral song, to Attic tragedy (uniting both the iamb and the chorus) and comedy (where the chorus performs, as we will see, the famous Schlegelian parabasis). The high point of this ironic disjunction between the natural and the artificial in Aristophanes's work also characterizes the end of Greek literature and the beginning of the Roman satire.

That the Roman satire is the only genre with which, according to Schlegel, the Latin poets managed to enrich the realm of art is due to its furtherance of Greek comedy through an evocation of discordant elements, such as poetry and urbanity, fantasy and social reality, wit and seriousness. Saturated with (the Latin *satura* means "medley") colliding dictions of the high and the low, the poetic and prosaic, Roman satire increases the sublime disharmony first introduced by Attic comedy.

From Horatius onward European literature increasingly assimilates what is different—the "charming fairy tales of the Orient" for instance—until in the Middle Ages "modern" literature finds its first dignified expression in the religious, but vernacular, poetry of Dante. Combining vision and realistic detail, mysticism and earthly love, Christianity and antiquity, Dante stands at the beginning of a literary tradition that becomes increasingly formless as it unites different genres and styles in its linear progression. A parody of the abundance of nature, modern art could be said to be as natural as it is artificial, as unifying as it is disjunctive. The development of modern literature as Schlegel describes it in his early essays on Greek art stages the uncontainable growth of the sublime perversion that he first recognizes in Greek comedy. This autonomous, contaminating force, presenting the absolute freedom of the imagination to incorporate its own historical context, threatens the beauty of what it brings forth—Dante degenerates into Ariosto's grotesque—until in the art of the Renaissance beauty and ugliness become inseparable: here the peak of modern art—also the death of classical beauty—takes place in a return to antiquity. Prime examples of this untenable unity between the classical and the modern are, of course, Cervantes and Shakespeare. Their works give expression to that subversive, chaotic power which doubles the reality of what is created into a sublime appearance, a fragment indeed, of the infinite fullness of life: the life of man among men. If

Cervantes holds a special place in Schlegel's aesthetics it is because he is the first to translate his comic precursors into a full-length novel (*Don Quixote*)—a novel, moreover, the second part of which constitutes a critical judgment of the humorous events in the first part. This kind of fusion between the comic and the serious leads us directly to Cervantes's dramatic counterpart, Shakespeare. As Schlegel's *Studium* essay explains, Shakespeare's tragicomic "modernization" of classical drama breaks with the harmonious totality of Greek tragedy by staging its a priori, abstract conflict between the hero and his destiny as a personal struggle inside the protagonist: with Joyce's words in mind, drama becomes an "interplay of passions to portray truth" between or within common men:

> Überhaupt ist in Shakespeares Dramen der Zusammenhang selbst zwar so einfach und klar, daß er offnen und unbefangnen Sinnen sichtbar und von selbst einleuchtet. Der Grund des Zusammenhanges aber liegt oft so tief verborgen, die unsichtbaren Bande, die Beziehungen sind so fein, daß auch die scharfsinnigste kritische Analyse mißglücken muß, wenn es an Takt fehlt, wenn man falsche Erwartungen mitbringt, oder von irrigen Grundsätzen ausgeht. Im HAMLET entwickeln sich alle einzelnen Teile notwendig aus einem gemeinschaftlichen Mittelpunkt, und wirken wiederum auf ihn zurück. Nichts ist fremd, überflüssig, oder zufällig in diesem Meisterstück künstlerischer Weisheit. Der Mittelpunkt des Ganzen liegt im Charakter des Helden. Durch eine wunderbare Situation wird alle Stärke seiner edeln Natur in den Verstand zusammengedrängt, die tätige Kraft aber ganz vernichtet . . . Es gibt vielleicht keine vollkommnere Darstellung der unauflöslichen Disharmonie, welche der eigentliche Gegenstand der philosophischen Tragödie ist, als ein so gränzenloses Mißverhältnis der denkenden und der tätigen Kraft, wie in Hamlets Charakter. Der Totaleindruck dieser Tragödie ist ein *Maximum der Verzweiflung*. Alle Eindrücke, welche einzeln groß und wichtig schienen, verschwinden als trivial vor dem, was hier als das letzte, einzige Resultat alles Seins und Denkens erscheint; vor der ewigen *Kolossalen Dissonanz*, welche die Menschheit und das Schicksal unendlich trennt.[12]
>
> [In Shakespeare's plays, the correlation is altogether so simple and evident that it is immediately and automatically clear to

> any open and unbiased mind. The foundation of that correlation, however, is often hidden so deep, the invisible ties, the relationships are so subtle that even the most shrewd critical analysis cannot but fail when it shows lack of tact, when it starts from false expectations or from fallacious principles. In HAMLET, all parts necessarily develop from and, conversely, react on one common center. Nothing is out of place, superfluous, or accidental in this masterpiece of artistic wisdom. Its center is in the hero's character. Owing to some curious situation, the strength of his noble character is concentrated in his mind, whereas his power to act is completely paralyzed ... Such a boundless discrepancy between reflection and deed as portrayed in Hamlet's character may be the most perfect representation of the insoluble disharmony that is the true subject of philosophical tragedy. The overall impression of this tragedy is a *maximum of despair*. Every single impression, which in itself seemed great and important, shrinks into insignificance when compared to what emerges here as the ultimate and only result of all existence and thought, the eternal *collossal dissonance*, endlessly dividing humanity and fate. (My translation)]

The confusion that emerges from *Hamlet* is instigated by the gap between the whole of the work and the individual character in which the totality finds its concrete, fragmentary form—a discrepancy that is simultaneously overcome and intensified in Hamlet's interior struggle between theory (reflection) and practice (deed). It is this "interest" in the reality, or individuality, of the work—this typically modern drive toward the subjective and the particular putting an end to the Kantian disinterested pleasure of beauty—that is responsible for the total loss of Greek unity (beauty) and the concomitant yearning for that lost ideal on the part of Shakespeare's characters. In modern drama, then, the hero's strife embodies the "colossal dissonance" between the real and the ideal, necessity and freedom, which in Greek times was supposed to be timeless.[13] Only in comedy did this dissonance find a particular outlet. With this transition from antiquity to the Renaissance the conflict that was so far the domain of comedy becomes an integrative part of tragedy, which Schlegel redefines as "philosophical tragedy": the contemplative enactment of the abyss.

From Shakespeare onward, modern literature runs the risk of developing into two extremes—into an art form concerned only with the beauty of its exterior form (the particular) or, alternatively, into a philosophy about lost aesthetic ideals (the universal). Hence, it is, according to Schlegel, the task of romanticism to contain this double threat to art by overcoming its schism in a third phase in which the disjunction between the particular and the universal—that eternal "colossal dissonance"—becomes the inexhaustible source of an art form that is as unifying as it is disjunctive. The distance of this ideal is what has driven Schlegel's own literary writings into a continuing, theoretical digression on the need for a new genre that will combine the "intrusion into life" characteristic of modern drama with a philosophical view of the whole. He claimed to find that genre in the romantic novel and wrote *Lucinde*.

It will be clear that Schlegel's essentially "modern" category of the sublime is closely linked to a deeply historical understanding of literature. His recovery of ugliness at the heart of classical beauty identifies that moment in literary history when a critical awareness of the inadequacy between content and form, life and art, was first—unknowingly—articulated. This anti-mimetic rupture at the very core of Greek *adaequatio* sets into motion an alternative development in which the *natural* growth of art, by transgressing its own laws of beauty, is seen to embrace the plurality or fullness, rather than simply the unity, of nature. From this perspective, the sublime unleashes a creative, particularizing, *historical* power that no artistic form can contain. While in Greek art this (at that time still natural) self-transgression coincides with the emergence of a multiplicity of genres—comic drama staging the dissolution of epic, lyric, and tragic poetry—in modern art, it leads to the (by then subjective) dramatization of finitude by means of "philosophical tragedy," until in romanticism the *knowledge*, or idea, of this self-transgressive power paves the way for a future reunification of all genres in what the young Joyce would later call "[t]he great human comedy in which each has share, giv[ing] limitless scope to the true artist, to-day as yesterday and as in years gone."[14]

Undoubtedly, Schlegel's interest in the ugly and the comic was articulated in response to the emerging "realist" concern of his contemporaries, concern that had found its first significant expression in the rise of the eighteenth-century novel. His own reflections on the novel as the genre of all genres in which the becoming of art as such finds a suitable—albeit fragmentary—form leaves little doubt about Schlegel's indebtedness to Sterne, Fielding, and, to a lesser extent, Richardson. But the connection between comedy and realism runs deeper than the fascination with the contemporary and the banal expressed by the early, realist novel. In fact, in Schlegel's view, the eighteenth-century novel fails to translate into prose what Greek comedy accomplished on stage: to make of art the expression of nature's abundant powers, that is, ultimately the life of man among men. His own novel *Lucinde* was to artfully order the chaos of surrounding nature as Aristophanes's vital comedies had done many centuries before: "Sollte es nicht ein Dichtungswerk geben können das zugleich Roman und classische Komödie wäre . . ."[15] [Should it not be possible to conceive a poetic work that is at once a novel and a classical comedy . . . (my translation)]. Or again, "Jedes Gedicht, jeder Roman soll eine festliche Verschwendung sein, eine aristoph[anische] Komödie und ein Glücksspiel wie Trag[ödie]"[16] [Every poem, every novel should be a festive extravagance, an Aristoph(anic) comedy, and a game of chance like trag(edy) (my translation)].

In his essay "Vom ästhetischen Werte der griechischen Komödie,"[17] Schlegel traces the origins of Aristophanes's comedy back to the "holy joy" that the Greeks experienced in their celebration of Dionysus (God of drama and wine) or that the Romans felt during their Saturnalia, the feasts in honor of the God of agriculture (Saturn). These religious rituals, characterized as they were by a mixture of the high and the low, demonstrate joy to be the highest, natural power of mankind. A limitless expression of the abundance of nature, joy transcends the boundaries among individuals and unites them at the highest point of their vital powers. Love is what Schlegel calls this religious loss—or doubling—of self in absolute pleasure, while the mode of expression most suitable to it he recognizes in the all-encompassing depths of the lyric:

> Eine bloße Äußerung des Gefühls, die lyrische Darstellung der Freude, kommt nicht so leicht in Gefahr, ihre äußre Freiheit zu verlieren,—desto mehr die dramatische. Sie nimmt den Stoff zu ihren Schöpfungen aus der Wirklichkeit, ihre Bestimmung ist eine öffentliche laute Darstellung des Lächerlichen, und ihre Freiheit ist dem Laster, der Torheit, dem geheiligten Irrtume fürchterlich. Aber eben dadurch wird sie einer neuen hohen Bedeutung, einer neuen Schönheit fähig; wenn die Freude, wo wir Schranken erwarteten, uns mit Freiheit überrascht, so wird sie das schönste Symbol der bürgerlichen Freiheit.[18]

> [A mere expression of feeling, the poetic representation of joy does not so easily run the risk of losing its external freedom,—this applies even more to dramatic representation. The subject matter of its creations is taken from reality, its purpose is a public, loud representation of ridiculous situations, and its freedom has no mercy on vice, folly, and hallowed error. But that is the very reason why it becomes capable of transmitting new meaning, a new beauty; when joy surprises us with freedom instead of restriction, it becomes the greatest symbol of civil freedom. (My translation)]

Since the freedom of the lyric is inwardly oriented, since it is produced by a subject that under the aegis of its sentiments incorporates everything beyond itself, the joy inherent in it is unifying and hence harmonious and beautiful. Drama, on the contrary, is less an expression of subjective feelings than it is an imitation (*Nachahmung*) of the real. Here, the artistic freedom of the subject is limited by an external power—that of reality—which the dramatic form never ceases to face. Thus caught in a perpetual strife between the freedom of fantasy and the demand for realism, drama takes the freedom of the artist less for granted and, in fact, lays bare before us the incongruity of artistic representation. It is this inner conflict at the heart of drama that threatens the art form with extinction. At the same time, however, the very fact that drama is able to affirm itself over and against its destructive forces adds to its creativity a sense of exuberance that reduces all traces of negativity to a harmless illusion. Precisely here, in this re-affirmation of subjective freedom, lie the roots not only of drama's democratic power (Attic comedy was written at the time of Athenian democracy) but also of its comic force: "Fast alles Komische beruht auf dem Schein von Selbstvernichtung"[19] [Nearly everything comic is based on the illusion of self-destruction (my translation)]. In laughter the exterior and destructive limits to freedom—as well as the irruption of ugliness and evil accompanying them—are demolished, the dissonance reduced to a mere illusion. In it the conflict between art and reality is stripped of its impact and recuperated as part of the play. Through this process of ironization ugliness loses its purely negative function and becomes the condition under which a *playful* contact with reality—and hence drama itself—is possible. "Familiarization" is what Bakhtin calls this humorous simultaneity of distance and closeness in his essay "Epic and Novel."[20] In Schlegel's terms, the real is made unreal so that the audience may approximate (but never enter) the stage.

Prime agent of this dialectic between art and reality as well as between play and audience is the Greek chorus: "Der Chor besonders deutete auf das Athenische Volk, welches in der Schönheit eines Spiels seine eigne Heiligkeit erblickte"[21] [Especially the chorus referred to the people of Athens, beholding their own sanctity in the beauty of a play (my translation)]. In tragedy the chorus is made up of twelve or fifteen players who, in the name of the citizens of Athens, including the dramatist himself, comment upon the actions on stage, often in the form of a dialogue. The locus of both action and reflection, the chorus is situated at once inside and outside the play, in that zone where the fantasy of the maker and the reality of the audience meet. In this respect, it is important to note that the chorus consists of ordinary Athenian citizens who are yearly trained to perform in both tragedies and comedies. Hence, a large number of spectators must at one time or another have participated in the plays that they attend. Thus it is that the chorus represents the locus where actors and audience—tragic heroism and comic everyday life—coincide. While in tragedy this dialogic constituent contributes to the education of the public, in comedy it draws the audience into a vertiginous play of contrasts between the real and the unreal that annihilates whatever easy recognition may have come about. This sublime part of comedy is called "parabasis":

> In der *Form* ist die alt-atheniensische Komödie der Tragödie ganz ähnlich. Sie hat von dieser einen chorischen und dramatisch-dialogischen Bestandteil, auch Monodien. Der einzige Unterschied besteht in der Parekbasis, einer Rede, die in der Mitte des Stücks vom Chor im Namen des Dichters an das Volk gehalten wurde. Ja, es war eine gänzliche Unterbrechung und Aufhebung des Stückes, in welcher, wie in diesem, die größte Zügellosigkeit herrschte und dem Volk von dem bis an die aüßerste Grenze des Proszeniums heraustretenden Chor die größten Grobheiten gesagt wurden. Von diesem Heraustreten (*ekbasis*) kommt auch der Name.[22]

> [In its form the old-Athenian comedy is completely similar to tragedy. From the latter, it has adopted a choral and dramatic-dialogical constituent, also a monody. The only difference lies in the parabasis, a speech that in the middle of the play is addressed by the chorus to the people in the name of the poet.

> Yes, it was a total interruption and adjournment of the play, in which, as in this one, the greatest licentiousness reigned and in which the rudest things were said to the people by a chorus that was stepping out to the edge of the forestage. From this stepping out (*ekbasis*) its name is derived. (My translation)]

In parabasis the play is interrupted, the masks taken off, and the audience addressed in an aside as offensive as it is ugly. If we attend to this violent rupture extending from the background of the stage (the chorus stood at the back) to the very edge of the forestage, what we are made to see is the rejection of fictional illusion in favor of the *reality* of the play: its existence as a fiction, its performativity, its gesturing actors, and, last but not least, the living interaction between actor and public that makes a work of art theatrical in the first place. Parabasis is to drama what the sublime is to beauty: a significant deviation that sets into motion a running commentary on the dynamics of art. In this "dialogical" structure (the word is Bakhtin's), art is seen to generate its own counterforce, that of reality, a force that at once questions and affirms the freedom of the imagination to incorporate whatever resistance it experiences. The presence of the audience is, of course, the first sign of this otherness intrinsic to the infinite freedom of the play—and parabasis the answer of an authority (an author) that wants to claim this disruptive presence as its own. What is heard in parabasis and in the laughter it provokes is a play stepping out of itself into the real world of the viewer, who at first feels overcome by this crude contact but then laughs it back to where it belongs: the world of play. This continuous hovering between the stage and its audience makes of drama a permanent deviation that destroys whatever fictional illusions have been built up, only to speak of another level where fantasy and reality unceasingly meet: that of theatricality—the essence of drama—as such.

To discern in the ironic duplicity of parabasis the image of drama as such is to read into comedy the internalization of its own framing devices, a procedure known as *mise-en-abîme*. In its fullest extension, this implies viewing the work both as an enactment of and a reflection on its own production. Hence, when Schlegel praises Attic comedy for questioning the tradition of Greek art, he is pointing out the beginnings of a self-reflexive mode of art, the dynamics of which depend on an internal dramatization of an exterior—critical—view of the whole. In other words, Attic comedy is regarded as the primal expression of the kind of self-reflexivity, theatricality—or again in Bakhtin's words, dialogism—that is to characterize, and problematize, postclassical poetry. What was previously defined as the sublime self-transgression of beauty can now be reformulated as beauty acting itself "out" on stage, that is, out of itself and into the world of the viewer.

What the reflections Schlegel offers on comedy, and on parabasis in particular, bring to light is the fact that his interest in the "natural abundance" of art is above all an attempt to integrate into art the living presence of an audience. In comedy he hears first and foremost *the real world of the audience*—its expectations, its habits and thoughts, and, of course, its aesthetic receptivity. With this in mind, it is hardly surprising that in his essay on Greek comedy he sets up a distinction between tragedy and comedy on the basis of the public to which it is addressed. While the former intends a sophisticated audience, the latter has in mind the man in the street. Hence, the former can stage lofty and abstract types, while the latter must make its presentation realistic, local, and detailed enough to excite even the least receptive viewer.

> Das Komische richtet sich, weit mehr als das Tragische, nach dem Grade der Reizbarkeit und der Fassungskraft seines Publikums; und diese hängen wieder von dem Maße der geselligen Ausbildung und aller Seelenkräfte ab: daher der Unterschied unter dem Niedern und Edlen Komischen. Um eine nicht so reizbare Empfänglichkeit zu beleben, werden stärkere Reize, heftigere Erschütterungen erfordert; die Widersprüche und Kontraste, überhaupt die Verhältnisse, welche der ungebildete Verstand fassen soll, müssen gröber und faßlicher sein.[23]
>
> [To a much larger extent than tragedy, comedy takes its cue from the degree of the audience's sensitiveness and its powers of comprehension; these, in turn, depend on the degree of social development and of all powers of the soul: hence the distinction between lower and higher comedy. In order to enliven a rather inert receptiveness, stronger incentives, more intense commotions, are required; the contradictions and contrasts, quite generally the relationships the uneducated mind should be able to grasp, need to be rougher and more comprehensible. (My translation)]

Reading comedy as an address to an uneducated public allows Schlegel to account for Aristophanes's crude realism as the effect of a distant, uninterested viewer. If Aristophanes wants to attract his audience's attention, then he must overcome the space between the stage and the people by a realism that becomes the more dramatic—and grotesque—as the audience proves to be untouchable. As said before, sublime ugliness is above all the sign of the subjective disposition of its viewer: it is the negative dramatization of a noncooperative, perhaps hostile, interlocutor whose only interest lies in reality rather than art. The self-destructiveness that Schlegel recognizes at the heart of comedy thus signals not only the infinite freedom of the maker but also the autonomous desires of an audience against whose lack of receptivity the play must wage a never-ending battle. In the sublime conflict between drama and life, we hear the exuberant violence of a writer who believes his pen to be mightier than the sword. Thus, if a comic like Aristophanes is also a realist, it is because he has no illusions about the communicability of his intentions and, in fact, prefers to laugh at whatever easy impact he claims to have on the outside world. In his comic gestures lies outlined—and therefore temporarily bridged—the distance between himself and the public. To be a realist in this manner implies not simply adherence to the principles of mimetic representation but also criticism of the very possibility of ever establishing a meaningful connection between art and the world, artist and public. One becomes a realist by being an ironist. And by making comic use of a tragically given.

Comedy is the effect of the disjunction between text and reader, as much as, conversely, this dissonance is the source of an exuberant, rhetorically convoluted style of representation that aims less at an imitation of reality than at the production of a subjectively involved readership. To engage his public's attention, Aristophanes could never say, or demonstrate, enough. At the same time he always said too much. Once put on stage for the sake of the common people, his comedies were either shocking or uninteresting, depending on the viewer. It is this arbitrariness—this inherent finitude—of Attic comedy that Schlegel wanted to begin to understand by transforming the contingency of the empirical reader into a theory of ugliness, in which the irruption of the formless was considered the first sign of the history of modern art, and of the modern, bourgeois reader—a history that the romantics thought to be evolving toward a new kind of beauty, but which Joyce was to rewrite into a hilarious farce.

Schlegel's sublime—comic—art negatively contains the presence of its reader. More specifically, its infinite lack and disharmony disclose the point at which is situated a (spatially and temporally) distant viewer, who, at once inside and outside the work, destroys the unity imposed by the author. Rather than passively undergoing the conditions set out by the artist, the reader is made to negotiate the terms on which the dialogue is taking place. The sublime confusion of the work thus points to an unceasing production as well as reformulation of what counts as the ultimate beauty, even meaning, of the work. Contrary to what Schlegel's contemporaries (Kant, Wordsworth) experienced as the ineffable grandeur of nature paradoxically signaling the superiority of the artist's ego, Schlegel's sublime reminds us that this superiority is an illusion insofar as it hinges on the encounter between two oppositional voices, both of which represent mutually exclusive interests: while the author's sole aim is to give a definitive shape to his fantasies, the reader confronts him with the exigencies of daily existence. The result is that the author's expression derails as he—ironically—takes into account the historically differentiated contexts embodied by his audience. Here, in this effective interaction, borders are crossed between beauty and ugliness, fiction and reality, text and context. Although this hybrid mixture, to the extent that it results from the artist's *conception* of a varied public, in a sense prescribes the conditions under which our own critique can be formulated; although Schlegel's irony is to a certain degree setting the terms on which our dialogue with his texts is to take place, it would be a mistake to interpret his reformulation of the sublime as just one more way of reinforcing his own authority. Rather than giving in to him, we are expected to keep resisting the format he hands down to us and alter it in a way he could never have intended. Having authorized us to speak, Schlegel's sublime is to be in turn subverted to contribute to a discourse that far surpasses that of the male subject. What emerges at the end of the line is not an egotistical, masculine "I" but an intersubjective, androgynous "we."

THREE

Gender and Genre in Aristophanes

If Schlegel interprets the subversive force of the sublime as the counterpresence of the reader against which the freedom of the maker first becomes—grotesquely—visible, then it is all the more significant that in his own writings (*Lucinde, Gespräch über die Poesie,* "Brief an Dorothea") the reader is female. One of Schlegel's greatest merits is, indeed, the fact that in his emphasis on the dialogical production of beauty, he also highlights the gender relations involved in this process. His more explicitly feminist essays evolve around the question as to how his insights in the workings and history of art can contribute to the emancipation of his female counterpart. What is especially interesting in this context is his essay "Über die weiblichen Charaktere in den griechischen Dichtern,"[1] in which the changing representation of women throughout the history of Greek drama constitutes the parameter with which Schlegel evaluates the various periods of Greek civilization. Whereas the inner and outer beauty of Sophocles's female protagonists attests to the perfection of his whole work and surrounding culture, Homer's domestic women are indicative of the immaturity of the Greeks, while Aristophanes's ugly women are the carriers of the first signs of Athens's degeneration. As before, drama functions as the pivotal genre with which to read the surrounding world. But what is different is the importance of the female figure, who assumes the role that the chorus was previously made to enact: woman becomes the living image of reality drawing into itself not only the relation between stage and audience but, much more significantly, the whole makeup of the artist's culture. In another essay written around the same time, "Über die Diotima,"[2] Schlegel further explores the consequences of this intimate link between woman's status in a particular context, on the one hand, and the value of the surrounding culture, on the other, by reconstructing the growth and decline of Greek civilization on the basis of certain significant emancipatory moments (such as the school of Pythagoras, in which men and women received equal education).

In the essay on the female characters in Greek poetry that we are concerned with, he explicitly focuses on the *artistic* representation of women as the place where Greek poetry internalizes, as said, the taste of its audience and of its culture at large. In Sophocles, women are, like their male counterparts, close to perfection. Here both sexes symbolize richness, harmony, and completion. In this ideal world every part is naturally integrated with the whole, and what shines through this unity is the fulfillment of mankind: a stage where man and woman are two equal halves of an androgynous whole. Aristophanes's comedies, on the contrary, are less concerned with the perfection of natural beauty than with the imperfections of everyday, public life. Concretizing what in Sophocles remained for the greater part an ideal, Aristophanes puts on stage androgynous females that overtly cross traditional sexual or gender-related boundaries:

> Sehr viele Gründe lassen uns im voraus vermuten, das allgemeine Verderben des Zeitalters habe sich bei dem weiblichen Geschlechte vorzüglich frühe und heftig geäußert. Aber der Grad von weiblicher Zügellosigkeit und Verderbtheit, den uns Aristophanes darstellt, überrascht uns und übersteigt allen Glauben . . . Aber dennoch ist die Komödie des Aristophanes eine Kopie der Natur, oft sogar Portrait eines individuellen Originals; enthält unzählige Züge, die aus der Wirklichkeit entlehnt sind, und ist ein unverwerfliches Dokument für die Sitten-Geschichte. Vollständig durchgeführte weibliche Charaktere fanden in der alten Komödie nicht statt, und finden sich nicht in ihm; aber die Sitten der Weiber, die er aufführt, so manche einzelne Züge, das Kolorit des Ganzen geben ein nur zu vollständiges Gemälde weiblicher Zügellosigkeit. Der bloße Inhalt einiger Stücke mag erraten lassen, was unsre Sprache nicht genau ausführen darf. In einem derselben rot-

tieren sich alle Weiber einer Stadt zusammen, unzufrieden über den schon lange geführten Krieg, verschwören sich zu einer heroischen Enthaltsamkeit und zwingen ihre Männer Frieden zu schließen, durch das große Mittel, durch welches kluge Frauen sinnliche Männer zu beherrschen pflegen. In der weiblichen Volksversammlung bemächtigen sich die Weiber, als Männer verkleidet, durch List des Marktplatzes und der Regierung, dekretieren die Herrschaft der Weiber und Gehorsam der Männer, Freiheit und Gleichheit auch in der Liebe, Gemeinschaft der Güter und der Männer; durch ein andres Dekret erhalten Häßlichkeit und Alter (vermutlich die Majorität) gleiche Rechte auf die Liebe und den Besitz der Männer, als Schönheit und Jugend.[3]

[For a great many reasons, we assume in anticipation that the epoch's general corruption became apparent in the female sex at a very early stage and in quite an intense way. But the degree of female licentiousness and corruption Aristophanes portrays, surprises us and exceeds all belief . . . Nevertheless, Aristophanes's comedy is a copy of nature, often even a portrayal of an individual original; it has innumerable features that are borrowed from reality, and it is a valuable document for the history of life and customs. Fully developed female characters did not occur in the ancient comedy, and do not recognize themselves in it; but the manners of the women he does portray, the many particular features, the color effect of the whole portrayal give a remarkably complete picture of female licentiousness. The mere content of some of his plays may give a hint at what our language cannot express precisely. In one of these, all the women of a city band together, dissatisfied with the sustained war situation; they conspire to force their husbands to conclude a peace treaty by means of heroic abstinence, the mighty weapon with which intelligent women tend to dominate sensual men. In the female assembly, the women, dressed up like men, take hold of the market place and the government, decree the power to women, male obedience, freedom and equality also in love, community of property and men; another decree stipulates that ugliness and old age (probably the majority) are as much entitled to love and possession of men as beauty and youth are. (My translation)]

As much as Schlegel praises Aristophanes's comic genius in another context, when it comes to the debate on women's rights—in which the conservative comedian stood on the antidemocratic side—serious treatment in Sophocles's manner seems to be called for. Aristophanes's parody of women's struggle for equality in *Lysistrata* is, Schlegel regrets, a far cry from the harmonious, tragic representation of the beautiful, wise, and brave women in plays like *Antigone* or *Electra*. It seems that the philosopher here has lost the kind of superb ironic wit with which he normally unravels his opponents' texts. If he had read Aristophanes's comedies seriously, as he wants us to, then what he would have ended up with is laughter as a significant political gesture. For what else is Aristophanes's portrayal of women's degeneration if not the refusal on the part of his female characters to be "naturally" beautiful in the way Sophocles conceived them. In contrast to the latter's idealizations, the former's ugly females stage real, "immoral" women—immoral in the sense that they exuberantly offend the old tastes and expectations. I would argue that Aristophanes's grotesque figures are the negative signs of the real disrupting the beautiful ideal. With them he has unwittingly dedicated himself to making visible what in Sophocles remained invisible (according to Schlegel, did not exist): the necessary distance between the real and the ideal, the women in the audience and the beautiful types—played by men!—on stage. Fifty years after *Antigone*, Sophocles's ideals have long been lost and have been made to give way to figures who refuse to reflect what has by then become a lie. Dissimulating beauty, they put on one mask while discarding the other. This exchange of masks keeps Aristophanes's women hovering between reality and spectacle, the beautiful and the sublime. This, in turn, leads to a critical indeterminacy that endows them with the power to highlight the illusory nature of the dramatist's fantasies: in reality women have never climbed the public stage. But this is not all, for no longer beautiful the women in *Lysistrata* can pose as men, "act" (in a double sense) as men (as the male actors that they are), while turning the tables against them: women gain the power to see rather than be seen, to choose their mates and rearrange love in such a manner that freedom and equality reign.

In different ways, Aristophanes poses the problem of how to "contain" a work of art that in its vacillation between reality and image lays bare the inadequacy as well as injustice of mimetic representation. His dramas explicitly demonstrate the crisis in Greek beauty to be associated with the political crisis in democratic Athens: just as the cycles of natural poetry give way to an autonomous power that no Greek beauty can adequately frame, so the democratic reforms of the male rulers have unleashed an emancipatory process that threatens to deprive them of their own authority. In fact, the changes in Greek poetry and the emergence of drama in particular would not have been possible without political changes in the public arena: the chorus as medium of criticism was, after all, the product of a democratic climate, as much as Schlegel's own theory and practice of criticism were inspired by the democratic ideals of the French Revolution. As for the conservative Aristophanes, if we read his comedies seriously, then they too become democratic statements, not only in the sense that their subversiveness presupposes a liberal context but, above all, because his female figures, inasmuch as they openly insist on being taken seriously, gain the autonomy to counter the maker's mocking and conservative vision with a tale about freedom and equality. Viewed from a seriously feminist perspective, their actions on stage confront the male audience (women had a separate section in the theater) as well as actors and author with the limits of their patriarchal power. Refusing to be determined by the male gaze on and beyond the stage, Aristophanes's women claim their bodies as well as their rights. Through abstinence and by literally hiding their sex, these women change war (Athens was involved in the Peloponnesian War) into peace and, as men would, enter parliament to vote oppression into equality, possession into community (*Gemeinschaft*) of property and men. Absence (through abstinence) in the private sphere thus becomes a mode of presence in public, while invisibility in parliament becomes visibility at home.

These women's vertiginous manipulation of the contrast between reality and appearance instigates a challenge to gender-based, hierarchical divisions between men and women, public and private (husbands become public property), male viewers and female spectacle, masculine fantasies and feminine realities. Theirs is a vital transgressive presence in which, contrary to Aristophanes's and Schlegel's intentions (*was unsre Sprache nicht genau ausführen darf*), opposites merge, bodies are doubled, playful illusions become the occasion for a serious truth.

In the period that follows Aristophanes's works, during the so-called new Attic comedies (Menandros), drama, according to Schlegel, loses its explicitly political impact. No longer concerned with public issues, it concentrates on the representation of domestic life. (Many critics have identified it as the beginning of realism.) Paradoxically, Schlegel remarks—and here he has regained his taste for irony—this interest on the part of the artist in women as purely domestic beings results in plays in which married female citizens are particularly absent. Rather than picturing married women as one would expect from these new comedies, they focus on courtesans (*hetares*), because the latter, in contrast to their domestic counterparts, are educated and enjoy the company of wise men. It is this peculiar digression at the heart of new Attic comedy that once again reveals the imposture of mimesis to be closely linked to the invisibility—and political oppression—of the female. Reading those "realistic" comedies as a fraud allows Schlegel to detect what would otherwise remain hidden: the women in their homes, "[d]enn nach den Sitten der Alten waren diese von der männlichen Gesellschaft abgesondert, und lebten unter sich"[4] [(f)or according to the ancient customs, they were separated from the male community, and lived among themselves (my translation)]. Once the surface of Menandros's comedies has been broken, once their fictional frames have been laid bare—in short, once the form has been made the content—reality is allowed into the picture, and what is absent becomes present: women's place in the home.

Now in order to better understand Schlegel's own view on the sexual politics of art, we should turn to one more text by him: "Über die Philosophie: An Dorothea."[5] Written in the form of a fictive letter to his beloved, the essay enacts the kind of emancipatory dialogue that it has as its theme. The letter is written with the intention of introducing Dorothea to the workings of philosophy. In it Schlegel starts out from the binary opposition between man and woman as involving the difference between philosophy and poetry: by nature a rational being, man is active on the public front (engaged with politics and science) while his favorite means of reflection is philosophy. Woman, in contrast, is an emotional creature because her natural disposition is that of motherhood. Hence she expresses herself in poetry. Now the fact that woman is "naturally" destined to be a mother, does not—for Schlegel—imply that she should be restrained to the home. Instead of remaining a *häusliches Wesen* as she so often is in eighteenth-century Germany, it is woman's task to develop the maternal that she embodies beyond her original nature. Woman's ultimate destination is "religion," which in Schlegel's early thinking is not so much a matter of having faith in one God as it is a kind of Dionysian deliverance to the natural joys of humanity, to physical and spiritual love. In other words, woman's fulfillment lies in the transcendence of motherhood—that natural germ that all women share—into the living powers of universal love. She must at once develop *and resist* the maternal inside her by transforming the natural cycles of motherhood (and the sensitivity this implies) into a religion of physical and spiritual love. For Schlegel this continuous vacillation between the maternal and the religious, between the natural and the spiritual enables women to break with the stereotyping of their sex as well as with the consolidation of socially constructed gender roles:

> Nur sanfte Männlichkeit, nur selbständige Weiblichkeit sei die rechte, die wahre und schöne. Ist dem so, so muß man den Charakter des Geschlechts, welches doch nur eine angeborne, natürliche Profession ist, keineswegs noch mehr übertreiben, sondern vielmehr durch starke Gegengewichte zu mildern suchen, damit die Eigenheit einen wo möglich unbeschränkten Raum finde, um sich nach Lust und Liebe in dem ganzen Bezirke der Menschheit frei zu bewegen.[6]
>
> [Only gentle masculinity, only independent femininity would be the right, true, and beautiful kind. If that is true, one should by no means put extra emphasis on the different characteristics of the sexes, since these are only innate, natural qualities, but rather attenuate them by means of strong counterbalances in order to allow the individuality to find—if possible unrestricted—room to move freely as one pleases in the vast area of humanity. (My translation)]

This rupturing of stereotypes through Dionysian love coincides with a reversal of roles in such a manner that women are initiated into philosophy, while men learn to express themselves by means of poetry. For just as women must overcome the limits of their sex, so men must transgress theirs by substituting the abstractness of their thought by a communication with the world. Combining his penchant toward philosophy with the poetry of his female counterpart, man fulfills his ethical destination. Language (*Mitteilung*), woman's domain, is the necessary instrument for a practically involved philosopher. Hence, Schlegel can conclude his letter with the ironic observation that, contrary to his intentions, Dorothea is the one who has introduced him to philosophy: for in his dialogue with her he has found the means to shape his thoughts such that they are ready for publication. What first appears to be an episode of truthful communication between a man and a woman turns out, in the end, to be the occasion for the philosopher to perfect his own writing as much as to prove himself a poet of sorts.

In his letter on philosophy, Schlegel's emancipatory concerns hide the truth of the matter: what he is seeking is the means to find the right word. "Vielleicht tätest Du gut, von der Philosophie selbst auch nicht mehr zu erwarten als eine Stimme, Sprache und Grammatik für den Instinkt der Göttlichkeit, der ihr Keim und wenn man auf das Wesentliche sieht, sie selbst ist"[7] [Perhaps it would be better if you would not expect more from philosophy than a voice, language, and grammar for the instinct of divinity which is its germ and—in the main—its essence (my translation)]. Since the success of his philosophy on the interdependence between the two sexes depends on the degree to which he can involve—persuade—the female reader, what Schlegel needs is a rhetorically effective style of writing. He must, in other words, *produce* the truth of what he is saying, by bringing forth the reader who can prove him right. Since the addressee is still caught up in the reality of the home, since her interests do not exactly lie in the wisdom of her beloved, Schlegel's struggle to find the right vocabulary is essentially a battle against woman's daily existence. To read his letter rhetorically—as he himself does at the beginning and the end—is to make visible the practical constraints of the home. This anti-theoretical thrust of his writing, expressed as it is by Schlegel's poetical interests, is the sign of woman's public absence. In it lies hidden the portrait of a secluded, domestic being whom Schlegel never ceases to elevate to a figure of style: the trope of apostrophe. Writing philosophy in the form of a rhetorically convoluted letter, Schlegel makes tangible the unsurpassable distance that must be crossed before men and women can become equal partners. By thus thematizing and re-inscribing the boundaries between philosophy and poetry, by practicing philosophy as apostrophe, Schlegel allows women's reality to enter his essay and make of his apparent monologue a political dialogue.

It is in his sublime mixture of disciplines and genres that Schlegel raises questions about gender. Situating himself in that zone where literature and philosophy—fiction and theory—intersect, he highlights the artificial, conventional, gender-related limits of his profession. Adopting the position of both writer and philosopher, Schlegel reveals the *work* that goes into the establishment of truth (such as the one about the sexes): man's rhetoric, of course, but also woman's domestic labor. In fact, one might go as far as saying that it is the absence of the female addressee—her work in the house—that has turned his search for truth into a rhetorical enterprise in the first place. Woman is thus made duplicitously present as the principle of figuration, which by undermining the distinction between content and form, the literal and the figural, praxis and theory, guarantees that the male philosopher always thinks about how he says what he is saying, thereby opening the debate on how things are traditionally framed: what is included, and who is left out. In this manner, to read Schlegel's philosophical texts as a rhetorical address or apostrophe is to engender a (philosophical) genre that encompasses other (literary) genres, while raising doubts about the way they have traditionally been divided. In the "Letter on Philosophy," more specifically, he dissolves the opposition between philosophy-for-men versus poetry-for-women. Equally, he annihilates the division between the public (by extension, masculine) genre of the essay, on the one hand, and the private (and hence feminine) genre of the letter (the epistolary novel), on the other. Renegotiating these gender-based hierarchies between genres and discursive strategies, Schlegel's genre of all genres can be regarded as a challenge to what Anne Mellor, borrowing Eagleton's description of the eighteenth-century literature of sensibility, has recently called the "benign patriarch's" "feminization of discourse." For if we follow Mellor's argument that the development of eighteenth-century literature "could be construed as locating the genre of the novel, in some meaningful sense, within the private or domestic sphere assigned to the feminine,"[8] then Schlegel's reformulation of the novel as the genre of all genres (see next chapter) also constitutes a significant attempt to liberate this so-called feminine format from its domestic ties. Rather than affirming the novel as woman's private, autobiographical mode of expression—as Richardson and Fielding have done—Schlegel refuses to appropriate this stereotype and instead elevates it to a parody of all traditional genres, including that of the feminine novel. As we will see, *Lucinde* is Schlegel's ironic but deeply suspicious response to the sexual stereotyping characterizing the eighteenth-century sentimental novel. Its vertiginous dialogical form debunks such gender-based distinctions as the ones between private and public, sentiments and fantasy, fiction and theory, the natural and the spiritual. This deployment of the novel as the site of political subversion brings us close to the theory of the novel Bakhtin articulates and, even more so, to his analysis of Rabelais's laughter as the expression of an all-encompassing vital force: a kind of organic flux in which individuals forget their boundaries. What is heard in the laughter of Schlegel's hybrid novel is a Dionysian celebration of art's freedom from fixed categories, a comic—and above all "realistic" (in its ironic sense)—address to women's occluded presence in the home. An ode, finally, to the abundant powers of the female body, pregnant as it is with its own redemption.

FOUR

THE ROMANTIC NOVEL: *LUCINDE*

INTRODUCING LUCINDE

When Friedrich Schlegel's *Lucinde* was first published in 1799,[1] the book caused such a scandal that it was not reissued until the 1830s, when the public erroneously began to view it as a celebration of free love. The book's reception has been characterized by hostility and misinterpretation ever since.[2] The novel—ironically subtitled "Confessions of a Blunderer"—presents a semi-autobiographical portrait of Schlegel's physical and spiritual love for his mistress Dorothea Veit. But, as we will see, it is exactly the notion of "autobiography" that Schlegel's writing puts into question.[3] The novel—which was never completed—consists of a series of fragments representative of a variety of genres, such as the fantasy, the idyl, the epistolary novel, the dithyramb, and the allegory. The majority of these fragments are written in the form of a dialogue between an "I" (Julius) and a "you" (Lucinde) and are structured around the central and longest piece called "Apprenticeship for Manhood." In contrast to the other fragments, the "central" piece is narrated in the third person, an ironic move indeed given that this impersonal narrative is the most straightforward (auto)biographical or confessional portion of the novel: it deals with Julius's past amorous affairs, his many failures, his gradual education toward manhood, and his final rebirth in the arms of his beloved Lucinde. But besides the fact that this most personal story is written in the least personal form, there is yet another ironic twist in this central piece, namely, the fact that it chronologically precedes the beginning of the novel. For the moment Julius discovers true love in Lucinde is also the moment when he picks up the pen and addresses his beloved at the opening of the book. This strange narratological dislocation leaves us with an autobiography whose autobiographical centerpiece precedes the opening of the book. To this ironic situation is added the fact that the centerpiece ends with a switch to a first-person narration and the fact that Julius meant to place this autobiographical flashback much earlier in the novel, if only he had not been forced to delay his account by a series of external interruptions.

The question, then, arises: how do we read this fragmentary novel whose structure hinges upon the interruption and decentralization of its center? And how do we relate the *form* of the novel to its *content*, that is, to the love between Julius and Lucinde? For a preliminary answer we need to return to fragment 116 (cited earlier), where, we remember, romantic literature is described as being to the arts what sociability, friendship, and love are to life. In a curious way, then, romantic literature calls for an understanding by way of analogical inference: it is to the arts what love is to life. In order to know what the *Roman* is—what kind of art—we need to comprehend the function of love or romance in life.

For Schlegel, love as the synthesis of self and other is a fragment through which the ideal subject ("I") presents itself in instants of self-annihilation, absence, or otherness.[4] It is a form of self-presentation that finds its fulfillment at the very moment the "I" coincides with what lies outside itself, the beloved: "Nur in der Antwort seines Du kann jedes Ich seine unendliche Einheit ganz fühlen"[5] [Only in the answer of its "you" can every "I" wholly feel its boundless unity[6]]. In this ironic interplay between self and other, or completion and depletion, love resembles Schlegel's transcendental poetry as the unity of art and philosophy. Love synthesizes the chaos of life "just as" romantic literature unites the different genres of art. However, does this analogy between love and romantic art not bring together life and art in a manner that repeats the very essence of Schlegel's romantic literature? Simply put, isn't the resemblance between Schlegel's *Roman* and *romance* conducive to much more than simply an understanding of romantic art? Doesn't it also imply a practical, creative component? Isn't, in other words, Schlegel's analogical understanding of transcendental poetry itself a mode of creativity? What all this means is that to "understand" romantic poetry in terms of love, and, conversely, the latter in terms of intellectual intuition[7]—the way Schlegel repeatedly does—is as much a theoretical as a practical enterprise. Thus, by relating love and the romantic novel in his amorous novel *Lucinde* for instance, Schlegel theorizes as much as he creates. No sooner does Julius pick up his pen to put his love into words than his self-expression escapes what was originally intended and turns into a self-reflexive theory of the novel.

To the extent that Julius's romance functions as a theoretical apprehension of the work, and the expression of his love is indissociable from the positing of a theory, *Lucinde* is less about the attempt to unite physical and religious love, as has traditionally been argued,[8] than about love as a mode of artistic self-theorization. It now remains to be seen in what way Julius's amorous writing theoretically legitimates itself in its practice and, conversely, what role this self-theorization assigns to the participants of the discourse: are we dealing with a traditional sexual contract between active lover and passive beloved, male addressor and female addressee? Or is the assignment of positions not that clear? Are we, as readers, perhaps drawn into a book that triumphs over our theoretical view in—precisely—*sublime* exuberance?

Dear reader, before we engage in a dispute of phrases, let me explain to you why I can no longer theorize the sublime. The reason is that . . . (Long silence. The reader gets uncomfortable. Then impatient. Finally angry: "What does she think she is doing*?" At his [sic] wit's end he picks up a pen and writes: "I don't need this grand metaphysical gesture about The Anti-Narrative. Get on with the writing.") I like your style.*

When Julius first meets Lucinde—and here we are at the end of the centerpiece—we are told that what attracts the young man to her is the "wonderful similarity" between their personalities. Like him she has suffered from an unhappy love life, like him she loves music, like him she tries her hand at painting. It is clear that what he discovers in her is the eloquent and beautiful expression of his own inmost thoughts. Julius's fascination with the woman coincides with a narcissistic devotion to the *living image* of his own self. What he discovers in her is his own self-reflection, a reflection that transports the man beyond himself and introduces an irreducible gap in his life. For the instant he discovers himself in her is accompanied by a radical break with his past. We are told: "Auch er erinnerte sich an die Vergangenheit und sein Leben ward ihm, indem er es ihr erzählte, zum erstenmal zu einer gebildeten Geschichte" (53) [He, too, recalled his past, and by telling her about it saw his life for the first time as a connected whole (98)]. By thus completing the past, Julius leaves behind his old self and enters the present as an image of himself. (The "present" of course cannot be dissociated from the text before us.) However this image is not simply one that finds its outlines in the presence of the beloved: it is one that—and this is important—has been actively created by her. The man he becomes looks, indeed, much like the figures in her paintings. She belongs, after all, to "denen, die nicht in der gemeinen Welt leben, sondern in einer eignen selbstgedachten und selbstgebildeten" (53) [that part of mankind that doesn't inhabit the ordinary world but rather a world that it conceives and creates for itself (98)]. If the man's rebirth as Lucinde's work of art leaves him a reflection of himself, herself, and her painting, then Lucinde, in turn, does not escape the transformative powers of love and becomes no less an image. For no sooner does Julius adopt the artistic talents of his beloved than he depicts her charming presence on the canvas. Lucinde now brings to life his paintings which used to be "stiff and rigid" and "almost monstrous":

> Sie teilten ihre Neigung zur Kunst und Julius vollendete einiges. Seine Gemälde belebten sich, ein Strom von beseelendem Licht schien sich darüber zu ergießen und in frischer Farbe blühte das wahre Fleisch. Badende Mädchen, ein Jüngling der mit geheimer Lust sein Ebenbild im Wasser anschaut, oder eine holdselig lächelnde Mutter mit dem geliebten Kinde im Arm waren beinah die höchsten Gegenstände seines Pinsels. (56)

> [They shared an inclination for the arts. Julius finished some paintings: now they came to life, a stream of inspiring light seemed to spill over them, and the real flesh glowed in living colors. His favorite subjects were girls bathing, a young man looking with furtive pleasure at his own image in the water, or a fond, smiling mother with her darling child in her arms. (101)]

As this passage suggests, Lucinde's presence offers the man the opportunity not only to express himself—via a self-expression that reduces her to an image—but, in this expression, to reflect upon himself. Hence his self-portrayal as the man looking at his own image in the water. It is clear that the love between the two people has put into motion a series of reflecting images that carry the lovers into a higher mode of self-awareness as well as into an increasing artificiality. Thus, the progression of their love—as this "medium of reflection"—toward the unity of the "I" and the external self originates an increase of artistic images in such a way that at the height of the lovers' union Julius sees himself and Lucinde in a colorful vision of multiplicity and difference:

> . . . und nun mußte er von Tage zu Tage neue Verschiedenheiten [between himself and Lucinde] entdecken. Zwar gründeten sich selbst diese nur auf eine tiefere Gleichheit, und je reicher ihr Wesen sich entwickelte, je vielseitiger und inniger ward ihre Verbindung. Er hatte es nicht geahndet, daß ihre Originalität so unerschöpflich war wie ihre Liebe. (56)
>
> [. . . and now he was forced to discover new differences every day. To be sure, even these differences were based on a fundamental similarity, and the more richly her character revealed itself, the more various and intimate did their communion become. He had not suspected before that her originality would be as inexhaustible as her love. (101)]

In Schlegel's terms, this is the moment of the sublime, this scene in which the harmony between lover and beloved yields a vision of chaos. As their love is a *Verbindung* through which the lovers reflexively determine themselves and each other in their opposition, their symmetrical co-determination cannot but disclose itself to be pervaded by a radical disharmony. And it is in this revelation of their differences, of their loving communion as a mere appearance, that lies the truth of the matter. For by thus affirming its irreality (plurality), their "fundamental similarity" asserts Julius's (and Lucinde's) artistic creativity at its origin. For what is announced in this breakdown of unity (at the height of their union!) if not the manner in which the two lovers were originally drawn together and their differences overcome by their common interest in art, a love of art that at once reduced their lives (and their love) to a work of the imagination. At stake here is the growing synthesis of love and art out of the intensifying communion between self and other. As the two characters become one and lose their identity in one another, the boundary dissolves between unity and duplicity, between what is life and what has been artfully created.

Surely it is because Julius's expression of love cannot but attest to its artifice that the man's love story is a parody at best. Conversely, we might well say that the fictiveness of his confessions becomes expressive of the gap that separates him from his beloved. In its irreality, Julius's love story presents us with a portrait of their differences. In other words, the cracked mirror here held up simultaneously reflects the separate lives of the "I" and the "You," of the subject and the object. Out of the fragmentation of Julius's text, that is, out of the confession of his blunder, appears the text of Lucinde: *Lucinde.*

To the extent that Julius inadvertently lets his confession of love slip into a novel about Lucinde, he accomplishes Schlegel's search for the romantic novel as the unity between the work and its theory. It is, indeed, in the digression embodied by Lucinde that we are given Schlegel's view on art, namely, that insofar as the writer does not control his creation, the fictional frame gets broken and the (ironic) truth irrupts. This radical indeterminacy between the theory and the reality of the work of art explains not only the novel's sudden switch from first-person narration to the use of the impersonal (reflexive) "he" in the centerpiece, but also the switch from that third-person narrative—a third person in its fullest sense, that is, written from a near-Hegelian synthesis of Julius and Lucinde[9]—to a first-person critical reflection upon it:

> Andeuten will ich dir wenigstens in göttlichen Sinnbildern, was ich nicht zu erzählen vermag. Denn wie ich auch die Vergangenheit überdenke, und in mein Ich zu dringen strebe, um die Erinnerung in klarer Gegenwart anzuschauen und dich anschauen zu lassen: es bleibt immer etwas zurück, was sich nicht aüßerlich darstellen läßt, weil es ganz innerlich ist. (58–59)
>
> [I want at least to suggest to you in divine symbols what I can't tell you in words. For as much as I think about the past and try to penetrate into my ego to examine my memories in the clarity of the present—and let you examine them as well—still something is always left that can't be described outwardly because it is wholly inward. (104)]

What is affirmed in this transition from the third-person narrative about the past to the first-person reflection on its impossibility, is the fact that in Julius's text recollection and fantasy, reflection and writing have become indistinguishable. Thus abolishing the boundary between the truth and the lie, Schlegel's novel declines the imposture of autobiographical representation for the sake of a more truthful approach to itself: the writing subject that alone can guarantee the authenticity of autobiography is the outcome rather than the origin of the text. Hence for Julius to write to Lucinde is already to be written by her. This is what one could call her auto-fiction.

From what has been said so far and at the risk of pushing Schlegel to his (deconstructive) limits,[10] we can conclude that Lucinde makes possible Julius's self-expression—also the verbalization of his love—exactly because she is the man's other. However, as the exteriority of Julius's inner self she also confronts him with what is purely outside or surface in his love and thus with its extreme artificiality. Hers is the critical glance that, in the same breath, exposes the irreality of their love, while giving that love a visible form. In the same way as art and philosophy for Schlegel mutually determine each other in their reciprocal destruction, so do Lucinde and Julius, art and love, *Lucinde* and "the Confessions of a Blunderer," come about in their mutual exclusion. The result is a text—this text, *Lucinde*—that gives voice to an increasing self-consciousness on the part of the lover. It is a self-awareness through which he is made to view his expressions of love, criticize them, and in this critical reflection further improve them. The manifestation of his love thus takes place along a path of art and criticism, the coexistence of which leads him to a stronger sense of self as well as to a hyperbolic expression. (Hence his ultimate resort to his excessively rhetorical "divine symbols.") The more intimate the relation between Julius and Lucinde, and the further developed his selfhood, the more the lover becomes an aesthetic object to himself. The end of the process is the moment when—in his unity with the beloved-critic—Julius is able to view (reflection) his own love or life (praxis), becomes a living image of himself, and in this way loses himself in his own fiction making, the life of the text: *Lucinde*.

> Wie seine Kunst sich vollendete und ihm von selbst in ihr gelang, was er zuvor durch kein Streben und Arbeiten erringen konnte: so ward ihm auch sein Leben zum Kunstwerk, ohne daß er eigentlich wahrnahm, wie es geschah. Es ward Licht in

seinem Innern, er sah und übersah alle Massen seines Lebens und den Gliederbau des Ganzen klar und richtig, weil er in der Mitte stand. Er fühlte, daß er diese Einheit nie verlieren könne, das Rätsel seines Daseins war gelöst, er hatte das Wort gefunden. (57)

[Just as his artistic ability developed and he was able to achieve with ease what he had been unable to accomplish with all his powers of exertion and hard work before, so too his life now came to be a work of art for him, imperceptibly, without his knowing how it happened. A light entered his soul: he saw and surveyed all the parts of his life and the structure of the whole clearly and truly because he stood at its center. He felt that he would never lose this unity; the mystery of his life had been resolved and he had found the Word. (102)]

We are at the end of the centerpiece. Julius's life—his love for Lucinde—has found its completion in the man's autobiographical word. We can now return to the opening of both this piece and of the novel as a whole and begin to read Julius's word. What will arise is a reading of what the novel cannot present: its own origin, or in the words of the text, "the mystery of a momentary beginning or transformation." The origin is a mystery because it does not lie at the origin of the text[11] but is situated at the *end* of the center, namely, at that fleeting moment in which Julius's love, life, and art are one. The mystery of the origin is then the fact that Julius's beginning—occurring as it does in the retrospection at the center of the novel—is already past while yet to come. Or again, the riddle at the origin is "the transformation" between the past reality and the future text. It comes as no surprise therefore that the development of the novel, as the development of its impossible incipience and thus of its own absence, is characterized by a growing fragmentation and a series of increasingly interrupted dialogues that dazzle the reader with their ironic reversals. Trying to read *Lucinde* amounts to nothing more—or less—than an exegesis of the synthesis of art and criticism, an exegesis then of the presence of theory in the absence of the work. In its fullest extension, this implies a revelation of the manner in which the fragments structured around the centerpiece—those fragments that begin where the center left off—function as a theoretical contextualization (in a literal and figural sense) of its incompletion. Indeed, to the extent that Schlegel's theory arises in the absence of the work, one has to read the rest of the work (or center)—a "rest" in the sense of a deliberate *Fragment* rather than an unintended *Bruchstück*—as a theoretical development of the center's suspension between origin and end. Out of the center's ironic doubling, out of its presentation of absence, grows the whole of the novel whose movement reiterates the circularity at its origin. This self-theorization of the centerpiece in the remainder of the novel stages a movement from a factual autobiography (representing the life of the narrator) to a fictive one (presenting the life of the text). In his *Gespräch über die Poesie* Schlegel defines this motion as a transition from confessions to arabesques:[12]

> Besonders die Confessions geraten meistens auf dem Wege des Naiven von selbst in die Arabeske, wozu sich jene Romane [by Fielding and Richardson] höchstens am Schluß erheben, wenn die bankerotten Kaufleute wieder Geld und Kredit, alle armen Schlucker zu essen bekommen, die liebenswürdigen Spitzbuben ehrlich und die gefallnen Mädchen wieder tugendhaft werden.[13]
>
> [Confessions, especially, mainly by way of the naive, develop of themselves into arabesques. But at best those novels (by Fielding and Richardson) rise to the arabesque only at the end, when the bankrupt merchants regain their money and credit, all the poor devils get to eat, the likeable scoundrels become honest, and the fallen women become virtuous again.[14]]

That the arabesque is here put on a par with the confessional novel is due to the fact that both are characterized by a combination of "eigner Anschauung und dargestelltem Leben"[15] [self-reflection and represented life[16]], the absolute synthesis of which constitutes Schlegel's ideal romantic book. What separates the two genres, however, is the way in which this synthesis is achieved: While the confessions present the life (the objectivity) of the narrator (the subject), the arabesques present the life (the subjectivity) of the work (the object). In the latter case, the synthesis of *Geist* and *Buchstabe* is essentially objective—what the arabesque presents is exactly the inner coherence or *Geist* of the novel—while in the case of the confessional novel, the synthesis concerns the writing subject: it presents the becoming-*Buchstabe* of the writer's inner self. The two genres are thus complementary. Together they represent the romantic novel as the synthesis of two irreconcilable opposites: of reflection and historical reality, of subjectivity (cf. the sentimental novel as practiced by Richardson or Fielding) and objectivity (cf. the fantastic or "naive" novels of Hoffmann or Ariosto), of subjective content (love) and objective form (art).[17] What emerges from this paradox is a work suspended between the mystery of love and the capriciousness of fantasy, as well as between the reality of the subject (Julius) and the fictiveness of its objectification (*Lucinde*).

If, as should be clear by now, the fragmentary arabesques framing the central autobiography originate from what the "Lehrjahre" has left unsaid—remember that Julius was incapable of expressing the love that was "totally inward"; if, in other words, these (objective) arabesques arise in the breakdown of autobiographical (subjective) representation, then it leaves no doubt that they take their place only as the absence of the subject (and his love) at their center. They mark, in other words, the realization (in a double sense) of the failure of self-representation and of what is identical to it: the recognition of the artificiality of the expressions of love. Theirs is a rhetorical force at the literal and figural "heart" of the novel. However, by thus asserting the limitation of Julius's project—his intention to exteriorize what is interior—by giving shape to this sublime moment of chaos, the arabesques also contain, resist or, indeed, *frame* the breakdown of the man's autobiography. Ironically, then, they save Julius's narrative exactly by narrating his incapacity to control it. No sooner does the text refuse to be controlled than it asserts its freedom to control itself. In fact, as we will see, its structure or inner coherence derives exactly from the repetitive failure, on the part of the narrator, to successfully complete what he set out to do. Contrary to all intention, and only in contrast to Julius's intention, the development of the textual arabesques is made possible by the fact that the novel never moves beyond its (autobiographical) origin.

Not only does this mean that the temporal progression of the novel is countered by an atemporal or spatial force—one that reduces the narrative to a repetition of its center or lack thereof—but it also implies that the course of the novel is characterized by a continuous departure from itself, a sublime difference within that abolishes any temporal progression and transforms the novel into an ongoing parody of itself. This motion-as-interruption or permanent deviation doubles Julius's narrative into a dramatization of what in chapter 2 was called "parabasis" or the demystification of illusions.[18] In the parabasis of Greek comedy, we remember, actors take off their masks to address the audience in a direct manner. Hence it functions like a *mise-en-abîme,* a mirror in the play that reflects the drama on stage. But whereas parabasis in Greek comedy generates a violent confrontation between art and reality, in the romantic novel the disruption must be more subtle: "Die Parekbase im Rom[an] muß verhüllt sein, nicht offenbar wie in der alten Komödie"[19] [The Parabasis in the nov(el) must be hidden, not openly visible as in the ancient comedy (my translation)].

In Schlegel's romantic novel, parabasis becomes a mode of narrative development (along a horizontal axis) that reflects upon itself (along a vertical axis) and in this way is suspended as it proceeds in a spirit of continuous self-irony. The vacillation between continuity and discontinuity that is thus engendered conjures up a narrative that has as its theme the illusory quality of the unity of the text. Since the text is caught in a permanent disjunction or fragmentation, every affirmation of narrative progress is simply a ruse. At the same time, however, it is in this ongoing negation of development, or plot, that the illusion of the novel is able to sustain and even further develop itself. As a result, the fragmentary unfolding of the text is one that leads toward a perfected development of the ruse or *Einbildungskraft* at its origin. The fiction gets completed, the whole of the novel achieved exactly to the extent that the work never develops beyond its origin, and what appears to be progressive is simply a deception. That is why the fantastic novel as the expression of unlimited fantasy constitutes the end point that every work of fiction, for example, the sentimental novel, already "contains" (in a double sense) at the beginning. The fantastic novel thus becomes the space or frame of the development of the novel: "Auch die Gesch[ichte] des Romans läßt sich nie vollenden; ist also selbst nur Gegenstand eines F[antastischen] R[omans]"[20] [The his(tory) of the novel cannot be completed either; is therefore itself only the object (or subject) of a f(antastic) n(ovel) (my translation)]. Or again: "Die Parekbase muß im F[antastischen] R[oman] permanent sein"[21] [The Parabasis must be permanent in the f(antastic) n(ovel) (my translation)].

And just as the fantastic novel is shaped by a dialectic between progression and disruption, organic unity and fictive suspension, so too does the arabesque perfect the synthesis of praxis and reflection constituting every imaginative act of (self-)presentation. Indeed, Schlegel explicitly equates the arabesque and the fantastic by defining the former as "die älteste und ursprüngliche Form der menschlichen Fantasie"[22] [the oldest and original form of human imagination[23]]. Perhaps we can now begin to explore the way in which the novel's arabesque-like frame and its falsely progressive character do not simply point up but also complete this "most original form of [Julius's] imagination."

It could be said that this is the essence of *Lucinde,* this revelation of Julius's boundless fantasy, this unlimited creation of the "I" in the novel's failure to present anything at all, except then itself as a self-generating blunder. If the novel as a whole fails to be a whole as such (remember that it is made up of a series of fragments that were never completed), it is because it has no single center (an "I") from which the whole could originate. In reality, then, the development of *Lucinde,* no less than Julius's conception thereof, is a figment of the imagination. More correctly, the mystery of the momentary beginning and its development throughout the novel takes the form of a *turning away* (parabasis) from origins and a *re-turn* to a more fundamental notion of origin, namely, one that takes itself the form of a reversal or reflection in which the work projects its own non-being. This *Ursprung* can best be defined as an ironic twist in which, according to Schlegel, the fullness of consciousness grasps "itself as void, and apprehends the void as the infinite excess of chaos."[24] It is the backward leap into the future in which the gaze turned to the past creates a vision of the whole still to come.[25]

Because of this notion of origin as a mediation between past and future it is not surprising that *Lucinde* stages the question of its origination in terms of a dialogue between addressor as origin and addressee as destination. As stated above, the course of Julius's autobiography stages a continuous interruption in which arises an abundance of fantasy. This notion of a vacillating movement between autobiography and fantasy parallels what was said before about the dialectic between love and art. It was argued then that the breakdown of the loving communion between Julius and Lucinde unfolded a vision of art, and that, conversely, this revelation of fiction was linked to the gap between the two lovers. From this we concluded that Julius's artistic self-portrayal became the locus of a double portrait: that of Julius and of Lucinde. One can now re-interpret this concept of a double autobiography in terms of Julius's dialogue with Lucinde. From this perspective, the female addressee arises as the figure interrupting Julius's confessions of love while transforming them into an evocation of pure fantasy and ultimately into a vision of the whole: *Lucinde.* Thus no sooner does Julius pick up his pen to communicate his deepest sentiments to his beloved than the text's inscription misses the mark (*Buchstabe*) and slips into an image (*Figur*) of itself. The visionary text that grows out of it gives shape to Lucinde—or *Lucinde*. The female figure here functions as the rhetorical force of the text subverting Julius's confession into an excessively poetic construct. In her absence she unleashes a pure flight of the imagination hovering on the wings of reflection between the inscription and the inscribed, form and content, or in Schlegel's words, between "Band der Ideen" and "Einheit des Buchstabens."[26]

Lucinde is the feminine power of figuration interrupting Julius's sentimental address with a vision of its irreality. Countering his illusion of intimacy with the reality of her absence, she instigates a hyperbolic flux of words that says more about the man's gifts as a writer than about his feelings as a lover. Echoing the Socratic art of conversation, according to which the philosopher exhausts the answer in the formulation of the question,[27] question and answer or addressor and addressee are here united in what remains a purely rhetorical address on the part of the narrator (one that does not elicit a response). That is why the addressee remains mute for the greater part, makes her appearance twice (in "Fidelity and Playfulness" and "Yearning and Peace") and solely, it seems, in order to dramatize her status as a mere "figure" of speech or as the personification of Julius's self-figuring, rhetorical address. Lucinde to Julius: "Du bist's, es ist die Wunderblume Deiner Fantasie, die Du in mir, die ewig Dein ist, dann erblickst, wenn das Gewühl verhüllt ist und nichts Gemeines Deinen hohen Geist zerstreut" (78–79) [You are that person. When the turmoil has died down and nothing mean or common distracts your noble soul, then you see reflected in me—in me who am forever yours—the marvellous flower of your imagination (126)].

It will be our task in what follows to illustrate the intricate ways in which the absent Lucinde confronts the writer with the limits of his text and to reveal how in the counterdiscourse thus set in motion lies hidden not only the portrait of the reader—but also the autonomous development of *Lucinde*. Hers is the novel that Julius no longer controls. Reducible neither to one genre (autobiography) nor simply to one text (*Lucinde*), Lucinde's "novel" initiates a collision between discourses and perspectives that problematizes the conventions of its form. The result is a permanent transgression of traditional boundaries between such genres as the epistolary novel, the idyl, the medieval allegory, the Socratic dialogue, the Goethean *Bildungsroman*, and so forth. In this mixture of formats, Schlegel is developing the rules of a new genre—the so-called romantic novel—that is to be nothing less than the genre of all genres: the genre of literature as such, or what I would call the literary genre par excellence, *the address,* always in conflict with itself for always reaching out for an as yet absent or disinterested reader. Intending what is yet to be made present, the addressor is already past himself, past that center from whence he can totalize the work as his own. Reading Julius's novel as an address—an indirect I-You dialogue—implies letting the reality of the reader into the picture. It means bringing into the discussion what ordinarily remains hidden: the social (in this case also sexual) contract and narrative conventions making the author's sound or scribble a meaningful utterance in the first place. Of course, turning the interaction between male writer and female reader into the topic of the conversation results in a permanent displacement of the ultimate meaning—and genre—of the text. In fact, in its endless deferral, Schlegel's text is at once developing the format—the rules or theory—by means of which it could be classified while legitimating itself in its production. *Lucinde* is Schlegel's creative and modern response to the fixed divisions of the classical art forms—the epic, lyric, drama—which were still prevalent in eighteenth-century Germany, at the expense of the "lesser," "effeminate" genres such as the romance and the novel. These conventional forms he wanted to bring toward their end in the production of something radically new: a future-oriented novel in which the male writer's word was to be pervaded by its female response.

But we should delay no longer. Time has come to begin reading the beginning, that is, the prologue. It is the moment at which the narrator—upon the completion of the text—glances back at the whole, situates himself before the text and addresses the reader:

> Mit lächelnder Rührung überschaut und eröffnet Petrarca die Sammlung seiner ewigen Romanzen. Höflich und schmeichelnd redet der kluge Boccaz am Eingang und am Schluß seines reichen Buchs zu allen Damen. Und selbst der hohe Cervantes, auch als Greis und in der Agonie noch freundlich und voll von zartem Witz, bekleidet das bunte Schauspiel der lebensvollen Werke mit dem kostbaren Teppich einer Vorrede, die selbst schon ein schönes romantisches Gemälde ist. (3)
>
> [Petrarch smiles with emotion as he surveys and introduces the collection of his immortal romances. Subtle Boccaccio

speaks politely and flatteringly to the ladies at the beginning and at the close of his opulent book. And even the sublime Cervantes—still amiable and full of delicate wit, though old and wracked by pain—clothes the colorful spectacle of his vibrant works in the costly tapestry of a preface that is in itself already a beautiful romantic painting. (42)]

Already from the onset the text presents us with a curious ironic switch. For here is a voice pointing to the novel and the prologue to come, precisely by describing the prologues of three other writers—Petrarch, Boccaccio, and Cervantes—whom Schlegel considers the precursors or prologues to his own writing.[28] We are asked, in other words, to read the opening of the novel—an opening that surveys a yet invisible novel—by reading the openings of other works that, in their turn, function as a prefiguration not only of the texts they introduce but also of the novel that we are about to read. The message is clear: this is a beginning reading beginnings of texts yet to begin. The opening renders provisional and interrupts what it sets out to do. (The narrator's *Rede* is indeed a *Vor-Rede.*) Or in Schlegel's terms, the parabasis has begun and the canvas has been stretched. Shall we enter its surface and let ourselves be engaged in the detours that an intimacy with the text involves? Or do we decide not to trust the narrator (indeed, what else is our reading of an invisible novel if not an act of faith or trust?) Shall we take leave (*Abschied*) and by doing so further develop the interruption that Schlegel's parabasis had already initiated? For how could our farewell or decision not to read be anything else but a reiteration (and hence reading) of the prologue's end and its self-reflexive *Bild zum Abschiede*? Opposing this text, pretending not to hear its croakings, we would only bring to life, indeed perform, Schlegel's metaphorical swan, who in the womb of Leda (*Lucinde*) breathes out its song of immortality:

> Nur ein Wort, ein Bild zum Abschiede: Nicht der königliche Adler allein darf das Gekrächz der Raben verachten; auch der Schwan ist stolz, und nimmt es nicht wahr. Ihn kümmert nichts, als daß der Glanz seiner weißen Fittiche rein bleibe. Er sinnt nur darauf, sich an den Schoß der Leda zu schmiegen, ohne ihn zu verletzen; und alles was sterblich ist an ihm, in Gesänge auszuhauchen. (3)
>
> [Only a word, an image as a farewell—not only the royal eagle can despise the croaking of the ravens; the swan too is proud

> and does not hear it. Nothing concerns him but to keep the brilliance of his white feathers pure. His only thought is to nestle in the lap of Leda without hurting her; and then to breathe out in song every shadow of mortality. (42)]

In this way, not to read becomes a mode of appropriating the text in the very act of turning away (parabasis) from it. The immortality of the swan's song is thus guaranteed in the end (swan song) of our reading.

THE END

The text can now begin.

Probably no passage is more explicit about this irreducible paradox—the fact that the work and the reader, praxis and theory engender each other in their mutual exclusion—than *KF* 112:

> . . . Der Synthetische Schriftsteller konstruiert und schafft sich einen Leser, wie er sein soll; er denkt sich denselben nicht ruhend und tot, sondern *lebendig und entgegenwirkend.* Er läßt das, was er erfunden hat, vor seinen Augen stufenweise werden, oder er lockt ihn es selbst zu erfinden. Er will keine bestimmte Wirkung auf ihn machen, sondern er tritt mit ihm in das heilige Verhältnis der innigsten Symphilosophie oder Sympoesie.[29]
>
> [. . . The synthetic writer constructs and creates a reader as he should be; he doesn't imagine him calm and dead, but *alive and critical.* He allows whatever he has created to take shape gradually before the reader's eyes, or else he tempts him to discover it himself. He doesn't try to make any particular impression on him, but enters with him into the sacred relationship of deepest symphilosophy or sympoetry.[30]]

Schlegel's inclusion of the reader's *Entgegenwirkung* in the composition of the text hints at the ambiguous status of the interpretive moment within the act of writing. At once unifying and disruptive the critic's theoretical glance hovers over and inside the text, thereby demarcating the absence in which the work comes to life, albeit in a fragmentary way. In the opposition of the critic's stance the fragment projects its future completion. For the prologue this implies not only that the reader's exclusion from the text posits the space where the text can affirm its self-production but also that the prologue itself—to the extent that it reads the whole of the novel in a backward glance—is necessarily excluded from the text it originates. This exclusion explains the prologue's deviations (its turning away as a mode of indirect inauguration) and its appearance in the form of a costly tapestry that hides the text onto which it opens the curtain. The prologue as this paradoxical union of the text and reader, of its originating act and the text separated from it, resembles Leda's fertilized germ as the yet-to-be-fulfilled product of the unification of Zeus's and Leda's bodies. More specifically, the opening address—characterized as it is by an originary fragmentation that involves the suspension of what it brings forth, including itself—enacts the Greek myth, according to which Leda's eggs, out of which Helen and Castor and Pollux hatched, initiated the fall of Troy and the foundation of Greece. In their synthesis of life and death the prologue's paradoxical opening gestures—their opening as a closing—coincide with the imagery of the final paragraph. The end's *Bild zum Abschiede* completes in a *finalizing* gesture the incompletion of its origin. Origin and end are one in their incompletion. At last, we can now begin to read Julius's word.

Dear reader, one more image before saying goodbye: Magritte's "The Human Condition I."

Between Me and You: In Pursuit of an Apostrophe

That Julius's first letter to Lucinde stages its opening address ("Dear Lucinde") in the form of its title ("Julius to Lucinde") already suggests the thematic concerns of the letter to follow. What we are about to read is, indeed, a letter in search of the addressee whose presence would guarantee the confessional genre of Julius's writing.[31] For only upon producing a reader does the letter become what it is—a confession to Lucinde—and can we (or Lucinde) begin to understand the document. However, the enterprise is self-destructive in that it involves a shift from Julius's autobiographical "I" to a portrayal of its critical other, Lucinde; from expression to reflection; from text to context.

Dear reader, if in my theory on Schlegel the time approaches that we will share this monologue, it is because in you I unfold my reflections. I desire to speak as only you would, for you are much more critical than me.

Viewed from an overall perspective, the letter stages an autobiographical account of the vision Julius once had of his beloved Lucinde. While the introductory part of the letter concentrates on the context from which the vision takes its shape—the voluptuous forms of nature and the narrator's wealth of feelings—the greater part concentrates on the vision itself: "Und so sah ich auch mit dem Auge meines Geistes die Eine ewig und einzig Geliebte in vielen Gestalten, bald als kindliches Mädchen, bald als Frau in der vollen Blüte und Energie der liebe und der Weiblichkeit, und dann als würdige Mutter mit dem ernsten Knaben im Arm" (7) [And so too with the eye of my spirit I saw the one and only and forever beloved in many forms: sometimes as a childlike girl, sometimes as a woman in the full bloom and strength of love and femininity, and sometimes as a worthy mother with her earnest little boy in her arms (43)]. It leaves no doubt that the protean format of the vision evolves from the multiplicity of impressions and associations to which the narrator has been subjected by his surroundings. But besides this interpenetration between the lover's emotions and his natural context, there is the equally important manner in which the appearance of the beloved projects the "textual" context, namely, the further development of Julius's novel. Accordingly, Lucinde as little girl represents little Wilhelmine, the woman in the full bloom of love symbolizes Lucinde as she appears in the "Lehrjahre," and the mother prefigures Lucinde's pregnancy in "Zwei Briefe." At issue here is Julius's vision of Lucinde as provisional portrait of *Lucinde*, or more simply: what we are dealing with is a vision of the text's inscription. Through the appearance of the beloved, Julius's autobiographical narrative becomes a visionary recapitulation and anticipation of its own production. What the addressee presents is the past and future history of the text's creation. In fact, by means of Lucinde Julius's account reflects a whole tradition of epistolary novels, from Rousseau's *La Nouvelle Héloise* to John Barth's *LETTERS*, insofar as this genre draws upon the writing process and its circumstances for its narrative content. In Schlegel, this convention needs, of course, to be interpreted in terms of his philosophy of art, according to which the act of writing (the autobiography) comes about in a provisional image of itself (the fantasy), an image that accordingly also functions as the locus of its incompletion (hence its preliminary, evanescent character) and its literary history.

Given that the vision of Lucinde completes and depletes Julius's autobiographical remembrance, it is not surprising that the beloved, soon after her appearance as a reflection of the novel, acquires the role of the absent addressee as *negative* index of Julius's discourse—negative in the sense that the "you" indicating the here and now of the writing is absent and that it subjects the "I's" story to a radical change into an address. A negativity emphasized by the fact that the "presence" of the addressee is caught in a series of descriptions all of which specify (for the first time) the vision in terms of what it is not:

> Ein feines Feuer strömte durch meine Adern; was ich träumte, war nicht etwa bloß ein Kuß, die Umschließung *deiner* Arme, es war nicht bloß der Wunsch, den quälenden Stachel der Sehnsucht zu brechen und die süße Glut in Hingebung zu kühlen; nicht nach deinen Lippen allein sehnte ich mich, oder nach deinen Augen, oder nach deinem Leibe. (7, my emphasis)
>
> [A subtle fire flowed in my veins; what I dreamed of wasn't just a kiss or the embrace of *your* arms; it wasn't just a wish to break the tormenting thorn of yearning and cool the sweet flames in surrender; I didn't yearn only for your lips or your eyes or your body. (44, my emphasis)]

The interdependence of Julius's autobiographical writing and his vision of Lucinde can be formulated as follows: at the same time that the vision reflexively generates Julius's writing—and the addressee as the marker of that writing—his writing also concretizes his fantasy, albeit in a negative way. Formulating this otherwise: whereas before the vision of the beloved staged the process of writing (the novel), we now see the written discourse (in the persona of the "you") specify the dream in a negative way. Fantasy and autobiography, fiction and reality, form and content—united as they are in the arrival of the beloved—cannot simply be separated, and any account that insists on doing so necessarily bears witness to a false start. Like Julius's. For it is not without reason that the lover cannot reproduce his vision until he has acknowledged the presence (or absence, for that matter) of his beloved addressee. Only then can he successfully "see" what the vision had to say: "[E]s war eine romantische Verwirrung von allen diesen Dingen, ein wundersames Gemisch von den verschiedensten Erinnerungen und Sehnsuchten" (7) [It was, rather, a romantic confusion of all these things, a wonderful mixture of the most various memories and yearnings (44)].

That the "truth" of the vision arises with the introduction of the addressee and the epistolary discourse that she inscribes implies that what the vision of Lucinde reveals is, on the one hand, the writing that gives it its reality (and reduces or elevates the image of the beloved to the status of addressee) and, on the other hand, the reflective or visionary moment (the "you") within the "I's" confessions. That also explains the fact that what Julius is made to see—the mixture of memories and desires—is nothing less than a reflection of the letter itself, at least insofar as the letter involves the remembrance of a dream about love and desire. So that we can say that in the very same moment, the "truth" of the vision is and is not the writing process at its origin—for how could we insist on their identity if the truth revealed here belongs to the past (as remembrance) or the future (as desire). Instead the dream points up the preliminary or historical quality of the letter (and the vision within). Or to phrase this temporary interdependence between form (letter) and content (dream) in yet another way: Julius's vision is as much about the (fictive) past in which it originated as it is a prophecy about the letter to come (in the sense that this letter is written *after* the occurrence of the vision). Thus, while the letter fulfills the dream's prophecy, thereby putting an end to the fictive nature of the vision, the description of the dream gives content to the autobiographical-epistolary frame, which as a result yields the actuality of its *practice* to the fictive nature of the vision (*reflection*) itself.

But this interrelation gets even more complicated as the dream progresses:

> Alle Mysterien des weiblichen und des männlichen Mutwillens schienen mich zu umschweben, als mich Einsamen plötzlich deine wahre Gegenwart und der Schimmer der blühenden Freude auf deinem Gesichte vollends entzündete. Witz und Entzücken begonnen nun ihren Wechsel und waren der gemeinsame Puls unsers vereinten Lebens. (7–8)

> [All the mysteries of male and female frivolity seemed to hover about me as suddenly your real presence and the gloom

> of blooming happiness on your face inflamed my lonely self. Wit and rapture alternated between us and became the common pulse of our united life. (44)]

Out of Julius's perception of the romantic chaos, which coincides with the impossible unity of Julius's writing (praxis) and its vision (reflection), arises Lucinde's *wahre Gegenwart*; more specifically, the moment Julius can make out nothing is also the moment he encounters his real vision. And what he sees is, ironically, Lucinde's presence as the unity of the two lovers (*unsers vereinten Lebens*). Lucinde thus stands for the synthesis of the two lovers—the *wir* of the address—or for the unity of opposites that Schlegel here defines as *Witz* or *Entzücken* and that we have earlier designated as *theory*. Again, what the vision shows the lover is the inseparability of the autobiographical "I" and its visionary "you," of writing and reading, all of which are brought together in the dynamic structure of this address.

If Lucinde's presence reveals itself as *Witz*, which Schlegel has elsewhere defined as "die Erscheinung, der äußre Blitz der Fantasie"[32] [The appearance, the outward lightning bolt of the imagination[33]]. If, in other words, Lucinde's "presence" confronts Julius with the exteriority or appearance of his own fiction-making, then the "truth" of her vision resides in the way in which the intensification of his fictive sexual intoxication grants itself the possibility of an awakening (rupturing of illusions). To locate Lucinde's *wahre Gegenwart* in the sense of an existence beyond the boundaries of the vision, we need to illustrate how the growth of the vision implies its intensification to the point of a self-transcendence or postorgasmic lapse into the reality of the epistolary discourse. The decisive moment can hardly be overlooked:

> Ich bat sehr, du möchtest dich doch einmal der Wut ganz hingeben, und ich flehte dich an, du möchtest unersättlich sein. Dennoch lauschte ich mit kühler Besonnenheit auf jeden leisen Zug der Freude, damit mir auch nicht einer entschlüpfe und eine Lücke in der Harmonie bleibe. Ich genoß nicht bloß, sondern ich fühlte und genoß auch den Genuß. (8)
>
> [I begged you that for once you might give yourself completely over to frenzy, and I implored you to be insatiable. Still, I listened with cool composure for every faint sign of bliss, so that

> not a single trace might escape me and leave a gap in our harmony. I didn't simply enjoy but felt and enjoyed the enjoyment itself. (44)]

It is ironic that at the point at which the lovers reach their Dionysian union—also, as we have seen, the moment of Lucinde's *wahre Gegenwart*—Julius addresses his beloved with frenzied devotion, imploring her to be insatiable, while listening attentively to her cries of joy so that nothing will escape him. For by interrupting the unity between Julius and Lucinde through a direct address or demand for the beloved's satisfaction, the dream suspends the lovers' delirium—and thus itself as presentation of that delirium—and slips into a reflection of the I-You dialogue by which it is contained. The implications are manifold: firstly, the dream is made to discover itself as dream, thereby gaining a self-consciousness that points up its irreality, which overlaps with the appearance of the address (the *wahre Gegenwart* of the addressee) in which the dream-narrative is couched. Secondly, in the very act of exposing its irreality, the dream also intensifies the fictiveness that constituted its dream-like nature in the first place. Thirdly, the lovers' mystical union that already constituted the suspension of their individuality is here suspended by a mock address, which as the suspension of suspension prolongs what it interrupts. The result of this suspension to the second degree is an increasing synthesis of self-consciousness and unconscious rapture on the part of the lover whose voyeuristic-critical gaze elevates his *jouissance* to the *jouissance* of *jouissance*.[34] His is a self-conscious pleasure (or in Schlegel's words, an intellectual intuition) the intensity of which could be expressed only through a sudden switch to an epistolary address: "Du bist so außerordentlich klug, liebste Lucinde" (8) [You're so extraordinarily clever, my dearest Lucinde (44)]. As the unity of praxis (the writing "I") and reflection (the reading "you") the address is, indeed, the intoxicating suspension or, if you wish, the textual pleasure par excellence. As is the realization that all that is being said is merely a dream: "dies alles sei nur ein schöner Traum" (8) [all this is nothing but a beautiful dream (44)]. For in this realization, Julius's epistolary discourse is eating its tale or tail by validating an illusion that, if confirmed, invalidates the truth of the discourse by which it is uttered. Thus, at every stage of Julius's awakening the reader is alerted to the pervasiveness of the fictiveness or figuring powers that produce it. We are never given the freedom, that is, to decide what is truth and what is fiction, what is autobiographical and what is hallucinatory. The text reflects as it proceeds, and it is in this impossible or fantastic objectivity that Lucinde's *wahre Gegenwart* arises.

We have reached the completion of the letter, that is, the moment in which the story coincides with the epistolary utterance at its origin. Hence the return to the opening lines: "[D]er Morgen verdient allerdings schön genannt zu werden, die Luft ist still und warm genug, auch ist das Grün hier vor mir ganz frisch" (8) [The morning certainly deserves to be called beautiful: the air is still and quite warm, the grass before me brilliantly green (44)]. The natural surroundings that were previously part of Julius's vision are now recuperated in their "reality": "Das Wahre an der Sache ist, daß ich vorhin am Fenster stand . . . Also ich stand am Fenster und sah ins Freie" (8) [The truth of the matter is that just now I was standing by the window . . . And so I was standing by the open window, looking out into the open (44)]. What concerns us here, however, is not so much Julius's insistence on his perception of reality—a perception (*Wahr-nehmung*, the capturing of truth) that stands in radical contrast to the hallucination at the opening of the letter—as the way in which that so-called reality stages a repetition of what came before. For if it illustrates any "reality" at all, then it is the reality of the text and, by extension, the manner in which the final portion of the letter is the result of the text's self-production. Julius's description, then, serves to expose the "reality" or autonomy of his fantasy as much as it functions to discard as unreal what was written before. Of course, the two gestures are interrelated and in their dramatization of fictiveness serve to convey the continuity (the life) of the illusion as well as the illusion of continuity.

The truth of the matter is, thus, that the end of Julius's letter—in its return to the opening lines—not only provides us with a model for *actualizing* what is merely hallucinatory, but also offers us a way in which to read the preceding dream and, indeed, to reread our own interpretation of it. It goes without saying that we are made to witness the necessary incompletion of all attempts at interpretation, including our own. At the supreme moment of understanding the reader finds herself excluded from the text, which becomes more and more autonomous, more illusory, more self-referential. How else, then, could Julius communicate this moment of deepest insight if not in the form of a yearning for a delicate balance between reader and text, beloved and lover. How else could his perceptiveness affirm itself if not in the form of a *clairvoyant* gaze ("ich sah ins Freie") that misses its focus and slips into an hallucinatory vision of the movement of the text:

> . . . und wie sich die weite Ebne bald hebt bald senket, so windet sich der ruhige, breite silberhelle Strom in großen Schwüngen und Bogen, bis er und die Fantasie des Liebenden, die sich gleich dem Schwane auf ihm wiegte, in die Ferne hinziehen und sich in das Unermeßliche langsam verlieren. (8)
>
> [. . . and the silvery stream, broad and quiet, winds its way—like the gentle rise and fall of the open plains—in great swinging arcs into the distance, bearing with it, as it slowly disappears into infinity, the imagination of the lover that rocks itself like a swan on its waters. (44)]

With the end of the metaphor we have reached the end of Julius's literal return to the opening scene of both the letter and the prologue (remember Leda and the swan)—and the vision of the beloved that it entails—and the text slips back into a reflection on the here and now: "Den Hain und sein südliches Kolorit verdankt meine Vision wahrscheinlich dem großen Blumenhaufen *hier neben mir* . . ." (8, my emphasis) [The visionary grove and its southerly coloration were probably induced by the sizable heap of flowers and oranges lying (*here*) *next to me* (45, my emphasis)]. Inspired by Julius's immediate context—the flowers and oranges beside him—the letter's fictive autonomy arises as a parody of the organic unity of its natural surroundings. But we already knew that much: this is a writing in search of its own *Gattung,* in the sense of genre and self-generation. Its development is also a quest for origins that would guarantee the unified (organic) progression in the first place. A parody of organic or autobiographical unity the man's narrative stages a *still life* in a literal and figural sense: one through which the story of Julius's life "stills" and portrays itself in a writing that is neither fact nor fantasy, neither text nor context, but the staging of their confusion—Julius's vision of Lucinde's *wahre Gegenwart.* Perhaps we can now begin to understand the "nature" of Lucinde's presence.

Dear Lucinde

The loving union that Lucinde's *wahre Gegenwart* guarantees, and that as we remember can be expressed only by the address, must now be written to Lucinde. Or rather had to be written, and even should have been written in the first letter, if not for that unspeakable, disagreeable chance occurrence that interrupted

Julius's profound feelings and tender ideas, and his intention to describe the *dramatischer Zusammenhang unsrer Umarmungen.* But, as Julius tells us, this second letter will do nothing less than seek compensation for what was left out of the previous one by providing a concrete form to the contingency that had made that concretization impossible. The *Zufall,* we learn, is indeed to be woven into the narrative fabric of this letter and, more specifically, into its "charming confusion" and deliberate lack of unity:

> Wäre es nun auch die Form, so würde dieser in seiner Art einzige Brief dadurch eine unerträgliche Einheit und Einerleiheit erhalten und nicht mehr können, was er doch will und soll: das schönste Chaos von erhabnen Harmonien und interessanten Genüssen nachbilden und ergänzen. (9)
>
> [If this were also the case with its (the letter's) form, then this unique letter would gain an intolerable unity and monotony and be incapable of doing what it wants and must: to imitate and complete the most beautiful chaos of sublime harmonies and interesting pleasures. (My translation)]

The most beautiful chaos of sublime harmonies and pleasures—meant to present the disruptive power of the *Zufall*—refers, of course, to the "dramatic cohesion of the lovers' embrace" and thus to that which the *Zufall* had made impossible to represent. It is curious, then, that this letter portrays the sexual union of the two lovers while it originally intended to picture the *Zufall* that had invalidated that portrayal in the first letter. The text is, then, more and less than simply an evocation of chance. No sooner does Julius intend to shape the chance that interrupted his previous intention (to describe their love) than he misses again, and what should have been a portrayal of chance becomes a representation of love. The two, of course, are not simply distinguishable. For how else could one shape chance if not through the presentation of that which chance had left unshaped? This ironic synthesis of chance and love—the fact that love arises in the breakdown (the shaping) of chance and vice versa—leads us back to our analysis of the ironic interdependence of love and art: the artistic expression of love was then considered to be possible because of the otherness inherent in the structure of love, while the love between Julius and Lucinde was said to be based on their communal interest in art. With this in mind, we can redefine the dynamics of this letter as the depiction of the suspension—or indeed the chance occurrence—within love: it is a moment in which is anchored the appearance of absence, the event of the non-event. The figural.

In his *Literary Notebooks*, Schlegel explicitly identifies *Zufall* with the process of poetic production: "Der wahre Zufall ist synthetisch; genialische Situazionen. Das Genie, die constitutive Macht in der P[oesie], das absolut setzende Vermögen, treibt sein Spiel recht in [dem] ph[ilosophischen] R[oman]"[35] [True chance is synthetic; situations of genius. The genius, the constitutive power in p(oetry), the absolute positing ability, plays its game right in (the) ph(ilosophical) n(ovel) (my translation)]. Chance as the arrival of interruption or of the non-event is the epitome of *Einbildungskraft*. At once creative and destructive, chance provides the ironic ingenuity necessary to hold together what is incompatible. It is an energy capable of denying the unity of what has been created by showing its duplicity. What Julius wants to achieve in his lacing of chance at the heart of his narrative is thus the conscious recognition of his limits.

In the face of this synthesis of beautiful unity and sublime chaos we are reminded of Lucinde's *wahre Gegenwart* as the presentation of plurality (of dream and autobiography, Lucinde and Julius). That the force of chance is inextricably intertwined with the absent presence of the beloved is clearly illustrated by Julius's insistence on the use of his "incontestable right to confusion" in order to better represent and thus control that particular moment in which Lucinde, by chance, had disappeared from her room:

> Ich gebrauche also mein unbezweifeltes Verwirrungsrecht und setze oder stelle hier ganz an die unrechte Stelle eines von den vielen zerstreuten Blättern die ich aus Sehnsucht und Ungeduld, wenn ich dich nicht fand wo ich dich am gewissesten zu finden hoffte, in deinem Zimmer, auf unserm Sofa, mit der zuletzt von dir gebrauchten Feder, mit den ersten den besten Worten, so jene mir eingegeben, anfüllte oder verdarb, und die du Gute, ohne daß ich es wußte, sorgsam bewahrtest. Die Auswahl wird mir nicht schwer. (9)
>
> [I'm making use, therefore, of my incontestable right to confusion and am inserting here—in quite the wrong place—one of the many scattered pages I wrote or scribbled on when I longed for you impatiently and couldn't find you where I thought you must be, in your room, on our sofa—these pages

> I wrote with a pen you'd just used, and filled with the first words that came to mind and which you kindly and without my knowing it carefully preserved. It's not hard for me to make a selection. (45–46)]

Given the fact that chance had already been associated with the disruptive power within love, it comes as no surprise that it is now likened to the otherness or absence of the beloved. Lucinde's *wahre Gegenwart,* grounded as it is in the presentation of absence, is the figure of *Zufall.* It now remains to be seen in what way her chance absence, and Julius's *unbezweifeltes Verwirrungsrecht* that goes with it, finds its expression in the letter before us.

In a strangely dislocating movement Julius proclaims that he inserts *here totally in the wrong place* one of the many scattered pages that he once wrote—with her pen—out of yearning for his beloved. His "right to confusion" thus seems to find its concretization in the radical disjunction between the indexical sign *here* and the instant of discourse that it denotes. Sign and reality or *Scriptum* and *Faktum* do not coincide. The text that occurs *here* really took place elsewhere. *Here* is the wrong place as much as *this* text points to another text, one that was written in the past but that will not be disclosed until the dithyrambic fantasy that follows. Thus, what *this* letter denotes is nothing more than the transition from the past to the future, from the previous fragment to the one to come. Or one might say that in contrast to Julius's insistence on confusion, *this* letter represents the narrator's active gathering (*gatten, gattieren,* to assemble) and ordering of pieces: the arbitrary selection of the page, the gap that it leaves behind in the *zerstreute Blätter* and its subsequent insertion *here* in *this* document. The letter's position in the novel is, then, simply provisional and indicative of the text that we are about to read: the dithyrambic fantasy, originally written when Julius could not find the beloved where he had hoped to find her. Here, as in the first letter, the text seems to herald its own past and future production. What is more, this self-generation captures not so much the unity of the text as the *Zufall* disrupting any claim at unity, and the absent Lucinde as the "origin" of that interruption. What is here conveyed is the text's unceasing construction of coherence out the *repetitive derangement* associated with Lucinde's absence: the text that once represented the dislocation of and concomitant desire for the beloved now indicates the displacement of and yearning for the ("original") text itself. So, if there is any self-generation in this text it is the self-reproduction of an originary moment of *dislocation* and thus of that which makes it impossible to speak of "autonomy" or "self-positing" in the first place. But then again, as was stated before, repeating the illusion of self-generation is just another way of affirming the continuity of the fiction before us. Be that as it may, one thing is certain: the proliferation of transfers *here* enacted results in an increasing decontextualization of the beloved whose absence is now omnipresent. Indeed, the transfer between this letter and the previous one—one of increasing objectification of absence—further develops the relation between the absent beloved and the fragmentary pages to which she gave rise, and the subsequent removal of the original scattered pages to the present novel. What emerges from this is a mosaic of representations that, through a series of arbitrary transpositions, supplant each other in order to better preserve the chance moment of their inspiration: the absence of the beloved. The arbitrariness of Julius's composition, to the extent that it is organized around its remote source of inspiration, becomes suspicious at best.[36] No sooner does Julius relinquish the motivation of his production than the *Zufall* is recuperated in a deliberately construed artifact whose disorderly layers of texts figure a cohesion of opposites: the unity of Julius's *right* to confusion and the *chance* absence of the beloved. It is left to the dithyrambic fantasy to illustrate how this synthesis of system (Julius) and chaos (Lucinde) makes present what has here been left out: the physical cohesion of the lovers or Lucinde's *wahre Gegenwart.*

◇

Dear reader, we are taking a lot of chances trying to reach an agreement on Schlegel. That is the essence, the being, the copula of our relationship: chancing copulation. Without it—without wit—we chance Blanchot's désastre.[37]

Love Shapes: Lucinde's Matrix

As pointed out before, Julius's dithyrambic fantasy hinges upon a series of chance dislocations or *Entfernung[en]*:[38] the absence of the beloved and the circulation of fragments that the absence inspires. Thus, to the extent that the fantasy marks the transference between the *zerstreute Blätter*, the two preceding letters and the document before us, *das heilige Blatt* signals the history of its (re)production. Julius's dithyramb is, more specifically, a

Dionysian hymn in honor of the fabric of textual production, insofar as this is reflected by the movement of sexual reproduction.[39] The most beautiful situation in the most beautiful world is the one in which the text that unites copy and original(s)—the fragment as loss of the original and space of reproduction—aestheticizes its inherent plurality into a celebration of physical love.

What is in question is, once again, the relation between art and love, textuality and sexuality, *Lucinde* and Lucinde. Once again, the beloved appears as the mistress of Julius's linguistic self. Once again, she transforms their unity into an intimation of her lover's imaginative productivity; that is, ultimately of the texts that are past and still to follow. Julius confesses that much when he exclaims:

> Ein große Träne fällt auf das heilige Blatt, welches ich hier statt deiner fand. Wie treu und wie einfach hast du ihn aufgezeichnet, den kühnen alten Gedanken zu meinem liebsten und geheimsten Vorhaben. In dir ist er groß geworden und in diesem Spiegel scheue ich mich nicht, mich selbst zu bewundern und zu lieben. (10)
>
> [A large tear falls on this sacred page that I've found here in place of you. How honestly and simply you've expressed the old, daring thought of my most cherished and secret intention. In you it's come to fruition and I'm not afraid to admire and love myself in such a mirror. (46)]

The "original design" (*Aufzeichnung*, sketch, "matrix" might be a more appropriate term) *that Lucinde, as absent source of inspiration, is said to have woven into the text* is the one that prevents the novel from being too easily closed off as a unified whole. Its "presence" thus speaks of incompletion. It is the man's *Einbildungskraft*, which, as the originating projection of consciousness in its reflection, is predicated on a radical involution. Because of this transformative-reflexive character of her nature, Lucinde first makes her appearance—or disappearance—in the form of a page that Julius happens to find "in place of you." It is a page the tangibility of which is first affirmed by Julius when he says that it reflects her spirit—as well as his—in a well-defined and perfected way: "Denn auch dein Geist steht bestimmt und vollendet vor mir; es sind nicht mehr Züge die erscheinen und zerfließen: sondern wie eine von den Gestalten, die ewig dauern, blickt er mich aus hohen

Augen freudig an und öffnet die Arme, den meinigen zu umschließen" (10) [For your spirit, too, stands well defined and perfected before me; no longer does it consist of features that appear and melt away. No: like one of those (shapes) that live forever, your spirit looks at me joyfully through noble eyes and opens its arms to embrace me (46, modified translation)]. But no sooner does Julius insist on the well-defined nature of Lucinde's appearance, than it becomes all but clear whether the "shape" here referred to takes its defined substance from the page itself, or from the inscription thereof. Does she appear *as* or *on* the page? The ambiguity is only one in a series of doublings here presented under the cover of an everlasting, durable *Gestalt*, whose reflexive nature we can describe as follows: Julius's mind is reflected in Lucinde, who in turn is reflected by the (scattered) page, which finds its reflection in Julius's convoluted writing. Whereas Julius appears to constitute the origin and end of the series of reflections, it will soon become clear that things are not that simple and that the distinctions here set up—Julius, Lucinde, page, text—cannot hold in the face of Lucinde's ever shifting, omnipresent absence.

That Julius and Lucinde are hardly separable in their (or her) *Gestalt* is due to the fact that Lucinde takes her shape from the productive powers of Julius's imagination as much as the latter is *inspired by the chance disappearance of the beloved.* Indeed, upon his confrontation with the fact of Lucinde's disappearance from the room, Julius remembers the illusion he once cherished: "Ja! ich würde es für ein Märchen gehalten haben, daß es solche Freude gebe und solche Liebe, wie ich nun fühle, und eine solche Frau, die mir zugleich die zärtlichste Geliebte und die beste Gesellschaft wäre und auch eine vollkommene Freundin" (10) [Yes: I would have thought it a fairy tale that there could be such happiness and such love as I feel now—and such a woman, at once the most delicate lover, the most wonderful companion, and the most perfect friend (47)].

Thus, no sooner is Lucinde's presence an illusion than the man recalls thinking the existence of such a woman a mere fairy tale (*ein Märchen*), than the thought or illusion (the two cannot be dissociated) transforms itself into a "real" dithyrambic fantasy. We could say that Lucinde's "actual" absence and the impression it leaves on the lover puts into motion a series of illusions, all of which are here united on the page before us. The final format of the page, in other words, is the result of the ever growing impression Lucinde's absence has left on Julius. Transformed as she is from a "real" absence into the "presence" of this text, Lucinde's *Gestalt*—as page or text, Julius or Lucinde—holds together the flow of time as well as the series of images or characters it generates. The "design" that she was said to have inscribed in the text and that we have now defined as "impression" cannot be confined to any particular moment or to any specific place.

It should be clear by now that the dislocation of the fantasy, which began with the writing of the two preceding letters, is spreading itself to a point where the production of the novel coincides with a continuous derailment: the page originally written in a context determined by the absent Lucinde (the *zerstreute Blätter*) here appears, via a number of detours in time (e.g., Julius's memories) and space (e.g., the previous letters) in the context of *Lucinde*. *We can thus further define the "design" of Lucinde* as the growth of Julius's impression *insofar as this reflects the growth of the context*—that is, the absence of Lucinde—which originated the impression in the first place, although admittedly in a very provisional, incomplete way. The development from the original context to the present one (*Lucinde*) is characterized by a growing synthesis of text and context, Julius and Lucinde, the confessions of Julius and the portrait of *Lucinde*. More particularly, we could say that on the one hand the development involves an increasing concretization (textualization) of an originally ephemeral context (Lucinde's absence), on the other hand that it implies a shift—as was already pointed out—from a "real" absence to an illusory-fantastic one. The more Lucinde's absence becomes "well defined," the more it is turned into a mere fantasy. After all, what is essentially absent (or context) can be made present (text) only at the risk of an irreparable distortion.

Julius realizes that much as he alternatively moves to hyperbolic heights of exaltation: "Die flüchtigsten und heiligsten von jenen zarten Zügen und Äußerungen der Seele, die dem, welcher das Höchste nicht kennt, allein schon Seligkeit scheinen, sind nur die gemeinschaftliche Atmosphäre unsers geistigen Atmens und Lebens" (10) [The slightest and holiest of those fragile features and expressions of the soul that seem like bliss to those who don't know the greatest joy are merely the everyday atmosphere of our spiritual breath and life (46)]. Only to fall back into a self-critical mode of discourse that annihilates the possibility of ever reaching a harmony between text and context, "I" and "you:" "Die Worte sind matt und trübe" (10) [These words are dull and turbid (46)]. Ironically, it is exactly in the man's failure to fully express his intention (i.e., Lucinde as the object of that intention) that he is offered the opportunity to transform this intention into an "ever living" flow of ideas and an infinite movement of creative rebirth:

> . . . auch würde ich in diesem Gedränge von Erscheinungen nur immer das eine unerschöpfliche Gefühl unsrer ursprünglichen Harmonie von neuem wiederholen müssen. Eine große Zukunft winkt mich eilends weiter ins Unermeßliche hinaus, jede Idee öffnet ihren Schoß und entfaltet sich in unzähliche neue Geburten. (10)
>
> [Still, amid this throng of impressions I can do no more than repeat and repeat forevermore the single inexhaustible feeling of our pristine harmony. A great future beckons me to rush deeper into infinity: every idea opens its womb and brings forth innumerable new births. (46–47)]

Lucinde as the unpresentable figure of Julius's poetic inspiration alters what her maternal womb (*Schoß*) brings forth, destroying ideas only to produce other ideas, de-creating Julius only to carry him into an immeasurable (*unermeßlich*) reproduction. Julius's self-creation, then, succeeds in the repetition of its blunders. *That is, indeed, the "inner design" that Lucinde has inserted into the textual arabesque:* hers is an inner coherence that can be given substance only through a repetitive outlining and dissolution of form. What Julius's narrative reveals is the continuity of its interruption out of which arises as much the "life" of the text as the "life" of the context that gives the text a preliminary form.

This problematic coincidence of text and context also instigates the novel's sexual allegory. The continuous suspension of the man's inscriptions by Lucinde's absence can be considered as the moments in which he "successfully" captures or penetrates her evanescent body. At the same time, these ruptures initiate a deviation that reduces the confessions to a mere fantasy: they turn the autobiography into something radically different, an allegory of sexual love. The novel now completes what the previous letter set out to do: to represent the *dramatischer Zusammenhang unsrer Umarmungen* that had been left out.

In reality, this is the "inner design" Lucinde represents: the performance of the two lovers as it arises in Lucinde's continuous interruption of Julius's confessions of love. However, we should not be mistaken about the immediacy of pleasure that this might seem to involve. For nothing is less true. Let us after all not forget that their cohesion is an *appearance* in the full sense of the word, their sexual activity no more than an *act*:

> [S]o ist uns die witzigste unter den Gestalten und Situationen der Freude auch die schönste. Eine unter allen ist die witzigste und die schönste: wenn wir die Rollen vertauschen und mit kindischer Lust wetteifern, wer den andern täuschender nachäffen kann, ob dir die schonende Heftigkeit des Mannes besser gelingt, oder mir die anziehende Hingebung des Weibes. Aber weißt du wohl, daß dieses süße Spiel für mich noch ganz andre Reize hat als seine eignen? Es ist auch nicht bloß die Wollust der Ermattung oder das Vorgefühl der Rache. Ich sehe hier eine wunderbare sinnreich bedeutende Allegorie auf die Vollendung des Männlichen und Weiblichen zur vollen ganzen Menschheit. Es liegt viel darin, und was darin liegt, steht gewiß nicht so schnell auf wie ich, wenn ich dir unterliege. (12–13)

> [(T)herefore the wittiest of all the shapes and situations of happiness is for us also the loveliest. One above all is wittiest and most beautiful: when we exchange roles and in childish high spirits compete to see who can mimic the other more convincingly, whether you are better at imitating the protective intensity of the man, or I the appealing devotion of the woman. But are you aware that this sweet game still has quite other attractions for me than its own—and not simply the voluptuousness of exhaustion or the anticipation of revenge? I see here a wonderful, deeply meaningful allegory of the development of man and woman to full and complete humanity. There is much in it—and what is in it certainly doesn't rise up as quickly as I do when I am overcome by you. (49)]

It leaves no doubt that the performative quality of the love scene parodies Julius's dithyrambic fantasy insofar as this stages the ongoing disruption by Lucinde's absence and insofar as, because of this, the unity of Julius's text is above all a *dramatischer Zusammenhang*. The unity of love, it seems, is as much a con as is the unified *Gestalt* of the page before us. That is, in fact, what constitutes the cohesion of love, this unity with its other—art—with which it shares the impossibility of unity. To perform love, exchange roles, and play at being lovers is to bring together love and art in their mutual exclusion and, in the same breath, stage the impossible incipience of Julius's artistic discourse of love.

In contrast to Julius's claim that the allegory is about the perfection of humanity—a view that has been mistakenly advocated by a host of Schlegel critics after him—the final scene of the dithyrambic fantasy is less about ideal love than it is about Julius's representative act in its fullest sense. At the same time however, the allegory—insisting as it does on making present the writing that is both presence and absence, praxis and reflection—is itself pervaded by absence or incompletion. Because of this, we might think of the final line ("There is much in it . . .") of the allegory—also the end of the fantasy—as annihilating what came before, namely, Julius's insistence on the presence of allegorical meaning ("I see here a wonderful, deeply meaningful allegory"). By thus destroying the seriousness of the allegory, the closing line rejects any claims at closure (cohesion) and instead re-affirms the only valid thing to do: the reduction of the allegory and of love to a playful reversal of roles between top and bottom, or surface and depth. Whatever much is "in" the text stands "up" nearly as fast as Julius when he is lying "underneath."

If, as the final scene suggests, the content of the allegory also lies "on top"—on the surface—then we need to explore this interdependence of *Geist* and *Buchstabe* a little further. But in order to better grasp this interaction between content and form, let us turn to those other letters that Julius writes to Lucinde much later in the novel and in which he offers her a possible reading of the *Geist-Buchstabe* dynamics of his text:

> Heute fand ich in einem französischen Buche von zwei Liebenden den Ausdruck: "Sie waren einer dem andern das Universum."—Wie fiel mir's auf, rührend und zum Lächeln, daß, was da so gedankenlos stand, bloß als eine Figur der Übertreibung, in uns buchstäblich wahr geworden sei! Eigentlich ist's zwar auch für so eine französische Passion buchstäblich wahr. Sie finden das Universum einer in dem andern, weil sie den Sinn für alles andre verlieren. Nicht so wir. Alles, was wir sonst liebten, lieben wir nun noch wärmer. Der Sinn für die Welt ist uns erst recht aufgegangen. Du hast durch mich die Unendlichkeit des menschlichen Geistes kennen gelernt, und ich habe durch dich die Ehe und das Leben begriffen, und die Herrlichkeit aller Dinge. Alles ist beseelt für mich, spricht zu mir und alles ist heilig . . . und was für andre

> nur etwas ist, dessen sie sich mit Recht schämen müssen, wird für uns wieder, was es an und für sich ist, das reine Feuer der edelsten Lebenskraft. (67)
>
> [Today I found in a French book this statement about two lovers: "They were the universe to each other." It struck me—and I was moved and smiled at the idea—how something that had been set down so thoughtlessly as hyperbole had become literally true with us! Actually it's also literally true for this kind of French passion. They discover the universe in each other because they've lost their sense for everything else. We haven't. Everything that we loved before, we love even more warmly now. It's only now that a feeling for the world has really dawned on us. You've come to know the infinity of the human spirit through me, and I've come to understand marriage and life, and the magnificence of all things through you. For me everything has a soul, speaks to me, and is holy . . . and what for others is only something about which they're justifiably ashamed becomes for us again what it is in and of itself: the pure flame of the noblest life force. (113)]

It is beyond doubt that the idea of love—the lovers are the universe to each other—is here being played out in the confusing vacillations between *Buchstabe* and *Figur*, but what exactly these terms stand for, and if they stand for anything other than each other, is less than clear. Indeed, the premise of a clear-cut difference can hardly be sustained in the face of Schlegel's theory that the philosophical *Geist* takes place in its absolute other, the poetical *Buchstabe*, and that their impossible unity affirms itself as a rhetorical-philosophical *figure* of speech: irony.[40] In Schlegel's view, the interdependence of *Buchstabe* and *Geist* is such that the latter presents itself through the former in a fragmentary way. The act in which the *Geist* posits itself is also an act of criticism that destroys what has been achieved and, in this fragmentation of the material letter, points up its essence: that it is unreal and a work of the imagination. In this annihilating gesture—in which, according to Schlegel, the spirit is negatively "compared" to the letter—the artist gives way to a critic who understands the creator better than he understood himself: "K[ritik] ist eigentlich nichts als Vergleichung des Geistes und des Buchstabens eines Werks, welches als *Unendliches*, als Absolutum und Individuum behandelt wird.-Kritisiren heißt einen Autor besser verstehn als er sich selbst verstanden hat"[41] [C(riticism) is actually nothing but a comparison between the spirit and the letter of a work, which is treated as *infinite*, as absolute and individual.- To criticize means to understand an author better than he has understood himself (my translation)].

Surely the gesture with which the critic destroys the work (*Buchstabe*) only to declare that he understands its *Geist* better than the artist himself is a *Figur der Übertreibung* at best. For how could one claim to possess insight in the midst of chaos, if not with an ironic smile that warns us not to take the claim seriously. In an act whose structure is that of a literally hyperbolic destruction—and it is literally hyperbolic because it transforms (Greek *hyperballein*: to throw over, to excel, to exaggerate, to traverse, to double) the original into a multiplicity of fragments—any claim at "truth" could be an exaggeration (a figural hyperbole) at best. Julius's attempt, in the long passage just quoted, to understand the French Book better than itself enacts this literal and figural status of criticism.

It is indeed Julius's aim to illustrate how, for himself and Lucinde, the expression "They were the universe to each other"—characteristic as it is of the hyperbolic nature of love—is more than simply a figure of speech. If the hyperbole has become literally true for them—as the man claims but not without an ironic smile ("rührend und zum Lächeln")—then of course that *Buchstäblichkeit* needs to be demonstrated. Julius offers two ways in which the *Figur der Übertreibung* can become literally true. First of all, in what he calls "French passion": the physical *Übertreibung* or orgasmic annihilation through which the two lovers literally lose their sense of reality and find themselves transported into a mystical union. Secondly, in the spiritual love between Julius and Lucinde, through which both discover rather than lose their sense of reality. In contrast to French love, German love is first and foremost a matter of *Bildung* through which the two lovers are literally the universe to each other because they gain a better understanding of the world in their love. As we know, for Julius this spiritual education results in the perfection of his art and ultimately in the novel before us. Here, in this text, their physical and spiritual love has taken on the form of a *literal Buchstabe*. What was previously designated as *Buchstabe*—their physical (French) and spiritual (German) love—becomes merely figural in the light of this all too literal letter of Julius's text. But is it all that literal? After all, the text (*Buchstabe*) before us is characterized by a series of (self-)reflections on the nature of *buchstäbliche* truth; reflections that, furthermore, prove to be untenable in the face of Julius's conclusions that the true *Buchstabe*—the truth of the letter—belongs to nature, "das heiligste Wunder der Natur." (This of course reminds us of Schlegel's belief that the ideal *Buchstabe* had only been achieved once, namely, in Greek *Naturpoesie*, and that the rest of literary history was no more than an attempt to restore that unity on a higher level of reflection.)[42]

If Julius's text is the literal counterpart to the French *Figur der Übertreibung* it is because, in its self-critical progression toward the final revelation that only nature can be truly *buchstäblich*, it literally enacts the *Übertreibung*. The result is, however, that the text ironizes itself as it is posited and in this manner reduces Julius's claim ("for us the hyperbolic nature of love is literally true") to a mere *Figur der Übertreibung*. The text is split, it seems, between what it intends to do—to show the opposition between the French and Julius's book, between the figural and the literal hyperbole—and what it actually does: to reiterate the French *Figur*. In its incapacity to keep the literal and the figural separate, Julius's argument about the literal quality of their love *is* an exaggeration: *Geist* and *Buchstabe*, love and letters, can be compared only at the risk of a hyperbole.[43]

In order to avoid any further exaggeration, we should perhaps return to Julius's fantasy and show how this text-*Buchstabe* literalizes the spirit of love—a *Geist* which in this case is that of the absent beloved ("Denn auch dein Geist steht bestimmt und vollendet vor mir"). The following passage will be crucial for our analysis:

> . . . so ist uns die witzigste unter den Gestalten und die Situationen der Freude auch die schönste. Eine unter allen ist die witzigste und die schönste: wenn wir die Rollen vertauschen und mit kindischer Lust wetteifern, wer den andern täuschender nachäffen kann, ob dir die schonende Heftigkeit des Mannes besser gelingt, oder mir die anziehende Hingebung des Weibes. (12, the English translation appears on p. 96)

Syntactically, the passage is overdetermined by a flow of subordinate clauses (hypotaxis)—"wenn wir die Rollen vertauschen . . . und . . . wetteifern, wer den andern . . . ob dir . . . oder mir . . ."—in a hierarchical system that is ironically marked by the distance of the main clause or phrase that would give this construction its unity. A distance signaled firstly by the colon separating the two syntactic levels, "Eine unter allen ist die witzigste und die schönste:" (12); and secondly by the elision, in this main clause, of the

"Gestalt und Situation," both of which constitute the antecedents that the (adnominal) subclauses modify. The full construction would have been: "Eine unter allen ist die witzigste und die schönste *Gestalt (und Situation)*." The double dislocation of *Gestalt* thus grammatically articulated might well be considered as the reason why the exchange of roles ("wenn wir, wer den andern, ob dir, oder mir") falls back into a "dangling" syntactic performance without an interior design (*Gestalt*). Indeed, what the grammatical structure (or positioning) articulates is the *literal* absence of the *Gestalt*, the presence of which would turn this open-ended order of words or *Buchstabe* into a meaningful whole. In fact, we might say that the syntax negatively presents the absent *Gestalt*, at least insofar as the dislocation of the latter (as superordinate antecedent holding the syntactical hierarchy together) coincides with the collapse of hypotaxis into parataxis, subordination into conjunction, order into disorder.

The play on Lucinde's *Gestalt* cannot be missed. It is Schlegel's translation of the (absent) *Geist* of the beloved into form or *Buchstabe*. Not that Lucinde's ephemeral shape could be mastered by anything as concrete as word order. That is, indeed, the point of the preceding analysis: the struggle between text and context, which was said to constitute the duplicity of the fantastic genre, also ruptures any attempt at syntactical ordering. Lucinde's ever changing *Gestalt* spreads itself on an increasingly concrete and fragmentary scale. The result is, on the one hand, a reduction of the lovers' vertiginous exchange of *positions* (top-bottom) to an allegory of the syntactical *positing* of words; on the other hand, a doubling of the *buchstäbliche* word order into a vision of the *Gestalt* of Lucinde as it hovers over her lover's self-portrait and re-arranges it into a most daring picture of love.

Dear reader, I see before me the bewildered reflections of your eyes. In them I assemble a multitude of forms with which I wreathe the turmoil of our love. Above me your trembling breath as your right hand runs along the edges of my body. Underneath the soft touch of your left hand. Together your hands outline the content of my existence. Spinning round. Constructing a system. Here we make sense. Here we oppose the chaos of time . . . Until you turn the last page of our lives, and thrust me aside. Picking another book, you leave me nothing but a white margin of indifference.

A Portrait of the Artist as a Little Girl

Julius's *Charakteristik* of the little Wilhelmine is an attempt—on the part of the lover—to illustrate to Lucinde the reason behind his repetitive blunders, namely, the fact that as an individual he belongs to the clumsiest of all "races": the male gender (at least, that is what Julius claims). However, since he does not want to be associated with masculinity in general, his apology will present nothing less than a portrait of an individual, Wilhelmine, who although or maybe *because* she belongs to the opposite sex will better exemplify his point: being of the male gender, Julius suffers from impertinence and clumsiness, including the insolence to portray himself as a little girl.

Julius's apology thus confronts us with a curious, multiple duplicity: as a portrait of masculinity, it offers a picture of femininity; as a representation of the male *Gattung* (whole), it draws out the individual (part); as a character sketch of Julius, it conjures up Wilhelmine; although a defense of his masculine nature, it permits Julius to dissociate himself from it; although an apology for his clumsiness, it also allows Julius to repeat his errors. In a sense, one could claim that this is indeed the essence of the text, this representation of the whole (*Gattung*, the male gender) through a misrepresentation, which, in its enactment of error, captures what is so typically male: clumsiness and audacity. How and to what extent the characteristics of this text and those of Julius's masculinity are intertwined need to be explored in greater detail.

What, then, is a *Charakteristik*? Schlegel's *Literary Notebooks* define it as follows: "Die Charakteristik ein kr[itischer] Mimus"[44] [The characteristic a cr(itical) miming/farce (my translation)]. Or again: "Die Charakteristik ist eine eigne specifisch verschiedene Gattung, deren Ganzheit nicht historisch sondern *kritisch* ist.- <Ein kritisches Kunstwerk.->"[45] [The characteristic is a particular, specifically distinct genre, whose wholeness is not historical but *critical*.- <A critical work of art.-> (my translation)]. A *Charakteristik* is an exemplary presentation which is itself characterized by the very features of the thing (or idea) to which it refers. A text, for instance, characterizes a genre when it has itself the properties characteristic of that genre. Presenting the general in a concrete and typical way, a *Charakteristik* is both typical and diverse: always different for always designating the essential properties in an immediate way.

To the extent that Julius's character sketch takes it upon itself to exemplify these characteristics of the *Charakteristik*, it illuminates both itself and the genre to which it belongs. A characterization of characterization, it imitates itself as standing for the genre of the *Charakteristik* as a whole. Its miming is, therefore, critical because never simply identical to what it imitates. At once *specifisch* and *Gattung*, this self-characterization projects the promise to be complete and identical to itself, as soon as practice and theory—this character sketch and the *Charakteristik* in general—are united. A *Charakteristik* is characteristically never finished. What it makes visible is the laws—or genre—by which it can be recognized as what it is. Julius might just as well have called this piece "a confession of a blunder" or the "impression of an absence." In fact, Schlegel suggests that much when elsewhere he states: "Zu der Char[akteristik] eines Menschen gehört auch der p[oetische] Eindruck den ein Mensch macht"[46] [Also belonging to the char(acteristic) of a human being is the p(oetic) impression that a human being makes (my translation)]. If anything, this maxim describes Julius's fictive character (or characteristics) as it arises from his confessions and the impressions they evoke within the reader. The confessions, as we know, themselves result from the loving impression that Lucinde has left on the young man. It is, therefore, not clear which impression "der poetische Eindruck den ein Mensch macht" stands for, or to whom "ein Mensch" may possibly refer: Julius or Lucinde. This indeterminacy, of course, belongs itself to the nature of the impression, at least insofar as this stands for the impossible unity of a sender and a receiver. Thus, to define Julius's *Charakteristik* in terms of an "impression"—the distinctive imprint—is once again to emphasize the sketchiness of his self-portrait.

Because of this interconnection between *Charakteristik* and impression, it comes as no surprise that Julius's portrayal of his clumsiness—the characteristic incapacity on the part of the masculine *Gattung* to be a unified whole, to be an unequivocal man—takes place in a literary genre that aims at shaping the reader's impression: the apology. Moreover, to characterize himself as a man, Julius has to outline the properties of his masculinity over and against the female reader. The success of his self-portrait depends on the degree to which he can sketch out—produce the imprint of—a man against the background of a woman. Thus, given that Julius's self-characterization cannot be separated from his attempt to exert a controlling hand over Lucinde's difference, we can even say that his apology is such that it wants to unite the characteristics of his masculinity and of this particular text with the female reader's criticism thereof. That is, after all, the characteristic of an excuse, this admission of an error by a self-critical subject in the face of the opponent who finds her judgment curiously prefigured—even transformed—in an act of self-forgiving. If Julius can combine his text with its critical perspective, then his blunder is at once excused in its characterization:

> Denn diese Charakteristik soll ja nichts darstellen als ein Ideal, welches ich mir stets vor Augen halten will, um in diesem kleinen Kunstwerke schöner und zierlicher Lebensweisheit nie von der zarten Linie des Schicklichen zu verirren, und dir, damit du alle die Freiheiten und Frechheiten, die ich mir noch zu nehmen denke, im voraus verzeihst, oder doch von einem höhern Standpunkte beurteilen und würdigen kannst. (15)
>
> [For this character sketch is supposed to portray nothing more than an ideal that I want to keep before me always, so as never to stray from the fine line of propriety in this little work of art, this work of lovely and elegant worldly wisdom; and to make you forgive me in advance for all the liberties and indelicacies I propose to take and commit; or at least to have you judge and appreciate them from a more elevated point of view. (52)]

The ideal which Julius has here presented and which he wants to keep before his own and Lucinde's eyes—the ideal as a unity of two visions, of text and criticism—serves two functions: it guarantees the proper character of the work of art and makes Lucinde a priori forgive the errors that are still to be portrayed. These two functions are, in fact, interrelated. For, as we have seen, the "proper character" of the work—its genre—is the *Charakteristik* staging its own characteristics. The "proper character" of this *Charakteristik* is, then, its lack of characteristics; the "proper" is the "improper," the incompleteness, the necessary error. Because this self-characterization by way of the improper is thus a necessity, the error is a priori admitted, and ultimately forgiven. Julius's guilt is annulled to the extent that he keeps the critical ideal before his eyes; to the extent that he is his own harshest critic and, accordingly, collates the beloved's perspective with his own.

And here lies the man's criminal twist: what the man is guilty of—and what cannot be excused without repeating the crime—is the dispossession of the reader. That is the unheard of error, unmentionable without becoming unheard, cancelled, or forgiven ("understood"). To speak in this way is to engage in the pleasures of self-projection (*verstehen*: to stand for [the reader]) or self-revelation, which Julius likens to Wilhelmine's shameless exhibitionism:[47]

> Und nun sieh! diese liebenswürdige Wilhelmine findet nicht selten ein unaussprechliches Vergnügen darin, auf dem Rücken liegend mit den Beinchen in die Höhe zu gestikulieren, unbekümmert um ihren Rock und um das Urteil der Welt. Wenn das Wilhelmine tut, was darf ich nicht tun, da ich doch bei Gott! ein Mann bin, und nicht zarter zu sein brauche wie das zarteste weibliche Wesen? (15)
>
> [And now look! This adorable little Wilhelmine quite often takes an inexpressible pleasure in lying on her back and kicking her legs up in the air, careless of her dress and the world's opinion. If Wilhelmine does that, what may I not do, since I am after all, by God, a man, and do not need to be more modest than the most modest of women! (52)]

The passage captures the link between Julius's confession of his blunder and his pleasurable desire to incorporate or eliminate the judgment of the outside world (Lucinde), which had instigated that confession in the first place. What the man aspires to is the sight Wilhelmine presents *auf dem Rücken liegend.* Ultimately this amounts to a total disregard for or annihilation of *Vorurteile.* Writing in this open—confessional—manner would imply that Julius blinds (or shocks) his audience and, by repelling it, gains an autonomy as powerful and pleasurable as the little girl's *Selbstzufriedenheit.* Eliminating the beloved reader, this text would achieve its ideal of self-characterization, in which the masculine gender posits nothing other than itself and becomes the only judge of its own activities.

The character sketch of Wilhelmine is thus less innocent than it appears to be. The text takes its substance from a peculiar turn or repression (of the error as of the female reader), which Julius ascribes to the *Ungeschicklichkeit* of the male gender, but which is perhaps much more disconcerting—or shocking—than that. For the reader finds herself altered, even incorporated, into a portrait of Wilhelmine. The text admits the violence of this transformation—maybe the result of Julius's resort to a different "order" of words, the order of the *Gattung* where part and whole are one in their fragmentation—when it describes the interaction between the artist and the world in terms of a literal decomposition:

> Ein himmlisches Lächeln blühte auf ihrem kleinen Gesichte und sie drückte gleich einen herzlichen Kuß auf die gefärbten Lippen von Holz. Gewiß! es liegt tief in der Natur des Menschen, daß er alles essen will, was er liebt, und jede neue Erscheinung unmittelbar zum Munde führt, um sie da wo möglich in ihre ersten Bestandteile zu zergliedern. (14)
>
> [A heavenly smile lit up her little face and immediately she pressed an affectionate kiss on the painted, wooden lips. Unquestionably there lies deeply rooted in the nature of man a desire to eat everything he loves and put every new object he encounters immediately into his mouth in order to break it down, if possible, into its primal constituents. (51)]

What the text (Wilhelmine) does to Lucinde and us readers is here presented as an act of destruction.[48] The nature of man—previously referred to as clumsiness—in the final analysis (*Zergliederung*) reveals itself as the annihilating powers of language, destroying the beloved object (the reader) only to leave it a shattered reflection of itself. Not unlike Wilhelmine digesting the world around her with a philosophical appetite (*gesunde Wißbegierde*), Julius's text possesses the force to "characterize" every appearance (*Erscheinung*) in its originary configuration (*ersten Bestandteile*), which is that of the contradictory unity between part and whole, text and context.

This is the story of our lives as critics: to be shaped and reshaped in our dramatic cohesion with a text that, for all its apparent clumsiness, takes on a life in our deaths. But let us not be confused about our own role in this tragedy of sorts. For if the reader finds herself penetrated or persuaded by Julius's speech, it is because she herself—in her downright grudge against the male species ("so habt ihr doch immer viel und vieles wider das Ganze der Gattung")—has engendered the conflict in the first place. Willing to assume the opposite stance, that of the passive beloved, she has actively participated in his crime. Hence Julius's self-righteous question: "Habe ich etwa unrecht, wenn ich die Sittlichkeit bei Kindern, Zartheit und Zierlichkeit in Gedanken und Worten vornehmlich beim weiblichen Geschlecht suche?" (15) [Am I wrong when I look for morality primarily in children, and for delicacy and elegance in word and thought primarily in women? (52)]. We know the answer already. Stereotyping the opposite sex as delicate and elegant, he wrongs both Lucinde and himself. The writer's error is exactly his insistence on portraying his masculinity in a rigid opposition to, and hegemony over, femininity. It is characteristically man's criminal blunder that he literally turns to an absent woman for a figurative answer to his questions.

According to the logic of the *Charakteristik*, this text exemplifies in microform the politics of representation characterizing *Lucinde* and, indeed, literature in general: man's desire for the whole is based on a conception of woman as absent. Moreover, since man's projection of his identity onto his surroundings subsumes all otherness as the living force of his creations, every moment of resistance on the part of the female reader becomes the occasion for furthering his self-aggrandizing masculine ego. This is what I identified in the introduction as the romantic "egotistical" sublime. It has been Schlegel's merit to self-consciously explore these patriarchal conventions of romantic literature in a novel that has as its theme the manner in which the subject's self-production is made possible by the objectification and the absenting (*Entfernung*) of the other. Needless to say, where a book explicitly reveals itself to be mediated by woman's absence, we are in for some critical reconsiderations of artistic representation. Julius's "Portrait of Little Wilhelmine" is one of those moments when the text most critically reflects on the conditions that have made the writing possible: not only the violence done to the female reader but also the ease with which women have cooperated in producing their own stereotypes constitute the focus of Julius's irony. "Am I to blame," he asks, "if I look for elegance and beauty among women?" The question is meant rhetorically: we know it offers him an excuse for continuing to write at the expense of the other sex. But it is through disruptive pauses like these that the surface of the text also gets broken and something else articulated. Beauty or art or, more specifically, this text turns out not to be without borders: it is governed by gender relations. In the same vein, man's creative freedom proves to be all but free from sexual stereotyping. Put simply: the universal is not without gender. For Schlegel it is overtly androgynous.[49] Hence his play on *Gattung*, which means both genre and (female or male) species. When in Wilhelmine Julius explicitly exemplifies the masculine whole as feminine, he is doing more than simply appropriating the voice of his beloved. He is also contextualizing his romantic yearning for self-completion while pointing to a possible alternative: to the conception of a self as situated in a social world governed by alterable rules (woman writes, man reads). Rather than being transparent to himself, in the abstractness of his universal thought, the male subject is shown to be born from larger structures, such as the dramatic conflict between the sexes. As a result, Julius's *Bildungsroman* also draws us a portrait of Lucinde. Not at all a master-piece in the tradition of *Wilhelm Meister*, it stages a much neglected critique thereof. *Lucinde* or "Wilhelmine" (*Wilhelm Miene*, the Wilhelm look),[50] is what we get to read when what lies underneath changes places with what has always been on top. That is Julius's unsightly error that we cannot but forgive.

Dear reader, your patient silence has been fruitful. If you will excuse me for saying so: I prefer absent readers because they allow me the freedom to achieve what I have always longed for. Be my own critic. Not that you can be dispensed with. Unfortunately not. I need the idea of your presence to be able to continue to write. Without the idea of you my view on the sublime would have remained unpresentable, the absolute gap between theory and praxis affirmed once more. Hence, with your approval, I display here in front of you the product of our most unreal chance encounter. This is my gift—and yours—this romantic confusion of two narratives, two articulations of the sublime . . . I cannot describe for very long. Let me therefore draw you a portrait of the young Joyce that, when coupled to Schlegel's, will explain the rhetorical nature of the sublime better than the latter could have intended.

FIVE

From Addressing to Cross-Dressing: Some Afterthoughts on *Lucinde*

As the preceding analysis of the first six fragments of Schlegel's novel illustrates, *Lucinde* is truly an intellectual and moral outrage. As a result, few readers in the nineteenth and twentieth centuries have read it closely enough to determine why it is that this "little monster," as Wilhelm Dilthey called it, has continued to offend the aesthetic and moral expectations of its audience. Neither beautiful nor comprehensible, the book is a downright refutation of the traditional concept of art. More a practical illustration of Schlegel's theory of ugliness than of his view on romantic love, the novel sets into motion the dynamics of the sublime as I have formulated them in my earlier chapters on Schlegel. This does not mean that *Lucinde* has nothing to say about love, but rather that love here functions as an image of the artistic form by means of which it is expressed. Julius's confessions of love are made to produce a Dionysian force of exultation that continuously disrupts his loving union with Lucinde by means of a view of the text itself. Through an at times serious and at times comic narrative medium, the book never ceases to throw into confusion the reader's carefully constructed distinctions between what is real (Julius's love) and what is fantasy (his hyperbolic expressions). What we are made to discover on the way is the truth about artists and lovers: both are deceived in claiming their authenticity. While the artist runs against the presence of a critical reader, the lover cannot overcome the absence of his beloved. The former is threatened by reality, the latter by his illusions. In this dialectic between love and art, both are demystified. The greatest achievement of Schlegel's combinatorial genius is that by bringing these (and other) oppositions together, he fuels a shock mechanism that explodes the structure of his novel into a demonstration, indeed performance, of composition. Situated at the juncture of unity and disintegration, Schlegel's fragmentary work deteriorates into a narrative of configuration revealing not so much the signature of a sublimely empowered genius as the trace of a self-critical laboring writer. In addressing the worklike character of his novel, Schlegel has reformulated the subject as being immersed in an autonomously evolving textual body outlining the contours of its absence: the female addressee.

This brings us to the problem of how to conceive of the connection between genre and gender in this novel.[1] I say *this* rather than *the* novel, for the latter would suggest that "the" genre of "the" novel already exists, while it is precisely Schlegel's intention to develop a novelistic genre that far surpasses the existing eighteenth-century format: "Ein individueller Roman läßt sich nie vollenden, da selbst der Begriff der Gattung, sein Ideal nie vollendet werden kann"[2] [An individual novel cannot be completed, because even the concept of its genre, its ideal, cannot be completed (my translation)]. The romantic novel, we recall, is always in the process of becoming, forever incomplete, while hovering on the wings of reflection. In the "Letter on the Novel" this is reformulated to mean that the theory of the novel must itself be a novel. *Lucinde*, then, needs to be read accordingly: as a novel reflexively formulating the rules with which it can be identified as such. Both more and less than a novel, Schlegel's text parodies the genre that it redefines in the process. Suspended between the past and the future, but also between one genre and the next, Schlegel's novel throws into relief the historical and arbitrary nature of what classical theorists, such as Goethe and Schiller, believed to be universal categories. As the originator of comparative literature and linguistics, Schlegel was of course well equipped to detect relations where his contemporaries preferred to see only differences. What unites the classical genres—the epic, lyric, and drama, all of which found their way into his novel in one way or another—is the (admittedly varying) degree to which they are concerned with a presentation in front of a reader. All of them are, in other words, addressing the reality of the audience. Highlighting this connection, or conflict, between art and reality, literature and theory, but also male writer and female reader, allows Schlegel to bring together what in classicist poetics had to remain strictly separated. That is why the structure of *Lucinde* evolves around the figure of the address. Conceiving of the novel as intending an addressee is to lay bare the generic skeleton of literature encompassing all genres in its generality.[3] Conversely, the novel as the genre of all genres is the novel that has as its theme and format the trope of apostrophe.[4]

Now what else does this mean than the fact that in the absence of Julius's female addressee, the man is given not only an intimation of his theory on the novel, and literature in general, but also a historical survey of the different genres: from the epic of the "Lehrjahre" to the lyric of the novel's reflections, to the drama of its allegories. This is not Schlegel's way of erasing the female voice through a multiplicity of texts and genres or, alternatively, of using her absence as an occasion for universalizing a male theory on literature. On the contrary, by continuously signaling this relation between Lucinde's absence on the one hand and the theory of the work, the history of literature, on the other, Schlegel is showing how women have been—and are still being—marginalized by the transcendental voice of Beauty and Theory. He is, in other words, pointing to the hierarchical dialectic between male subject and female object that governs the production of late-eighteenth- and early-nineteenth-century art. If understanding art means transgressing its borders—moving from presence to absence—then by the same token theory draws out the contours of that absence: gives it a (gendered) face, so to speak. It reveals who or what lies underneath: Julius calls it passionate love, but listening carefully to what the self-reflexive, rhetorical twists and turns of his text have to say about it, we know we should not take his words at face value. Love is only the mask with which the writer is legitimating what he is doing: keeping Lucinde out of the picture or, equally, presupposing her absence so that he may continue to write. It is only through a close reading of this complex dialectic between content and form, love and art, theory and practice, Julius's confessions and the epistolary discourse in which it is couched, that we have been able to unravel a totally different story. Contrary to Julius's amorous ejaculations, his narrative confesses to the distance, even conflict, that separates him from his beloved.

Reading the work in accordance with the logic of the fragment has enabled us to draw out the borders of the novel and locate the margins from which is articulated a critical response. Exactly by erecting his autobiography on the absence of the female addressee, Julius has integrated a "desublimating" force (in Weiskel's definition of that term) that reduces his ego (and his love) to an unstable, rhetorical category. Inscribing the absent addressee in his text, Julius is faced with the contingency of the context and made to reject the illusion that his novel is *his* in the first place. By thus relinquishing his authority in the presence of the *you*, the writer endows the freedom of his creation with the inevitability of its reality. Caught as it is in this transition from spirit to letter, from system to chaos, from freedom to necessity, from self to other, Julius's address stages the evanescence—or in the words of the text, the riddle—of its own origins.

In my reading of the novel, Lucinde is the figure inside the text raising questions about the validity of such concepts as origins, selfhood, freedom, beauty, genre, and indeed gender. Signaling the locus in which Julius's story of love produces its counternarrative, Lucinde makes arbitrariness an integral part of the novel. Specifically, she gives back (reflects) to Julius what she takes away and in this manner adds a text to an already altered one. Thus it is that on the one hand Julius's confessions of love are, self-reflexively, *emptied out* into an epistolary novel about writing, while on the other hand this metadiscourse, by internalizing the discursive strategy that conventionally lies outside the plot, also *adds* a text. In this unceasing transgression of boundaries between inside and outside, text and context, Lucinde destroys as she endlessly en-genders new narratives. Textual production is here explicitly linked to woman's sexual re-production. Two striking instances were mentioned: the reference to Leda in the prologue and the vision of Lucinde as a mother in the opening scene of the first letter. Both were identified as emblematic moments in which the novel issues forth a vision of the texts still to come. Hence, it could be said that Lucinde's regenerative powers are the driving force of this novel as it gives birth to a plethora of visions and internal plays, all of which, in their turn, further distribute images of textual self-generation. This process of multiplication and ironic splitting gives rise to a linguistic medium that, rather than simply expressing Julius's passionate feelings, ushers in what lies at its basis: the work of the artist based as it is on a mother's labor.

The womb out of which the writing spins itself, I argued, lies in the middle of the book ("Lehrjahre"). Consequently, the narrative *development* of the six fragments preceding this center is also a *return* to origins, while the story of Julius's gradual social integration presented in the final six pieces—his friendship with Antonio, his marriage, his house in the country, his yearning for death—

is not much more than a regressive continuation of the little *Bildungsroman* that came before. Schlegel's romantic novel is admirable for the way in which the author never ceases to recuperate woman's age-old exclusion from art as an immensely self-critical principle of style.

Because of Lucinde's absence, Julius's confession is in a sense superfluous—a duplicity that the novel describes as its "dramatic cohesion." In this simultaneity of absence and excessive presence, she embodies the figurality of the man's speech and of his masculine self. This explains why Julius, speaking as a man in the portrait of little Wilhelmine, for example, appears in the guise of a woman. As he indicates in the sexual comedy of sorts, while he is lying on top (on the surface) there is always a woman underneath challenging him to exchange sexual as well as social and discursive positions.

Lucinde, then, is Schlegel's playful contribution to the debate on sex and gender, a contribution he had started a couple of years earlier in a much more serious vein. Undoubtedly inspired by his love for the liberated Dorothea Veit, daughter of Moses Mendelssohn, Schlegel time and again calls for a critical re-consideration of stereotyped gender roles. In his view, women are to use their sexuality, which he often equates with motherhood, for their own emancipation. Carrying in their bodies the fruit of another life, women have to develop this synthetic-metaphoric principle against the analytic, masculine modes of thinking. Unifying what man's logical reasoning keeps separated, woman's (maternal) nature can help to realize the equality between the two sexes. For Schlegel this implies, among other things, equal education, a liberation from the constraints of the home, and a rejection of those attributes considered to be typically feminine, at least insofar as they prevent women from becoming equal partners. What was her destination at birth—to be a mother inside the house—woman can pervert into freedom from prejudice and injustice.

Perversion is the key term here, as it recalls what was said earlier about the sublime: Schlegel's sublime emerges when beauty incorporates its borders (the reality of the audience) and makes of its material conditions the occasion for a radical change. If Schlegel's novel prefers the "right to confusion" of the moderns to the harmonious beauty of the early Greeks; in short, if it claims for itself the right to be ugly, then what this implies is above all a more modern, future-oriented, vision of (Greek) natural beauty as this is intimately linked to woman's capacity to develop her natural disposition into freedom from social stereotypes. To lace what I have called the feminine sublime into the workings of the novel is to seize on the limits of so-called natural beauty as the occasion to lay bare, and subvert, the gender-related conflict that makes it possible: what starts out as a stereotypical dialogue between an active male writer and a passive female reader becomes the source of a series of reversals in which the addressee writes her own novel about the limits of established (op)positions. Not only does *Lucinde* question traditional, gender-related expectations—Julius writes the kind of sentimental letters that we associate with Clarissa, while Lucinde proves to have left the house—but it also develops a lexicon of tropes that function as markers of the distance that continues to confront the author with his goal: to make of art the dramatization of the highest form of life, that of men among women.

Apostrophe, hyperbole, and allegory (or symbol) are the main representatives of Lucinde's distance and the corporality of text that it, perversely, induces. All three rhetorical figures are closely related: in Julius's address to his absent beloved, the directness of the I-You dialogue becomes an exaggeration as well as an allegory of artificial production. Curiously deviating as it is being written, layering a multiplicity of genres on its way, Julius's text gives rise to a literal metadiscourse offering him (not without irony) the tools and material which must make his writing possible in the first place. Hence, it is not altogether strange that we see the man write his novel with a pen that was already used by Lucinde. This androgynous confusion of two authors is also explicitly hinted at in Julius's "Lehrjahre," where we are told that he does not begin to reconstruct his life story until he has heard Lucinde's own confessions about her being a mother of a son who died soon after birth. And if we listen carefully to Julius's autobiography, we realize that his story is, uncannily enough, nothing but the echo of Lucinde's words: for, as we learn toward the end of the novel, the son that she bears him will die as well. The most startling feature of the text before us is that it repeats a more primordial narrative design that causes Julius's originality to evaporate as it is born, so to speak. Anticipating Joyce's "mother of all things" giving life to, while destroying, her son's creations, Lucinde here appears as a maternal figure inspiring—and in that prefiguration also destroying—the origin of this novel. Julius's failure to be the source of his own writing forms the occasion for lavishly confessing to his blunders. But addressing Lucinde he finds himself addressed—even cross-dressed—by an autonomous force which he cannot unveil without reproducing another. A dazzling simultaneity of tones and styles—from exuberant joy to despondency—is the outcome. Imposed by the past and by the outside world, Julius's words weigh him down by their accreted materiality as much as they lift him up on their intangible wings of reflection. In this multiplicity of sub- and metadiscourses, what gets articulated (considering the distance involved we should perhaps say "addressed" or "read") is the voice of a grotesquely cross-dressed reader: two-in-one, "Lucinde."

SIX

Joyce's Drama and the Conflicts of Realism

Toward Modern Drama

The question of how to control the scene of writing haunted Joyce throughout his life. No modern writer can be said to have been as obsessed with the fate of his texts as he was. The most telling instances of Joyce's incapacity to release the control over his work are, of course, the pioneering studies delivered by Stuart Gilbert (*James Joyce's* Ulysses) and Frank Budgen (*James Joyce and the Making of* Ulysses), both of which were to a great extent directed by Joyce himself. As for *Finnegans Wake*, it is well known how during the writing of his text Joyce was already trying to determine its public reception by putting together a collection of essays that twelve of his admirers—among them Samuel Beckett and William Carlos Williams—had written along the lines of research that their master had determined. Having originated the works, Joyce then went on to engage publishers, translators, and critics in procuring the kind of readership that would affirm the success of the artistic goal that he had set himself: to "forge the uncreated conscience" of his race. As exile, silence, and cunning did not suffice to realize his artistic mission, another medium had to be used: literary criticism. Handing out keys and schemes to his critics, Joyce laid out the norms of our communication with his texts—codes that had to reconstruct the connection to the outside world that his art had violently shattered. But Joyce never gave without taking much in return: providing his audience with useful structures of interpretation, he also, in a manner of speaking, usurped its position and made its critical enterprise into a mimicry at best. Consider, in this respect, the painful servitude with which Stuart Gilbert acknowledges Joyce's approval of his "study" on *Ulysses*:

> Several of the books Joyce mentioned in the course of our talks together are cited in the footnotes of the pages that follow. All of them can be read to advantage by those who wish to deepen their understanding of *Ulysses*, and as a course of reading "on the side" for an appreciation of the aesthetic climate of Joyce's art—I would also recommend the works of Walter Pater (especially the "Conclusion" of his *Renaissance*) Flaubert, Meredith and generally, the writers of the 'nineties. Finally, it should be mentioned that in the course of writing this Study I read it out to Joyce, chapter by chapter, and that, though he allowed me the greatest latitude in the presentation of the facts and indeed encouraged me to treat the subject on whatever lines were most congenial to me, it contains nothing (with the exception of chapter v, written for this new edition) to which he did not give his full approbation; indeed there are several passages which I directly owe to him.[1]

What resounds from this self-legitimization is the peculiar absence of that authority that one can expect from a critic. Gilbert's study can claim its legitimate genealogy to *Ulysses* only by the word of the Father-Artist, who in turn needs the recognition of the son in order to gain the public status of procreator. In this oedipal dialectic, Joyce emerges as the self-made artist, reproduced in the image (or portrait) of the same, uniting the status of writer and reader in his patriarchal posture. The Father's reputation is guaranteed as long as the son-reader agrees to be an emanation of his writerly gift.

Joyce's stance vis-à-vis his audience can best be understood in relation to his view on drama, as this is articulated in his early writings: in his critical essays as well as in *Stephen Hero*, that novel that the artist never publicly recognized as such, perhaps because it gave away much more than the Father was willing to reveal about himself. Reading those youthful texts might give us the key with which to open the locks that have kept us much too close to Joyce's other texts. My interpretation of Joyce's theoretical stance, voiced as it is through the mouth of a real and fictive teenager (the young Joyce, Stephen Dedalus), explicitly intermingles life and art, but also theory and practice, because such a (problematic) mixture will prove to be the core of our theory on drama.[2] To neglect the extent to which Stephen echoes—or fails to echo—the views of his maker would amount to overlooking the dramatic stature of his pronouncements. Detecting these cross-references, on the contrary, will enable us to reconstruct a theory that goes far beyond the youth's intentions. It will be clear, then, that my approach does not imply that we simply identify the Father with his youthful son. Instead I will set up an oedipal dialogue between the mature Joyce (as we know him from *Ulysses* and *Finnegans Wake*), the young Joyce (from *Critical Writings*, *Stephen Hero*, *A Portrait of the Artist as a Young Man*, and *Exiles*), and Stephen-the-hero in such a way that their respective attempts at male self-begetting cannot but resound a cacophony of voices: at times the voice is recognizably Ibsen's, Aquinas's, Aristotle's, Vico's. At other moments, however, the origin cannot be checked (in its double sense): this is when the speaker is the most dramatically engaged with self-production, and as such unwittingly close to Friedrich Schlegel's sublime as the unlimited autonomy of art. Having located this indeterminacy at the core of Joyce's theory and practice in terms of a modernization of the sublime, we can then reformulate it as a new version of the kind of *Querelle des anciens et des modernes* in which Schlegel was already involved one century earlier: the debate over what modern (drama) is cannot be properly conducted until one faces the real stakes of the issue, namely, the question of how one breaks the surface of a received tradition—draws out its limits—such that a transposition between the old and the new becomes possible. Whereas Schlegel situates this break at the juncture between Greek tragedy and comedy, in the works of Aristophanes (a break that culminates first in Shakespeare's tragicomic plays, then in Schlegel's novel *Lucinde*), the young Joyce recognizes it in the passage from romanticism to realism enacted by Ibsen's plays, which in *Stephen Hero* is likened to the innovations that Menander's new realist comedies introduced (after Aristophanes).

As was the case with Schlegel, Joyce's commitment to the modernization of literature begins with a reconsideration of the dramatic genre: "Literature is kept alive by tonics, it flourishes through conventions in all human relations, in all actuality. Drama will be for the future at war with convention, if it is to realize itself truly."[3] Since drama depends on the presence of real people, objects, and events, it has since Aristotle been regarded as the mimetic art form par excellence. In contrast to the novelistic form, dramatic representation takes place in real time and place and is, for that reason, constrained to the here and now of the performance. This means that the dramatist (and for the young Joyce, this includes a painter like Munkacsy[4]) is faced with the problem of translating his characters' states of mind in observable, spatial bodies on the one hand (as in Munkacsy's "Ecce Homo"), in momentary gestures and actions on the other.[5] The conflict, then, between inner soul and exterior form that we find in every form of art is here both more real and more short-lived. Like music—the analogy will become more significant as our discussion progresses—drama hands down the maker's (and the characters') intentions to the audience through the mediation of living performers, who while being real also add an element of impermanence and contingency to the contract set up between the dramatist and his spectator. Seen in this light, the dramatic genre, rather than being confidently mimetic, raises questions about the representational metastructures in which Western art has been couched from the start. Drama may relate to the world of its audience in an immediate fashion, in the same breath it highlights the distance that continues to separate the crowd from the players. After all, "No man, said the Nolan, can be a lover of the true or the good unless he abhors the multitude."[6] This emphasis on the untenable synthesis between art and reality has led critics such as Friedrich Schlegel to focus on the living, but non-mimetic, quality of the dramatic performance. If for both Schlegel and Joyce, drama is the primordial art form, it is because it brings to life the artifice and gesturing involved in mimesis as well as in what we consider to be real. By concentrating either on the conflict between content and form (Schlegel), or on the strife of passions and perceptions (the young Joyce), these critics demand that drama be seen less as a trustworthy imitation of human action—as Aristotle had claimed—than as a struggle to portray truth: "It may be asked what are we to do, in the words of Tolstoi. First, clear our minds of cant and alter the falsehoods to which we have lent our support."[7] While for Schlegel drama's unmasking of reality was for the first time articulated in the transition from Greek tragedy to comedy, Joyce recognizes its anti-mimetic force in the symbolic complexities of Ibsen's realism.

For Schlegel as well as for Joyce, the dramatic form is highly duplicitous. Through drama we get an image of the contingencies involved in the transaction between artist and work as well as between the fictive universe of art and the reality of the audience: "There are some weighty truths which we cannot overpass, in the relations between drama and the artist. Drama is essentially a communal art and of widespread domain. The drama—its fittest vehicle almost presupposes an audience, drawn from all classes."[8] As the art form most visibly based both on movements of exteriorization and on the encounter between the scenes of representation and reception, drama offers us the literal counterparts to the mental processes involved in the production and consumption of art. This way, the theatrical stage becomes the most suitable place in which to start conceiving new modes of expression and representation. As it is the physical embodiment of the process of aesthetic apprehension, the theater offers the young Joyce the right setting in which to think through what kind of artistic unity may take place between the subject and the object of perception in modern-day art: what he has learned from Bruno of Nola is that "every power in nature must evolve an opposite in order to realise itself and opposition brings reunion."[9] In Joyce's mind, the redefinition of literature has to start with a reflection on the subject-object dichotomy visualized in drama—its roots "struck in earth, but through [its] higher leafage the stars of heaven are glowing and astir"[10]—because it is around this dichotomy that the logic of artistic expression as well as perception evolves. Reconsidering this polarity between the spiritual and the material will eventually lead to a totally new mode of aesthetic apprehension on the part of the audience, of artistic production on the part of the maker. In fact, as we will see during our discussion of *Finnegans Wake*, the positions of subject and object are to merge in a kind of Derridean intermediary ground, where diffraction takes the place of binary reflection.

In what follows I will demonstrate that the young Joyce's concern to alter the conventions of literature in order to bring "real life" on stage is based on what one could call a "pragmatist" approach to reality and to the sublime. It is in his search for a modern—time-imbued and dramatic—unity between the subject and the object that Joyce construes a definition of reality as it is based on the communal structures of thought and feeling by which a society constitutes itself. Not an objective, timeless, Kantian category that man strives to attain without ever achieving it (the basis of his theory on the sublime), reality here appears as a fluid category the boundaries of which are socially and dramatically constituted. For Joyce, then, to define real life in his essays on drama is already to address—by means of what many critics have recognized as a highly convoluted rhetorical style—the community of affections and expectations on which his definition of reality is based. Drama is Joyce's model for the kind of reality he is trying to articulate because it is, more than any other genre, based on construing a world in an effective and affective communication with an audience, whose passions and aspirations he is going to probe "with no scrupulous knife."[11] Furthermore, what Ibsen teaches the young Joyce is that once one lets real life on stage, there is no way to contain it because the definition that would enable us to do so is being generated in the performance itself, that is, in the play's address to a specific audience, its collective as well as private tastes. Because of this immeasurable format, Ibsen's realistic drama becomes "of universal import."[12] The conflict in drama that Joyce calls "the interplay of passions to portray truth"[13] concerns this affective status of reality, the fact that any definition of reality involves not only a communal interpretation (of artist and audience, for instance) but also, and more importantly, an increasingly heterogeneous spectrum of tastes and feelings. Reality for Joyce takes place in a discourse with a public, the community of which is primordially affective and hence contingent. Reality defined as/in passion (in its double sense, *Ecce Homo*) is at once a source of conflict and communality, contingency and universality, individuality and community. Its exemplary configuration is found in Ibsen's drama, whose characters' private feelings are interesting for what they tell us about the community at large: "Ibsen's plays do not depend for their interest on the action, or on the incidents. Even the characters . . . are not the first thing in his plays. But the naked drama—either the perception of a great truth, or the opening up of a great question, or a great conflict . . ."[14] In its address to his culture as a whole, Ibsen's symbolic realism offers Joyce the opportunity to formulate a theory about art that, I will argue, has far-reaching political implications: the paradigmatic object of conflicting passions, not surprisingly, turns out to be the female body. The politics of Joyce's drama will be the focus of the next chapter. Let me first disentangle his belabored writings on drama, art, and life, concerned as they are with finding the right form and diction by which his views could be immediately put into practice. And in keeping with Joyce's distrust of a purely theoretical definition of drama, let us read his essays side by side with *Stephen Hero*.

Realism versus Symbolism: Detailing the Sublime

Joyce has often been praised for masterfully imitating the kind of unusual mixture of realism and symbolism that Ibsen's controversial plays first introduced on stage. However, when it comes to envisioning the relation between these two contradictory poetic modes, we are all too often left in the dark.[15] Joyce sets the tone for this obscurity when, in his early essays on Ibsen, he praises the dramatist in vague terms for on the one hand letting "real life" on stage, while on the other hand substituting the action to "a great conflict which is almost independent of the conflicting actors."[16] What Joyce admires in Ibsen becomes somewhat clearer in his review of the French translation of *Catilina* (a play dating from 1849): it is the complex manner in which the dramatist succeeds in confronting his "romantic" interest in great truths with a "classical" taste for "the things present to him."[17] Written at a time when the romanticism of Victor Hugo was competing with the realism of Balzac, Ibsen's first play is remarkable in its fine ear for the transition between the old, subjective and the new, objective forms of art. Comprising the prime instrument of Ibsen's analysis of this conflict are the play's characters, who, as Joyce puts it, are less interesting as realistic individuals than as dramatizations of a larger strife. In this concern with the synecdochal (symbolic) quality of art—art as the presentation of the opposition between subject and object—Ibsen proves himself loyal to the kind of romantic project that Friedrich Schlegel had started to evolve in his reflections on Greek drama, and with which the young Joyce too was trying to come to terms as he set out on his artistic journey.

As I substantively argued in the previous chapters, at the heart of Schlegel's philosophy of art is the analysis of artistic freedom. Free aesthetic production occurs when the subject projects itself in the object conceived to such a degree that the two merge in one *living* (dramatic) image. At that moment of synthesis, the subject loses itself in what it brings forth. What started out as a subjective conception on the part of the artist turns into an uncontrollable objective concretization: the work of art is, like nature, totally autonomous within its transgressive boundaries. This contradictory transition from subject to object Schlegel describes as a self-generative ironic process, one in which the unity of subject and object intensifies as the disjunction between them becomes all the more evident. At the height of its self-realization, the subject encounters its own finitude. In Schlegel's romantic vision, the beauty of a harmonious unity and the joy it inspires is marred by sublime disharmony. With the introduction of the sublime at the very heart of beauty—because of this relatedness the philosopher prefers to speak of ugliness—Schlegel develops a theory of aesthetic consciousness in which Kant's disinterested, objective dedication to beauty is shown to be limited by a subjective, at times conflictual, interest in the world. In this manner, romanticism stands for the revelation of finitude in the midst of artistic freedom. This moment of sublime "arrest" (to use a Joycean term) in the face of what one has created is, as it were, an ambiguous instant in which lies fragmented what has been unified or completed. From this perspective, the sublime points to the moment when what has been left unshaped (unpresented) interferes and the crisis of beauty, its irreality, becomes visible: what we are made to see is that the beauty we perceive is an illusion at best. "In truth, this is not what it seems." For Schlegel, this dissenting, sublime voice is first heard in the transition from Greek tragedy to comedy: turning his attention from the harmonious construction of the plot to the performance of his characters in front of an audience, Aristophanes is, more than anything else, consciously playing with masks. From now onward, European literature, and drama in particular, takes us under the surface of its literal language to point out the scene, the (social) reality of its production. While Shakespeare's "philosophical drama" (the words are Schlegel's) could still openly claim that all the world is a stage, Ibsen no longer has these rhetorical ejaculations at his disposal and, instead, sees himself faced with the task of combining the symbolism of romanticism with the demands of realism: he has to *show* that *this* world is a stage. It is this conflict of perspectives—what we could call the opposition between (mimetic) realism and (anti-mimetic) symbolism, but which in reality lies at the very core of the romantic sublime itself—that the young Joyce experiences as the major inheritance from the past, and which he is trying to resolve in a "modern" way.

Ibsen's realism provides Joyce with an example of how to invest art's tendency toward the universal with the concreteness and multiplicity of the detail. The demand that art imitate the ugly, prosaic, and deceptive reality of the nineteenth-century bourgeoisie, forms the occasion for disciplining the romantic sublime—an ideal category—into a "preoccupation with the things present to him." A preliminary intimation of what Joyce's reformulation of the sublime entails is delivered by *Stephen Hero*, where Stephen counters the headmaster's argument that Aquinas's reflections on art intend "the sublime—that which leads man upwards," with the cynical observation that this "would apply to a Dutch painter's representation of a plate of onions."[18] To continue in the words of Joyce's review of Ibsen's *Catilina*: "For the imagination has the quality of a fluid, and it must be held firmly, lest it become vague, and delicately, that it may lose none of its magical powers."[19] The implication here is, of course, that by concentrating on the banality of everyday life the artist finds in reality the finitude that has traditionally been associated with the sublime operation of a self-conscious spirit. With the increased particularization there emerges a deeper tension. Within the limits of concrete scenes, rooms, and characters, each object, each gesture becomes invested with a highly concentrated energy that would evaporate into nothingness without this realistic limitation. In Joyce's ideal drama, the part and the whole, the phenomenal and the spiritual coincide to such an extent that the smallest element of the play already encompasses the dynamics of the whole. This leads him to declare that the driving force of drama is necessity, "mere animal instinct applied to the mind."[20] What holds Ibsen's play together, for instance, is not some conventional abstract form imposed from above but a structure developed from within, such that all the reviewer "can hope to do is to link some of the more salient points together in such a way as to suggest rather than to indicate, the intricacies of the plot."[21] The unity of Ibsen's drama lies in the artist's careful relating of individual images and actions, which give the inner plot such an immensely dense and richly layered cohesiveness that the plot disintegrates as it becomes visible. Such are the formal laws of drama: while they serve to set up the experiment, and gradually assume a particularized form, the detail that they generate is of such abundance that they are threatened with dissolution. In the process, the play disintegrates into "a supple rhythm."[22] The realism that emerges from the growing specificity of the play's structure is one that addresses not only the loss of the whole but in the end also the radical limits of man's attempt at creating a recognizable picture of reality.

In *Stephen Hero*, this mode of pushing "lawlessness to its extreme limit"[23] is identified as an experiment with the "veritably sublime process of one's nature," one in which no room is left for the well-known theories about the good, the beautiful, and the sublime. All that the setting allows for is the happening of the work, still developing the communal laws (conventions) that will allow the audience to identify the work as what it is:

> For Stephen art was neither a copy nor an imitation of nature: the artistic process was a natural process. In all his talk about artistic perfection it was impossible to detect an artificial

> accent. To talk about the perfection of one's art was not for him to talk about something agreed upon as sublime but in reality no more than a sublime convention but rather to talk a veritably sublime process of one's nature which had a right to examination and open discussion.[24]

For Stephen, the greatest enemy to the sublime is the old concept of sublimity, "in reality no more than a sublime convention." In fact, the traditional concept of the sublime shares with ordinary realism its adherence to conventions. Kant was the first to suggest this intimate link between the sublime and realism to the extent that he interpreted *das Erhabene* as man's experience of the absolutely real (the *noumenon*). What lay beyond (in) Kant's mind was the objective and divine reality that also founded philosophical mimesis (the imitation of an autonomous reality). In contrast, Stephen's search for "the veritably sublime" entails a rejection of this kind of sublimity and mimesis as outdated language games. Stephen's (sublime) conflict will be with a tradition rather than with a transcendental reality. In this he approximates Schlegel's art-historical reformulation of the sublime. Not unlike Schlegel, Stephen realizes that the category of the sublime, and by extension our relation to reality, is a matter of changing social and artistic formats. The necessity to (continue to) violently break with the tradition handed down to us, in order for a new concept of sublimity to be articulated, is what directly relates Stephen's sublime to the creative process, which in drama is the moment of raising a play. Emerging in the transition from the old to the new, the "modern" sublime demarcates the (creative) linkage between the known and the unknown, audience and play, that makes the innovation of the sublime possible in the first place. Possible and hence not yet determinate: the sublime as mediator that in its immediacy designates the happening of art—an event that, since Lyotard,[25] includes many possibilities including the potentiality that nothing may occur at all. For Stephen this sublime rupturing of the old format of art leads us away from art and in the direction of its other: nature, or what he calls a "natural process," but also "the process of one's nature." For all its anti-idealistic rhetoric, Stephen's sublime still confirms the supremacy of (himself as) the modern artist. It is left to Joyce to divest this category of its solipsistic connotations. What will appear is the sublime as the flash of an insight into that habitual environment to which the artist belongs (a larger, no longer transcendent, order), and which he "represents" so closely or naturally that only *a change* of habit—the function of the modern sublime—can highlight this interconnectedness.

The sublime as the unfamiliar-at-the-heart-of-the-familiar unmasking the self's immanent relation to others is what Joyce in his essay "Drama and Life" calls the "symbolic presentment of our widely related nature" (see my discussion above in the introduction). This he goes on to describe as follows:

> Human society is the embodiment of changeless laws which the whimsicalities and circumstances of men and women involve and overwrap. The realm of literature is the realm of these accidental manners and humours—a spacious realm; and the true literary artist concerns himself mainly with them. Drama has to do with the underlying laws first, in all their nakedness and divine severity, and only secondarily with the motley agents who bear them out.[26]

In contrast to the "spacious realm" of realistic literature staging the accidents in and circumstances of individual lives, the space designated by the stage is non-mimetic and symbolic because intent upon laying bare the underlying laws of society: the communal structures of thought and experience by which a society erects itself and which, for all their "divine severity," are first and foremost characteristic of human nature—and hence open to a critical examination.[27] Joyce's confidence that the underlying, symbolic laws of society can be retrieved in art should, however, not blind us to the complexity of the dramatic form that he is trying to formulate here. Setting the scene of his play, the Joycean dramatist uncovers the hidden laws of society that become visible only as they direct the progression of the play. For Joyce, then, the determinant structure of "our widely related nature" is not what presents itself in the whimsical and isolated lives of the common people but what is in a sense evoked by the occasion of the play. By the turn of a paradox, the laws of society are less real than they are a performance brought forth by the scene of the drama (by analogy also the scene of writing). Conversely, drama turns out to be the basic framework within which the inner structure of our communal experience gains a concrete, visible form. Or, to put this in simple terms, Joyce seems to suggest that the importance of drama lies in the manner in which it teaches us that human nature or communal life is based on an intricate play of illusions and gestures. Drama sharpens our understanding of the fact that our daily engagement with each other involves a theatrical performance. Thus, attending *A Doll's House,* for instance, we are made to realize that the conventional marriage enacted before us hides a disturbing truth, which in turn reflects our own deceptive relation to the people literally and figuratively closest to us. By putting nineteenth-century life on stage, Ibsen's social dramas, so to speak, light up the darkened auditorium in which the spectator usually enjoys the illusion of total isolation. Forcing us to see his art not "with the lantern of tradition," as Stephen puts it in *Stephen Hero,* but "by the light of day,"[28] Ibsen illuminates both the stage and its circumstances. In one "arresting" glance, we, the audience, see the world of fantasy on stage as well as the presence of the fellow citizen next to us. In this social experience induced by the theater, life and art meet. The bourgeois marriage that ordinarily constitutes a false, for repressive, union between two people is here exposed and transformed into a "shattering" experience of human interrelationship.

It is clear that the young Joyce's search for "the symbolic presentment" of human nature aims at the recuperation of some minimal universal experience that, while rooted in the singular, also transcends the idiosyncrasy of the private life of the individual. This is what he calls the strife of passions constant in human nature: at once singular and communal. If he claims to find this transcendent structure epitomized in drama, it is because here the human conflict is *represented* (as content) in front of an audience that by its very distant presence makes possible the dramatic *presentation* (the dramatic form) in the first place. In other words, drama *appears in/as* the conflict that it *talks about.* It concretizes a communal conflictual experience prior to its fixation in a social order. Nothing here is yet fixed, while everything is still possible. Endowing the communal present with the uncertain status of improvisation, drama functions much like the myths by which a society first constitutes itself: "I believe further that drama arises spontaneously out of life and is coeval with it. Every race has made its own myths and it is in these that early drama often finds an outlet."[29] Just as myths come from real experiences of life and death, so drama evolves in a living encounter between a play and its inherently varying "audience, drawn from all classes."

This primordial structure of drama Joyce describes in terms of "strife, evolution, movement in whatever way unfolded; it [drama] exists before it takes form, independently; it is conditioned but not controlled by its scene."[30] The frames that the dramatist sets up to delimit the underlying laws of society are subverted into a demonstration of their impossibility to contain the (gestural) force that they unleash. No sooner does the play assume a visible form than it opens up a life-size conflict not only between the play and its circumstances, art and reality but also between the artist and his medium. As soon as the dramatist reproduces the larger structures that surround him and that constitute the actual situation of the play, he loses control and, in a sense, disappears in the symbolic diversion of his creation: "But here the artist [Ibsen] forgoes his very self and stands a mediator in awful truth before the veiled face of God."[31] Those of us who still believe that the impersonal stance of Joyce's dramatic artist approximates that of a God indifferently watching his creation while paring his fingernails—as Stephen triumphantly claims in *A Portrait*—should start thinking otherwise.[32] If there is anything being pared here, it is the superiority of the male artist, as he is projecting himself onto the independent development of an experiment in which communal experience—the discourse of the other—is assuming a major role.

Throughout Stephen's development as an artist, there remains an irreducible gap between his theory and reality. As so many Joyce critics have elegantly demonstrated, the conflict between the youth's alternatively appropriative and sceptical attitudes toward his environment is the cause of an immense suffering. What Stephen has to come to terms with is that the concretization of his theory on drama—"dramatic art is the art whereby the artist sets forth his image in immediate relations to others"[33]—involves him in a process of intensifying directedness toward the reality of his surroundings (the audience) that leaves little room for grand ideals. He will, in other words, have to learn to forsake his belief in the superiority of his mind and, instead, regard his performances in front of the world as something finite.

Stephen's authoritative utterances on the dramatist stage their own radical finitude and,[34] indeed, indicate the price the young man will have to pay in order for his theory to gain truth. A large portion of Joyce's later works will consist precisely in staging the ultimate test of Stephen's hypotheses: in *Ulysses* the young man faces the success of his theory, as he is aimlessly gesturing in the streets of Dublin—a tragic figure lost in the rhythm of the world's refuse. There Stephen is forced to exchange his position as an artist for that of a reader trying to interpret the signs of the surrounding world: "Signatures of all things I am here to read, seaspawn and seawrack, the nearing tide, that rusty boot."[35] In Stephen's dialogical stature, grounded in the conflict between spirit and matter, the authority structure inherent in the artist's originating act is eroded from within. A shared rather than an egotistical act, as it still was in *Stephen Hero* and *A Portrait*, Stephen's "dramatic" utterance in *Ulysses* is so much linked up with its surroundings that it becomes impossible to distinguish between his language and the variable contexts from which it takes its shapes. Consider, for instance, this passage in which Stephen is walking on the beach and feels the need to urinate:

> In long lassoes from the Cock lake the water flowed full, covering greengoldenly lagoons of sand, rising, flowing. My ashplant will float away. I shall wait. No, they will pass on, passing, chafing against the low rocks, swirling, passing. Better get this job over quick. Listen: a fourworded wavespeech: seesoo, hrss, rsseeiss, ooos. Vehement breath of waters amid seasnakes, rearing horses, rocks. In cups of rocks it slops: flop, slop, slap: bounded in barrels. And, spent, its speech ceases. It flows purling, widely flowing, floating foampool, flower unfurling.[36]

Whereas the first sentence seems to be spoken by an impersonal narrator, the next fragmentary sentences belong to Stephen as he senses his bodily needs and he cannot make up his mind about whether to relieve himself or not. This is hardly intentional thought or the kind of dramatic speech that we heard him deliver in Joyce's early works. At most, Stephen's language "reflects" his bodily feelings—feelings moreover that seem to be in unison with the flow of the sea. In the "fourworded wavespeech" this relation between Stephen's language and the surrounding sea is given a more concrete form. Or a fluid non-shape: "seesoo, hrss . . . rocks. In cups of rocks it slops: flop, slop, slap." Flowing along with the water of his body and the sea, Stephen's language—if it is his—freely associates and rhymes. More *stream* than *consciousness*, it designates nothing but its own autonomous transition in the world around it. One could say that, staging themselves in the flux of the sea, Stephen's words escape his control. What remains is a rhythm of speech exhausting itself in its deliverance to the world. Less than a dramatic utterance in its traditional sense, the word is the world is the movement of time: a mere sign of direction, a urinal trail: "It flows purling, widely flowing, floating foampool, flower unfurling."

Classicism versus Romanticism: The Art of Limitation

In his earliest essays, written when Joyce was not yet twenty, the young artist repeatedly emphasizes the importance of exerting "force," limits, over oneself, not in the sense of physical violence, which he abhors, but as a direct control over one's instincts, passions, and emotions. Joyce's concern with limitation, however, does not imply that he seeks the lofty powers of grand designs soaring above the world as Daedalus did when he escaped from the labyrinth (or Stephen when he left Dublin). On the contrary, too much inwardly directed, mental constructions yield the kind of unlimited force that he wants to keep at bay. The human spirit should set itself to work not above but amid (or perhaps right under, *sub-limes*) the unruly powers of (human) nature. Like Icarus, the artist must drop into the sea in order to steer, with Odyssean cunning, the vessels of his art along the storms of the ocean, using the strength of the wind as the drive that will bring him home to his wife. If you can't beat Aeolus, join him: with that in mind Joyce avoids the double trap of Scylla and Charybdis (the rock and the whirlpool) while working toward a new form of art that will precisely derive its energy from the combination of these two opposites. Joyce's art of limitation consists of a dialectical reformulation of what in his first essay on Mangan (discussed in my introduction) he calls two "constant states of mind,"[37] one occupied with materiality—the classical temper—the other with the whirlpool of emotions and ideas—the romantic temper. His literary examples are the New School of realist drama, Wagner, and, to a certain extent, Shakespeare.

In this essay on Mangan, Joyce compares his own method to Shakespeare's: "A song by Shakespeare or Verlaine, which seems so free and living and as remote from any conscious purpose as rain that falls in a garden or the lights of evening, is discovered to be the rhythmic speech of an emotion otherwise incommunicable, at least so fitly."[38] As rhetorically thwarted as Joyce's defense of Mangan may seem to be throughout the essay, there is a clear indication that what he aims at in 1902 is a redefinition of the *Querelle des anciens et des modernes* that had been dominating the literary field for more than two centuries. More precisely, the reference to Shakespeare harks back to a disagreement between Friedrich Schiller and Friedrich Schlegel: in his "Über naive und sentimentalische Dichtung" (1794–95), Schiller grouped Shakespeare among the classical writers, while Schlegel, in the *Studium* essay discussed above, described him as modern. While Schiller claimed that Shakespeare was nowhere visible in his work, Schlegel detected (parts of) his personality in all of his characters. For the former, Shakespeare was the epitome of objectivity, for the latter the prime representative of subjectivity. This paradoxical status of the Renaissance dramatist—situated in the transition from the old to the new—interests Joyce immensely, and it is the core of Stephen's algebraic theory on *Hamlet* in the "Scylla and Charybdis" episode of *Ulysses*. In fact, Joyce wants to position himself vis-à-vis his art as Shakespeare stood in relation to his own: at once above and inside it. To accomplish this, Joyce has to incorporate into both his theory and his art the two schools in a radically new way. As *Stephen Hero* (in an echo of Joyce's essay on Mangan) explains, his is the "classical" temper in the sense of "the slow elaborate patience of the art of satisfaction. The heroic, the fabulous, I call romantic. Menander perhaps, I don't know . . ."[39] This quote is crucial in that it stages the kind of paradox that Nietzsche was seen to perform in his search for modern literature two decades earlier (and to which I shall return). Just as the philosopher found in Greek drama (Aeschylus in this case) the concern with the present that he was trying to stimulate among his contemporaries, so Stephen finds in the new comedy of "Menander perhaps" his example of the modern spirit called the "classical" temper. In contrast to the classical writers and the romantics in a traditional sense—both of whom Stephen discards as concerned with morality, as well as with the heroic and the fabulous ("Eschylus is not a classical writer")[40]—Stephen's (modern) classicism aims not to instruct but to simply "satisfy" the audience by deriving its inspiration from the crowd's daily life and tastes. Classicism stands for the kind of immediate restraint only a dramatist aiming at the spectator can exert over his ideas and emotions. Addressing the reality of the audience enables realists like Menander and Ibsen to attain the objectivity that alone can save the artist from excessive self-absorption. It is, however, left to Joyce to put the theory of his idealistic alter ego into practice. Through a combination of careful writing and precise (realistic) observation of everyday life, as Menander had done in 300 B.C., Joyce unmasks Stephen's aesthetic stance as nothing but a remnant of "romanticism" (in Stephen's sense), an ironic reminder of the kind of heroism that the youth claims to have shed.

In the chapters to follow, I will argue that Joyce's reformulation of the conflict between the classical (objective) and romantic (subjective) temper harbors the seeds of a feminist critique of the way men have for centuries ordered the world around the self-serving opposition of male subject versus female object. It will be our task to analyze Stephen's theory of drama "in immediate relations to [his] others," that is, to the daily practice of the women around him. As Joyce's oeuvre develops, the borders of drama's spatial frame are penetrated by the temporal flux of women's daily lives. The theater gives pride of place to the novel. Interestingly, mothers will become the dominant figures in what Cixous, dicussing *Ulysses*, once called the "monstrous epiphany," in which the contours of the artist's vision are permanently fractured by the local and social particularities of its setting.

One of the major questions we will need to raise is, then: upon having reformulated the borders of traditional art (and beauty), upon having opened up the subject to the contingencies of the object, what does Joyce bring into the picture? "Real life," definitely. But such a term is empty now unless one specifies the subject: *whose* reality do we get to see? It is, again, to Ibsen's social dramas that we will have to turn in order to catch a glimpse of what Joyce's new dramatic mode is all about. What has traditionally been left excluded, uncompleted—Schlegel's term—is not some mystical, transcendent order in the tradition of Kant but something much more "present to us" (which is why it had to be distanced in the first place): while Stephen Dedalus, in his own seemingly neutral fashion, reformulates the sublime such that it produces "a plate of onions," Joyce, I have argued, addresses an explicitly social reality. For the latter, detailing or restraining the sublime involves bringing home to the reader the inadequacy and injustice of the traditional subject-object, artist-model dichotomy in which man's so-called disinterested search for beauty objectifies as well as violently removes the female body. One of Stephen's poems should illustrate my point:

> Stephen, after certain hesitations, showed Maurice the first-fruits [*sic*] of his verse and Maurice asked who the woman was. Stephen looked a little vaguely before him before answering and in the end had to answer that he didn't know who she was . . . he felt with a sweet sinking of consciousness that if the end came to him it was in the arms of the unknown that it would come to him:
>
> > The dawn awakes with tremulous alarms,
> > How grey, how cold, how bare!
> > O, hold me still white arms, encircling arms!
> > And hide me, heavy hair!

Life is a dream, a dream. The hour is done
And antiphon is said.
We go from the light and falsehood of the sun
To bleak wastes of the dead.[41]

For all her deadly connotations, Stephen's muse keeps alive the old threatening "mother of all things" that also inspired Mangan, Shelley, and a host of other romantic poets, as argued in my introduction. Artistic fatherhood in the sense of "conscious begetting" may be founded upon a legal fiction and ultimately upon the void;[42] in man's imagination death is too consistently female for that attribute to be mere coincidence or uncertainty. Conceived only in terms of a body ("the arms of the unknown"), woman is always already the artist's origin (as muse) and end (death). Upon this certitude Stephen's aesthetics is irremovably built: he can use the female body to his own ends and even ascribe to it the violence he himself has generated.

Perhaps, then, we should revisit this matrix of man's poetry and restore to it the arbitrariness on which it is based. I will illustrate that when female beauty radiates not with the "whatness of a thing"—the essence of Stephen's epiphany—but with the conditions at the marketplace; when, in contrast to what Stephen claims,[43] aesthetics is seen to be based on eugenics, art delineates the artifice of our conventions and unearths what ordinarily remains hidden. The refusal on the part of Joyce's women to reflect "the necessary phases of [man's] artistic apprehension,"[44] the precondition for beauty, is what brings forth the feminine sublime: it designates woman's critique of the social conditions that have reduced her to the passive role of the other-of-the-same, onto which the masculine gaze projects its fantasies of beauty, only to get them doubly beautiful returned. While the young Stephen Dedalus is still caught up in what he himself calls the "test of love,"[45] in which man gives only to (literally) see what he gets in return, the young Joyce is already coping with the inadequacy of this artistic logic and praising Ibsen for positioning his women characters outside the male-artist versus female-model framework.

SEVEN

The Gender Politics of Joyce's Theory and Practice of Drama

A Feminist Note of Protest from Ireland and Norway

As Ewa Ziarek has already said,[1] whether we choose to describe Joyce as feminist or sexist—a major point of disagreement in Joyce criticism—the growing number of participants in the debate testifies to the important role gender plays in the author's work.[2] That one cannot come to terms with the implications of Joyce's literary innovations until one has addressed the portrayal of the sexes in his writings can be explained in terms of the "modern" enterprise itself. According to Alice Jardine,[3] the search for new artistic territory implies that one incorporates what has thus far remained marginal; in a sexual context this means moving into women's space. While such valorization of the feminine as the horizon toward which modernity evolves partly underlies my own project on the feminine sublime, one should not, of course, associate femininity and modernity in such a general way. At issue are some crucial differences, not only between the nineteenth- and twentieth-century concepts of modernity, but also between two oppositional views on gender. While Schlegel's typically romantic approach subscribes to a universal, androgynous (conflicting and therefore gendered!) ideal that will ultimately emancipate us from accidental (biological) sexual divisions, Joyce's modernism declines such an idealistic view and prefers to emphasize the social reality of sexual differences. Although the latter considers the human subject as limited by the body and the temperament—something that is universally true—he never ceases to expose the narrow-minded way in which those limits are being socially prescribed. If the young Joyce is interested in the (classical) limits of our material existence, the mortal body in short, then by the same token he throws into relief the social nature of our physical boundaries, borders at which conflicting views interconnect (the theme of my chapter on *Exiles*). Hence his preference for drama, which according to him lays bare the underlying social laws. What Joyce finds in Ibsen is an example of how drama can (symbolically) open up "a great question, or a great conflict which is almost independent of the conflicting actors," while (realistically) integrating this universal strife within its social surroundings. The opposition between spirit and body, about which the young critic can theoretically claim that it is "the condition of all achievement," Ibsen places in a culturally specific context, such that the biological body—the cause of our finitude—is seen to be explicitly gendered. At the same time that it endows us with a universal feature, or situates us against a commonly held horizon, the sexual body divides and distinguishes between men and women.

Translating this into the romantic vocabulary that Dedalus adopts in *Stephen Hero*, we can say that Ibsen symbolizes the prophetic stance of the artist who "alone is capable of absorbing in himself the life that surrounds him,"[4] not to "[fling] it abroad again amid planetary music,"[5] but to confront this kind of idealizing fiction with the social reality that it hides. In spite of Stephen's triumphant defense of the Norwegian dramatist against the Catholic forces that censor him, the boy remains peculiarly blind to what his predecessor has to teach him about the social particularity of art. It is Joyce, not Stephen, who fully understands the *real* implications of Ibsen's revolutionary stance. To quote his famous dialogue with Arthur Power on this issue:

> . . . you do not understand him [Ibsen]. You ignore the spirit which animated him. The purpose of *The Doll's House*, for instance, was the emancipation of women, which has caused the greatest revolution in our time in the most important relationship there is—that between man and women; the revolt of women against the idea that they are the mere instruments of men.

> —And the more pity, I [Power] replied, for the relationship between the sexes has now been ruined; an intellectualism has been allowed to supersede a biological fact, and the result is that neither is happy.
> —The relationship between the two sexes is now on a different basis, but I do not know whether they are happier or unhappier than they were before; I suppose it depends on the individuals. But I do know that Ibsen has been the greatest influence on the present generation;[6]

In sharp contrast to Joyce's political investment in Ibsen (to be discussed in more detail shortly), Stephen's purely intellectual, high-blown allegiance to the dramatist serves as one more mode of diverting, even silencing, the social truths that Ibsen has to offer: art is not made by, nor is it meant for, bodiless souls soaring above the world amid planetary music; it is made by and for people whose biological nature has far-reaching social consequences. Joyce's ironic stance vis-à-vis his character's view on Ibsen becomes clear when we consider Stephen's eloquence in its concrete surroundings: his mother's kitchen. I will argue that what we get to see is a male artist seeking to prove himself at the expense of an uneducated woman, whose (sexual) body has condemned her to a life at home—far removed from the intellectual heavens that her son dreams of. The universal strife between spirit and body is here, not surprisingly, won by a man whose lofty reasoning enables him to integrate—use and abuse—woman's reality for the sake of his own development. For if it is true, as Stephen says in *A Portrait*, that when he comes "to the phenomena of artistic conception, artistic gestation and artistic reproduction" no predecessor passes the test,[7] then surely it is May Dedalus who must be tested. Only her reproductive body can stand as a model for what Stephen is trying to attain: to become his own procreator. For that purpose, he is willing to betray both Ibsen and the person closest to him.

Stephen's theory on drama touched upon in the previous chapter stages more than the refusal to honor the artistic inheritance of his classical and romantic precursors. Behind his search for the dramatic form we can detect a much more important, political strife: his fight for new literary ground is painfully waged on his mother's (and Emma's) territory. Stephen wants to claim for his drama what his mother believes to belong to her Church: the creation of a racial conscience. In contrast to the religious rituals of the priests, however, Stephen's public performance will not serve a mysterious

God. Neither will it seize the audience's attention through the nets of a received idea. "The general attitude of women towards religion puzzled and often maddened Stephen. His nature was incapable of achieving such an attitude of insincerity or stupidity."[8] The dramatist, in other words, will not expound old religious or political views to naive women. As it befits a true "classicist," Stephen's task will be limited to delivering new material, which the listener needs to bring alive by actively participating in his play. Rejecting all standing contracts between writer and reader, his art aims to incorporate the presence of the audience, such that—as at the night of the Whitsuntide play in *A Portrait*—it will be emptied into a "void filled with applause."[9]

Thus, in chapter 19 of *Stephen Hero*, we see the self-absorbed youth trying to engage his ironing mother, by reading out to her his essay on Ibsen with a rhythm and an emphasis that immediately bring about the desired effects: though beautifully written and performed, the essay means little to the uneducated woman, for whose sake Stephen now elaborates on his theories, "with many crude striking allusions with which he hoped to drive it home the better."[10] Nothing less than a rape of sorts, "the excesses of this [Stephen's] new worship" of beauty,[11] leave his mother a frail image of Ibsen's Hedvig Ekdal—"that poor little creature" in her favorite play, *The Wild Duck*, who committed suicide out of love for her self-indulgent father. Death is the condition under which Father Ekdal can love his daughter again, in the same way that May Dedalus has to sacrifice herself in order to play a role in her son's self-absorbed fantasies—that of the listener willing to enter the scene and bring to life Stephen's theory on life and drama. As she explains upon hearing his essay: "sometimes I feel that I want to leave this actual life and enter another [that of art]—for a time."[12] The mother is the other that must be tried, her attention arrested, if Stephen wants to "drive home" the point that drama penetrates to the core of life. Infusing his abstract thoughts with the tangibility of everyday life, her participation carries his theory from its transcendent heights to a direct engagement with the rest of the world: not only does she relate Ibsen's work to her own married life, but she also introduces Ibsen to her husband, who, as representative of "that class of society which in literature as in everything else goes always with its four feet on the ground,"[13] in turn associates the Norwegian author with the stockbroker in Dame Street. However, while this autonomous development allows the artist to withdraw from his creation and see it run its course, this contextualization—this variable doubling outlining the smugness of Dublin—fails to bring Stephen the kind of "respectability" and hence authority aspired to: "So that from neither of Stephen's parents did respectability get full allegiance."[14] If the son has succeeded in first deriving his fantasies from and then projecting them back onto his mother, then the latter does not necessarily reflect them in a self-assuring way.

It is this contingency inherent in his divided stature that fills the youth with fear. The price Stephen has to pay for taking his inspiration from his (procreative) mother—and since Shelley we know how limited she can make us feel—is that he can feel only "terror" in front of his own vast, self-generative powers. This demonization of the act of creation becomes particularly clear in that famous scene in *A Portrait* when, in the anatomy theater of Simon Dedalus's old school, the youth searches for his father's initials but only finds the word *Foetus*. This is his reaction:

> But the word and the vision capered before his eyes as he walked back across the quadrangle and towards the college gate. It shocked him to find in the outer world a trace of what he had deemed till then a brutish and individual malady of his own mind. His recent monstrous reveries came thronging into his memory. They too had sprung up before him, suddenly and furiously, out of mere words. He had soon given into them and allowed them to sweep across and abase his intellect, wondering always where they came from, from what den of monstrous images, and always weak and humble towards others, restless and sickened of himself when they had swept over him.[15]

What Stephen finds so repugnant in his confrontation with the word *Foetus* is the fact that what he has deemed to be an "individual malady of his own mind" already exists in the outside world. Here in this remnant of history, Stephen is shocked into the recognition that his own monstrous thought is simply the offspring (fetus) of a more original word outside himself. His horror is just this realization that his thoughts, the present ones included, grow out of a verbal vesture that he does not possess, but that encompasses him like a mother's womb.[16]

Having invaded the territory that belongs to his mother, and that is here explicitly linked to her life-giving powers, Stephen experiences his gift as a frightful necessity. In his hands, her natural procreative force is transformed into an artificially induced development that bereaves him of his originality. Hence, his birth as an artist sets into motion the story of his failure. Furthermore, as he feels incapable of claiming responsibility for this monstrous tale, he (comfortably) projects its black powers back onto the female other. While in *Ulysses*, this mainly gives rise to frightening dreams about his dead mother, in *Stephen Hero* and *A Portrait*, Stephen is still trying to "arrest" and "purify" this threatening presence in poems (about Emma Clery), epiphanies (the bird-girl), and idealizing theories on female beauty.

To conclude these introductory remarks on the political implications of Stephen's reflections on drama, I want to consider one significant moment in the course of May Dedalus's trial, when she gently tries to resist the violence her son is doing to her, by warning him that texts like Ibsen's "might do harm to some people—uneducated, unbalanced people. People's natures are so different. You perhaps . . ."[17] Stephen's mother is here seen to oppose her son's tribute to Ibsen—and himself—with a critical voice that reminds us that Stephen's theory on drama gains meaning only as long as he can engage his listeners. Claiming her adversary share in Stephen's dramatic performance, she confronts him, and us, with the distance that continues to separate his theory from her reality and that makes of the son's deliverance less a truthful engagement with the world than a theoretical, patriarchal gesture. By momentarily refusing to participate in his drama, May Dedalus reminds Stephen of the authoritative position from which he is handing down his essay to his subordinates: "You perhaps . . ." In this unfinished address to her son, his carefully constructed critique of aesthetic and religious authority is made to sound as one more paternal imperative. Hence his immediate response "O, never mind me . . ."[18] In order for his view on drama to be successful, the artist's transcendent position must disappear in a dialogical engagement with the world: "Do you think these plays are unfit for people to read?" "No, I think they're magnificent plays indeed."[19] The balance has been restored: May Dedalus again assumes the role of the cooperative reader whose subservience is to guarantee the validity of the son's self-serving theories. If Stephen had given his mother Ibsen's *When We Dead Awaken* to read, perhaps she would have found the means with which to carry on her critique of his paternal logic of artistic exchange. For in this play the artist's reflection is irreparably shattered by the cracked looking glass of a non-serving woman.

In "Ibsen's New Drama," his essay on Ibsen's *When We Dead Awaken*, Joyce articulates a deep suspicion of the power relations underlying artistic production. The essay in many ways prefigures the thematic concerns that the author will extensively deal with some years later in his own play, *Exiles*. Central to Ibsen's tragic plot is the conflict between Arnold Rubek, the professor-sculptor, and Irene, who served as the model for the man's masterpiece, "The Resurrection Day." An uncanny forerunner of Stephen's dead mother, Irene has come back from the past to confront the artist with his murderous act: "I exposed myself wholly and unreservedly to your gaze . . . and never once did you touch me . . . I gave you my young living soul. And that gift left me empty within—soulless [*looks at him with a fixed stare*]. It was that I died of, Arnold."[20] Having given up her body and soul for the sake of his work, Irene feels she has been moulded—arrested—into a shape that has literally and figuratively left her lifeless. Upon her dead, beautiful as well as maternal, body, Rubek has erected, resurrected, his fame. It is this patriarchal system of so-called exchange, in which she gives and he takes, that Irene violently disrupts. Refusing to be a pawn in man's self-serving economic structure, and determined to resist the fantasizing gaze that perceives her sexual difference only in terms of the logic of artistic (re)production, Irene enters the scene as the self-resurrected other, who confronts the sculptor with the irreducible gap between his art and her life. The statue that he used to perceive as the accomplished unity of his art and life literally comes alive to affirm its (her) independence from the maker. Irene's resurrection embodies the transition from classical art in its traditional sense—represented by the sensuous completion of Greek sculpture—to "classical" art as Joyce defines it in his essays on drama. In her postmortem appearance, the patriarchal unity between the self and his image dissolves: it becomes a living, truly limiting experience.

Ibsen's play demonstrates what happens when what was figuratively true for the sculptor, namely, that his work symbolizes Resurrection Day, assumes a literal life on stage. For what Irene represents is exactly the after-life of the statue, its rebirth after, or better *in*, its death. In this breakdown, the woman resurrects the original *beyond man's economy of reflection*. This means that Irene's appearance at once confirms and mimics the logic of rebirth or return underlying Rubek's specular system of representation. If she brings anything back at all, it is the life-size difference between original and copy, model and statue, artist and medium. From this position of non-identity, Irene can now claim Rubek's statue as her own child:

> Rubek's transgression has indeed been great. Not merely has he possessed himself of her soul, but he has withheld from its rightful throne the child of her soul. By her child Irene means the statue. To her it seems that this statue is, in a very true and very real sense, born of her. Each day as she saw it grow to its full growth under the hand of the skilful moulder, her inner sense of motherhood for it, of right over it, of love towards it, had become stronger and more confirmed.[21]

Irene's trial concerns the manner in which her life-giving force has been appropriated and reproduced in the deadly image of the paternal same. Thus, if she wants to reclaim the statue born from her dead body, she will have to bring it to life in a manner that emphasizes the distance between Rubek and his creation: "The Resurrection Day" will be *her* resurrection day. Since the only escape from his inheritance consists in making real what was for him only a figurative gesture, she first grabs a knife to violently repeat what he did when carving out her death in his image. Upon the failure of this act, she exploits the development of Ibsen's drama to subvert the positions between artist and model. While she assumes the role of the artist, he (Rubek, but in a sense also Ibsen) becomes the model delivering the material with which to complete the play. His work becomes the inspiration for her final act: the passionless Rubek will be brought to life, resurrected, not however in an act of exclusion but in love. Through this inversion of the man's murderous act, the players have far transgressed the original setting of Ibsen's play, which now ends in an apocalyptic flash of lightning: drama finds its consummation in that moment when the male artist yields his authority to his female counterpart.

It should be clear that what in Joyce's other works was identified as the dramatic autonomy of the work of art is here used as a critical strategy with which to raise questions about the traditional manner in which women are portrayed by men. With his essay on Ibsen, Joyce far surpasses the boundaries of Stephen Dedalus's theory on drama and life. In fact, it is *against* Stephen's superior theoretical stance that one should read Joyce's appraisal of Ibsen. Whereas Stephen's blind adherence to his masculine ego prevents him from putting into practice his theory on art—and hence from becoming the artist that he so much desires to be—Ibsen reveals himself the supreme artist precisely in his openness toward the reality of the female other. What separates Ibsen from his predecessors is the way he combines his sympathy for his (intelligent) women, with a critical "restraint" of the old artist-model framework:

> However perfect Ibsen's former creations may be, it is questionable whether any of his women reach to the depth of soul of Irene. She holds our gaze for the sheer force of her intellectual capacity. She is, moreover, an intensely spiritual creation—in the truest and widest sense of that. At times she is liable to get beyond us, to soar above us, as she does with Rubek. It will be considered by some as a blemish that she—a woman of fine spirituality—is made an artist's model, and some may even regret that such an episode mars the harmony of the drama. I cannot altogether see the force of this contention; it seems pure irrelevancy. But whatever may be thought of the fact, there is small room for complaint as to the handling of it. Ibsen treats it, as indeed he treats all things, with large insight, artistic restraint, and sympathy.[22]

No sooner has Joyce recognized Irene as the artistic spirit invisibly soaring above the players' and our own heads, than he reinscribes her into the text itself and considers how she has been represented, as if he is aware of the danger that such an equation between femininity and pure spirituality might entail. Irene is no simple ghost, whose death is the condition under which Ibsen's fantasies can be played out. Rather than being a transcendent model against whose absence his drama takes place, she is present as the stylistic principle of resistance to such romantic, speculative stance:

> Indeed, if one may say so of an eminently virile man, there is a curious admixture of the woman in his nature. His marvellous accuracy, his faint traces of femininity, his delicacy of swift touch, are perhaps attributable to this admixture . . . With a deft stroke, in a phrase, in a word, he does what costs them [Hardy, Turgenev, Meredith] chapters, and does it better.[23]

Both above and inside the text, Irene embodies the strife between romantic transcendence and classical limitation that for

Joyce is "the condition of all achievement." She thus functions as the figure of conflict without which aesthetic innovation is impossible. The figure of (problematic) transition between the old and the new, her presence—or should we say resurrection—in Ibsen's text releases an uncontainable drive that subverts traditional boundaries between male artists and female models. Her "aloofness from passion," together with her violent refusal to serve as Rubek's reflection, endows Ibsen's work with the mixture of affect and critical detachment that only a Joycean critic torn by passions could dream of: "When the art of a dramatist is perfect the critic is superfluous. Life is not to be criticized, but to be faced and lived."[24] Ultimately, then, Irene is the figure of life: not as an abstract idea, for to idealize life, as Stephen does, is to "arrest" it within an oppressive model; not as an object to be given by women and taken by men—to conceive (woman's) life in terms of man's economy of exchange is, as we will see in *Exiles*, to degrade it as a common possession; but life as it is lived by a woman and faced or seen by a man, generating a conflict of perceptions—between model and artist—where we least expect it, at the height (and end) of Ibsen's authoritative stance (*When We Dead Awaken* was Ibsen's final play). Authority, for Joyce, conjoins a maximum of romantic self-aggrandizement with a maximum of limitation, uncertainty, and self-criticism. What he recognizes at the end of his essay, "in the conversion of Rubek's views as to the girl-figure in his masterpiece,"[25] is that his own mastery as a critic (and artist) is built upon an immense debt to this female persona. Since she has already effectively criticized the work, Joyce is in fact superfluous. No longer a mirror, nor a mute model for the speaking subject, Irene has outgrown him as an eloquent predecessor. Joyce can only hope that one day his work will do the same for all of us.

Bertha in Exile(s): Viewing the Artist's Distance from Nearby

Exiles is Joyce's only published play, which, although it was never publicly recognized as a masterpiece,[26] the author never ceased to defend against his antagonists. Clearly influenced by Ibsen, the play continues to explore the social boundaries of the stage of representation that Joyce first uncovered and transgressed in his essays on drama. The preceding chapters have demonstrated that for all their aesthetic concerns and for all their emphasis on the independence of art from moral and religious laws, Joyce's early writings display a remarkably intense preoccupation with reality: with the need to let real life bring a "soul into the work of the artist."[27] It is this belief in the modern as being based on a renewed unification between the material (real life) and the spiritual (soul) that puts Joyce's project in the tradition of Schlegel's redefinition of the sublime. The conflict between reality and the subject, which Kant's sublime had recuperated as the victory of transcendental reason over the imagination, Schlegel reconsiders as the internal strife characterizing the workings of the imagination; that is, its power to transgress existing boundaries, bring opposites together, and thus construe an intuition of a larger whole carrying within itself the seeds of a radically new mode of differentiation in which spirit and matter are not yet singularly divided. This vision of a dynamic, conflicting whole, generated in the imaginary bridging of the Kantian gap between the sensible and the supersensible, posits an aesthetic rather than a rational idea, which is ultimately the idea of imaginary production itself. Accordingly, Schlegel's sublime concerns less the presentation of the absolutely unpresentable than presentation as the absolute itself: art as it cannot be produced without leaving many things unshaped, and hence art as it cannot exist without remainder or excess. The sublime marking both the infinity and necessary incompletion of beauty breaks through the borders of the work to articulate what art cannot take into account—its own absence. In poststructuralist terms, this can be rephrased to mean that the sublime romantic text is, in its very universality, generating a meaning that can no longer be expressed by the existing forms, or genres, of art. The romantic (symbolic) sign thus plays on a double level: it uses conventional modes of representation only to speak of another, new language, which is nothing less than the romantic work as such. Thus carrying the mark of its own production, the romantic text means only in relation to itself—which is to say that meaning (subjectivity) is here being produced in a movement of auto-generation, for which there is no economy of restriction, no final transcendental signified from where to draw a proper boundary to what we (can) know. With presentation as the absolute itself, truth momentarily shines through the arbitrariness of the sign.

Thus, to the extent that the sublime formlessness *inherent in* the production of the romantic work-subject points to its universality, transcendence here is radically limited. In my analysis of *Lucinde*, I have shown this gesture of transcendence to effectuate the dramatic instantiation of the novel in the here and now of (Lucinde's but also my own) reading. Meaning in *Lucinde* was seen to be inscribed in an excessive layering of scenes of writing and reading, which I described as the discontinuous space of presentation in which the figural continuity of the work takes place. The totality of the Schlegelian text thus emerges in the excess or the beyond of literature which is not yet the realm of the concept as in Hegel but that of the idea of beauty: beauty as it arises in a supplementary relation of otherness to itself. Beauty as sublimity or ugliness.

Thus it is that, at the height of its creative powers, Schlegel's (self-reflexive) subject is made to see the surplus of images that separates it from itself. In that intuitive vision, the theatrical nature of the subject's autonomy is pointed out and the "I" momentarily merges with its surroundings. In *Lucinde,* this doubling between the self and the other takes place between a man and a woman—which I argued to be Schlegel's way of countering Julius's autobiography with the disturbing alterity that it hides: the fact that he uses the image of an absent woman to legitimate his unceasing self-projection. If in order for the *idea* of beauty to exist the original must be epiphanized, then in a man's world it is the female other that must be sacrificed. Thus seen in relation to the absent Lucinde (to her violent displacement), Julius's amorous letters become false, if not monstrous. The destructive machinery that the man's text sets into motion perverts not only what we ordinarily call love but also the whole idea of beauty. The disinterested stance of the subject that founded Kant's concept of beauty is here unmasked as a way of covering up our ugly interest in—domination over—the female other.

And just as for Schlegel, "modern" romantic art counters the classicists' naive belief in the natural, objective, and purposeless harmony between subject and object with a critical view of the sublime disharmony that it leaves unsaid, so Joyce's modern drama confronts the clinical detachment of the dramatist with an experience of the conflicts underlying it. At the peak of objectivity, the dramatist's indifference—the authority that it inspires—dissolves, and his entanglement with the surrounding world becomes clear. As argued before, the synthesis between life and drama that Joyce searches for in theory amounts to a far-reaching critique of Stephen's patriarchal logic of representation in practice. The realism that the conjunction of life and art yields in imitation of Ibsen's drama unmasks the youth's stance as artistic complacency: when seen in its context,

Stephen's aesthetic distance is as little detached from the world as Richard Rowan's neutrality vis-à-vis his wife can hide the interest that motivates it. The issue at stake in *Exiles*: a woman's body.

As in *Stephen Hero* and *When We Dead Awaken*, *Exiles* stages the inner conflict of the artist (Richard Rowan) in terms of a complex struggle between himself and a woman, who is alternatively his mother, muse, and concubine. Richard's plight is that of a son struggling against the spirit of a critical mother, whose negativity confronts the artist with his own limits: "Can you not hear her mocking me while I speak?"[28] The whole play evolves around Richard's attempt to transform into art the hardness of that spirit which, he feels, betrayed him and drove him into exile. In a sense, Richard's staging of his own cuckoldry aims at gaining control over a conflict that has so far dominated and harmed his career as a writer. Now that his mother is dead, Richard can literally and figuratively return from exile and subjugate that strife to his paternal authority.[29] Or so he thinks.

Exiles is a play about conflict, infidelity, the falsity of truthfulness, and the truth of artifice. That nobody here simply is what (s)he appears to be is due to the fact that every character derives his or her identity from the other characters to which (s)he is opposed, while none of these oppositions can claim to be sufficient in itself. Richard's friendship with Robert, for instance, gets its full significance only when looked at in the light of his relation to Bertha, who, as we know, is being actively seduced by Robert. The latter's declarations of love, in turn, become less convincing when we remember that in the past he has wooed many other women, among them Beatrice Justice, who for the past eight years has acted as Richard's spiritual pen pal. It is this intricate network of conflicting passions that makes it impossible to detect the defining contours of every single one of them. Boundaries here are constantly shifting not only between but also within the characters. In permanent conflict with themselves, all characters suffer from internal exile and from the impossibility of finding that singular reflection in the outside world that would allow them to create an identity through mediation. Hence, rather than grounding the mechanism of (self-)reflection, language here ultimately poses as a sham double mimicking its traditional function of representation or expression. It remains to be seen to what extent this linguistic impasse presents us with an alternative view on "realism" that could accommodate the voice of the central woman in this text: Bertha.

Despite its unity of time (one day) and action (betrayal), which has led critics such as Ezra Pound to describe *Exiles* as a distinctively unified play, Joyce's drama presents itself as a remarkably divided work in which contradictory planes of action and acting intersect. There is first of all the romantic intrigue between Robert and Bertha, at first sight the scene of an extramarital liaison, but in reality the outcome of Richard's carefully directed scenario. The amorous subplot, we quickly learn, is hardly anything more than an exercise in the Aristotelian definition of drama as the "imitation of an action," an engagement in pretended or make-believe action within a carefully arranged set of events that leave little room for exploration of character or psychology. Whatever happens between Robert and Bertha is imbued with such a degree of theatricality that their love affair immediately deteriorates into a comical farce.[30] Robert plays the stereotypical ardent lover, wooeing his mistress by means of a "mass of overblown roses" and a whole register of outworn clichés. Bertha, on the contrary, is less comfortable with her role as the passively seduced beloved, a role she feels has been forced upon her by Richard for only one reason: to have complete liberty with Beatrice Justice. Hence it is with critical detachment that she carries out her husband's script. To Robert's question why she puts away the roses so quickly, she responds:

> [*Takes them from the table and holds them close to her face.*] Is this what you wish me to do with them?
>
> ROBERT: [*Watching her.*] Your face is a flower too—but more beautiful. A wild flower blowing in a hedge. [*Moving his chair closer to her.*] Why are you smiling? At my words?
>
> BERTHA: [*Laying the flowers in her lap.*] I am wondering if that is what you say—to the others. (35)

The overdetermination of the characters' words and gestures as well as of the roses serves to emphasize the duplicity of the love scene and to develop a counterplot that has as its theme the operation of the play, surveyed by an invisible manager: Richard Rowan. Indeed, what resounds from Robert's exaggerated speech and gestures on the one hand, from Bertha's sardonic remarks on the other, is the ironic distance that separates the two characters from their actions—a double consciousness through which the lovers reveal themselves to be playing at being in love in words clearly not their own. In this comedy of sorts, language openly functions as a mask, thereby subverting the seriousness of what is said. Moreover, overflowing the boundaries of any one of its formulations, the lovers' discourse becomes the site where their parts incorporate the other parts of the play. Hence, their positions as lovers are all but fixed and, in fact, function as anchoring points from which they can freely be distributed and exchanged. Thus, not only does Bertha see in Robert's past amorous life the reflection of her husband's escapades, she also hears in his stereotypical remarks the echo of other men's voices: "I think men speak like that to all women whom they like or admire. What do you want me to believe?" (37). Robert, in turn, will later confess to Richard that what he admires in Bertha are

> Not those qualities which she has and other women have not but the qualities which she has in common with them. I mean . . . the commonest. [*Turning over the stone, he presses the other side to his forehead.*] I mean how her body develops heat when it is pressed, the movement of her blood, how quickly she changes by digestion what she eats into—what shall be nameless. [*Laughing.*] I am very common today. (49)

Robert's comments confirm Bertha's unease: her role of the actively pursued beloved is the projection of a man, in whose gaze she exists, not as a person in her own right, but as a vehicle of connection with the outside world. For Robert, as for Richard (in this respect, the two are interchangeable), she is the representative of her sex, "the commonest" or nameless body, the possession of which allows them to have something in common with each other. From this perspective, Robert's and Richard's love of Bertha is literally and figuratively a "passing" thing: it far surpasses what it appears to be while it transforms its recipient into a thing to be passed on from father to son, from master to slave, from artist to character. For Richard and Robert to be more than alliterative allies by name,[31] they must appropriate the female body that alone is capable of transforming the word into flesh. Thus acting as the vehicle that brings about the transubstantiation between spiritual father (Richard) and earthly sons (Robert, Archie), Bertha's presence is continuously displaced by the men around her and, in this manner, comes close to signaling nothing but the metaphorical as well as theatrical economy of the play. This explains why Robert describes her in terms of a vessel that is consumed by what it carries inside itself—"how quickly she changes by digestion what she eats into." In his paternal economy, woman's substance (content) becomes the locus of her consumption. She exists, in other words, by virtue of the life that she gives (away) to others. The full meaning of her being lies in her capacity to dissimulate her presence and become a means of transference between men. This is particularly clear, for instance, at the opening of act 2, where Robert is waiting to meet Bertha in secret, but is visited by Richard instead. Not only does Richard take Bertha's place, he also wants to hear from his friend the word that—as the latter once wrote to her—he has "never dared to say" to her. This is Robert's reply: "I admire very much the personality of your . . . of . . . your wife. That is the word. I can say it. It is no secret" (75). Thus, upon having been dispossessed by her jealous partner, Bertha is then reduced to a "word" in the two friends' verbal exchange—a word that is to affirm her insignificance as an autonomous being: "wife." In man's symbolic discourse Bertha becomes what in reality she is not, Richard's "wife." Ironically, the legal bonds of marriage by which the artist has never wanted to hold her, despite her repetitive requests that he do so, are here, in the company of his friend Robert, established once and for all: she is Richard's possession—"your wife," "your work"—given away by the one and taken by the other, as a token of their homoerotic friendship. As Robert puts it: "She [Bertha] is yours, your work. [*Suddenly.*] And that is why I, too, was drawn to her. You are so strong that you attract me even through her" (78).

To the extent that Bertha's dispossessed presence thus opens up the space in which the two men are united, the woman functions as the icon of sexual transgression: she is the literal and figural intermediary who transfers the amorous liaison between herself and Robert onto the friendship between Robert and Richard. Furthermore, as the "word" who connects the subplot, in which she is the recipient of Robert's seduction, to the framing story, in which she is the product of Richard's plot, Bertha is also the figure of textual transgression. Through her, plots interlace, dialogues are recontextualized, roles get imitated, and words extensively cited:

RICHARD: Yes. I saw it. What else went on?
BERTHA: He asked me to give him my hand.
RICHARD: [*Smiling.*] In marriage?
BERTHA: [*Smiling.*] No, only to hold.
RICHARD: Did you?
BERTHA: Yes. [*Tearing off a few petals.*] Then he caressed my hand and asked would I let him kiss it. I let him. (58)

Bertha here is not simply the instrument with which Richard, the artist, appropriates his characters' lives—from a distance and in proximity, as befits a Joycean artist. She is herself the very property of drama itself, at least in Aristotle's definition of the term as the "imitation of an action." For what else is her report to Richard if not an imitation or repetition of what was said before? What else is this scene if not the declamation of a previously cited speech? An imitation of an action that was already a repetition of what so many other beloved had done before her, Bertha's performance is the agent of multiple doubling. Her words mimic the theme of the subplot—seduction—and the operation of Richard's as well as Joyce's play itself, both of which are modes of leading astray. She thus represents the possibility that Richard's presence to himself through the mediation of his characters does not come full circle but is blocked by the capacity of drama to signify something quite other than what is intended.

Once transgression has explicitly been made an integrative part of the play, once the stage of dramatic representation has become part of the plot, the distinction between framing and acting can no longer be maintained: Richard's objective posture collapses and in the self-generative pattern that follows he becomes the tragic hero victimized by his own production. As he threatens to actually lose Bertha to Robert, he must exchange his authorizing stance for that of a subjectively involved character. He now visits Robert to disclose his knowledge about the affair and plead him to carry out the scenario differently: "Robert, not like this. For us two, no. Years, a whole life, of friendship. Think a moment. Since childhood, boyhood . . . No, no. Not in such a way—like thieves—at night. [*Glancing about him.*] And in such a place. No, Robert, that is not for people like us" (77). Ironically, the effect of Richard's intervention runs counter to what he originally intended. For having witnessed the man's incapacity to control his unruly partner, Robert can now openly claim that Bertha belongs as much to him as to Richard. No longer simply Richard's work, Bertha functions as the site of contest between two authorities. Now that the boundaries of her body prove to be less securely policed than Richard thought they were, there is no reason why Robert should not attempt to reinscribe those borders and make her his own property. Bertha becomes a shared object, the final format of which is the stake of their battle.

Confronted with this radical invasion of his authority, Richard tells Bertha what the two men have agreed upon and, in a final attempt to recover control over his alienated work, commands her to consummate her love for Robert. But a shared authority is of course a deflated one: once the mechanism of division is set into play, Richard is hard put to contain it within a scenario the boundaries of which have shown themselves to be divisible and hence porous, or transgressive. In inverse proportion to Richard's defective frame, the play has gained an autonomy that neither Richard nor Robert will be able to recuperate. In every scene that follows, the two authors prove to be lost in a work that reflects, and feeds upon, its previous actions: the dialogue between Richard and Bertha becomes food for thought in that night of probable sin between Bertha and Robert, which the next day becomes the topic of conversation between Robert and Richard, Bertha and Beatrice, Richard and Bertha.

Thus, what emerges from the appearance of Bertha as the figure of textual transposition and transgression is a play that increasingly devours the very distinctions and conflicts that have made it work. No sooner does Bertha relate the subplot to the framing story by imitating in front of Richard what happened between her and Robert than this performance is seen to generate a series of self-reflexive imitations, in which the original configuration gets increasingly doubled and mimicked. In a permanent recontextualization of words and characters, the boundaries dissolve between artist and character, master and slave, plots and frames—boundaries on which hinged the structure of the play. If it is in Bertha that this double movement of substantiation and consumption finds its concentration as well as explosion, it is because she is the men's medium of reflection or exchange that, once it is set into play, need not be limited to any one character, nor to any one place or action. Through her expansive mediation the play both gives birth to and feeds upon itself: its action is also a mode of reflection, emptied as it proceeds. Topical and typical, singular and communal, Bertha's body opens onto the body of this text. In this permanent movement, it gains commonality on the one hand, whimsicality on the other. A common gesture such as giving one's hand to be kissed by Robert Hand, for instance, becomes a figural gesture of marriage when cited to Richard. Thus, while she lives by virtue of what she gives—literally to the possessive Robert, figuratively to the distant Richard—her present is of such abundance that it does not let itself be possessed by any means. In her self-less deliverance she offers as much as she retains, so that we might well say that her gift is also a way of delaying her final entrapment. (This refusal to give, in turn, allies her with the two other women in this play who also detain their gift of love: the dead Mrs. Rowan and the diseased Mrs. Justice). Thus, in Richard's presence we see her dreamily "agree" to stay with Robert, while in the company of Robert she prolongs her visit by recurrently insisting on going away. Eventually, she will do both or neither. Hers is a protean appearance that is a source of pleasure for Robert (the automobile), "a deep wound of doubt" for Richard (the automystic).

It is this arbitrariness of her position that at once confirms and problematizes her existence as the "tool" in her lovers' hands. The territory of a struggle between two opposites—the artist and the journalist, he who gives and he who takes, the spiritual and the physical lover—she cannot but carry the mark of the opponent. The reassuring symmetry between Richard and his autonomous creation, which was to guarantee his identity as a Joycean (dramatic) artist—his return to the home of his "sweet and noble" father—has been permanently disrupted. Bertha has proved to be unreliable as a medium of self-realization. Instead of consolidating Richard's return to the Ireland he once loved, she has led him figuratively, and Robert literally, back into exile, the land of haunting mothers and wandering Jews.[32]

If on the one hand Robert and Richard need Bertha's body as the "common" property against which to symbolically order their masculinity, then this "object" which they share with each other does not guarantee them the masculine identity aspired to. Rather than endowing them with that identity and hence authority, Bertha offers them an uncertain bond: a space of conflict and reduplication in which scenes produce their own doubles while losing their significance in an endless chain of mirroring images. By thus problematizing the field of identity formation, by inviting a reconsideration of subjecthood in terms not of fixed oppositions—male subject versus female object—but as involving a destabilizing process of transposition that far surpasses originating divisions, *Exiles* generates a counterdiscourse to Richard's and Robert's male-dominated dialectical exchange. Along with the two men's circulation of the female body, aimed at possession and identification, a movement of splitting irrupts: I mean the conflict of views between the two men that makes of Bertha's body less an object than a hybrid construct of collective but contradictory deceit.

So while on one level *Exiles* is a play about the patriarchal transference of female bodies according to man's give-and-take model, on another it deals with woman's body as a rhetorical topos, a hybrid commonplace, the heterogeneity of which problematizes Robert's and Richard's oppositional constructions of masculine identity. In the latter case, we are dealing with a critical revaluation of the body-mind dichotomy on which their contest as well as their supremacy toward Bertha is founded. In contrast to Richard's non-involvement and Robert's possessiveness, both of which are modes of affirming the hierarchical opposition between male subject and female object, Joyce's text points to a different kind of attitude: to a conception of the female body as a living artificial construction. If we want to restore Bertha in her role of *actor* (actress), then we need to reformulate her bodily contours, not as fixed, but as points of reduplication and conflict. Theaters of communion they are, marked by an excess of social bonds that are ruptured as they cohere—bonds between Bertha and Richard, Bertha and Robert, Robert and Richard, Robert and Beatrice, Richard and Beatrice, Bertha and Beatrice, Archie and Beatrice, Archie and his mother, Archie and his father, Archie and Robert, Brigid and all the others. Bertha's bodily presence is, thus, more than simply an object governed by Richard, pursued by Robert. Rather than a preexistent "given" to be "taken," unveiled, or represented, she is the site of a "communal art" (as the young Joyce once said about drama), of a complex web of relations that share with each other their oppositionality. The convergence of sameness and difference is the point here, because it makes explicit that we are not dealing with community in the sense of a global identity, neither are we dealing with a construction based on disengagement (objectivity), as Richard would have it, or on a re-establishment of bonds (subjectivity) in Robert's manner. Instead Joyce offers a radical re-inscription of the two: in Bertha these two stereotypical views on women find their simultaneous expression and radical limit.[33]

Exiles is, indeed, a play in which the conflict between two opposites—as this has structured the history of Western philosophy, art, or science—is shown to be a masquerade, and Joyce's articulation of an alternative. The play both installs and criticizes the classical drive toward objectification on the one hand, the romantic yearning for subjective involvement on the other. The natural daylight in Richard's parlor is weighed against the artificial shade in Robert's cottage—the mirror against the lamp—and both are found deceptive. As said, these limits find their ambiguous outlines in the figure of Bertha, whose function it is to transfer and thus counter Robert's and Richard's projections of herself. In contrast to Robert, whom Joyce's notes to the play describe as "automobile,"

Bertha, I would argue, is "mobile," an exposition of dramatic representation that questions what it presents and in this duplicity produces an "understanding of its own nature" (149). What we get to understand is that Bertha's "nature"—associated as it is with birth and earth—is the effect of a male-dominated practice aimed at objectifying the female other.[34] This, I would argue, is realism of the most radical kind. An articulation of "reality" founded not on a mimetic representation of the outside, nor on an expression of the inside, but on a critical revaluation of the boundaries between inside and outside: who is the subject, who the object, how does one decide who is included and who left in exile?

This brings us to the final point of my discussion of Joyce's drama, namely, the role of comedy. That *Exiles* is not to be regarded as a merely tragic play Joyce explicitly indicates in his notes where he recognizes his literary prototypes in, among others, Rabelais and Molière (the theme of the cuckold, the struggle between two men over a woman). While we will have to return to the Rabelaisian element of Joyce's writing during our analysis of *Ulysses*, for now let us try to formulate Joyce's view on comedy and its connection to the sublime.

EIGHT

"From the Sublime to the Ridiculous Is But a Step"

Comic Drama

As the young Joyce was well aware, in order to understand the complexities of comedy, we need to look back to the times when it was first articulated as a genre: to the Greeks.[1] In his essay "Drama and Life" Joyce follows Aristotle's definition of comedy as emerging from a phallic—Dionysian—rite: "Greek drama arose out of the cult of Dionysos, who, god of fruitage, joyfulness and earliest art, offered in his life-story a practical groundplan for the erection of a tragic and a comic theatre."[2] As to the ancient source of the comic and tragic theater, we are still left in the dark, but most theories seem to confirm Aristotle's conjecture that they arose from Dionysian fertility rites: the comic chorus from phallic songs, the tragic chorus from dithyrambs (choral poems) in honor of the Greek god of agriculture. In fact, Greek drama emerged when to these ritual songs, performed by a group of satyrs (hybrid beings half-goat, half-human) were added spoken lines, and, in time, two or three actors to carry the plot. In its typical form, the fertility rite evolved around the death and resurrection cycle: the past year (the old king) was killed by the new season (the young king) and a scapegoat sacrificed to purge the tribe of its evils. The sexual strength of the successor was then tested in a question-answer session, which, in turn, was accompanied by orgiastic singing and dancing. According to Sypher, whose interesting analysis of comedy heavily borrows from Cornford's classic study *The Origin of Attic Comedy*:[3]

> [T]he dramatic form known as tragedy eventually suppressed the sexual magic in this canonical plot, leaving only the portrayal of the suffering and death of the hero, king, or god. Comedy, however, kept in the foreground the erotic action, together with the disorderly rejoicing at the rebirth or resurrection of the god-hero who survives his *agon*.[4]

More than tragedy's involvement in sorrow, then, it was comedy's indulgence in erotic action and rebirth that was particularly suited to honor the god of fertility and of the theater, Dionysus.

In Greek mythology, Dionysus was the son of Zeus and the princess Semele. Upon Semele's request to see her lover in his divine form, Zeus appeared to her in a thunderbolt. She did not survive the encounter. However, Zeus rescued his son and sewed him up in his thigh, where he stayed until he had reached maturity. Having been born twice, the first time from a mother tragically lost, the second time from a father joyfully rejoined, Dionysus was then raised by the female Bacchantes, who became his followers and, in his honor, installed festive rites that varied from boisterous drinking and sexual communion to the sacrifice of human victims. Vitality in the midst of death is what Dionysus represents: the affirmation of nature's potency over and against man's mortal existence. However, since Dionysus's regenerative power derives its significance from the extent to which it is able to counter the disruptive presence of death with a *renewal* of life, the vitality that he stands for is one of transgression or excess: his is the corrective return of nature that must always be richer and more abundant than the original that it resuscitates. In a sense—and this is not unlike Nietzsche's use of the term—Dionysianism is a mode of saying yes to nature's capacity to outdo itself. In this religion, then, nature functions as a permanent movement of innovation or transformation in which no phenomenon simply "is." This amounts to saying that Dionysus embodies the principle of rebirth that turns life into the unceasing reduplication of a lost original. His is the realm of image making in which life masquerades as real. *Drama here emerges spontaneously from life* because the latter is already the imitation of a precedent. In this cyclical return, nature disintegrates into artifice, while the distinction of the self dissolves in a fusion with what is the same. Dionysus stands for this immediate transformation of life into communal rite and hence, according to Joyce, offers in his life story the groundplan for a tragic and a comic theater, depending on whether one regards the transformation as heroic loss or common gain, death, or rebirth.

It is in Nietzsche's *Birth of Tragedy* that one finds a full-length reflection on the Dionysian origins of modern drama.[5] Although, as Aubert also notes, Joyce had probably not read Nietzsche at the time he was composing his essays on drama, a brief detour via the German philosopher will clarify what is (not) at stake in Joyce's Ibsenite tragicomic play, *Exiles*.

Although Nietzsche repeatedly attempts to differentiate himself from his romantic predecessors, his early study on Greek tragedy proves itself an inheritor of that tradition in its definition of reality as an ongoing movement of artistic transformation. The birth of tragedy is here defined as the major effect of the twin forces of creation and destruction that make up the ceaseless striving of existence: while Dionysus personifies the frenzied and limitless urge for life, Apollo is the god of temperance and harmony. Together they initiate the conflict out of which the tragic vision of the Greeks emerges, a vision that for Nietzsche implies an awareness of the cruelty and inhumanity of nature's drives. The only way to forget and make bearable the suffering that accompanies this Dionysian wisdom is through the shaping powers of (Apollinian) art. That it is in tragedy, not in the epic, that Nietzsche finds the artistic model with which to counter the destructive depths of his insight is due to the fact that, unlike Homer, Sophocles and Aeschylus have performed, rather than hidden, the conflict of life. In contrast to Homer's naive fascination for the beautiful and idyllic illusions of the Olympian world, Greek tragedy readily arises from—and in fact makes tolerable—human conflict, suffering, and violence. Tragedy, in a manner of speaking, condenses, or temporarily unifies, the incompatible elements in life. It expresses the metaphoric essence of existence in which everything is related to (rather than in conflict with) everything else. This transferability or iterability of experience (in Nietzsche's later philosophy called "the eternal return") induces as much joy as pain in Greek tragedy. Against Schopenhauer's pessimism, Nietzsche celebrates the affirmation of life. Against the utopian view that Greek culture was a haven of harmony he defends its violent opposition of conflicting forces. Against art's service to verisimilitude he emphasizes its joyful creativity.

For Nietzsche, tragedy was doomed from the start because of the insurmountable strife that had characterized its birth. With the arrival of Euripides and Attic comedy, Greek drama lost its Dionysian insight into the workings of conflict in favor of an Apollinian concern for logic and reason. Socratic dialectics ushered in the spirit of a new, rational age in which the tragic wisdom generated by a group of dancing satyrs (the original chorus) was no longer possible. It is important to note that Nietzsche's critique of comedy—that degenerated art form filled with "Socratic optimism"—is aimed at Menander's new Attic comedy, not at the old Attic comedy of Aristophanes, whose incisive attacks on Euripides and Socrates he repeatedly quotes in support of his own view. In contrast to the highly fantastical, polemical, and satirical plots of Aristophanes (discussed above), Menander's comedies took their subject matter from the erotic lives of the Athenian middle classes. Highly improbable romantic events were integrated into a simple plot with generalized characters that, although drawn from real life and pictured in detail, soon deteriorated into empty, predictable types: the greedy father, the unresourceful lover, the impudent slave, the unreliable soldier, the innocent daughter . . . all of them clothed in recognizable outfits and stereotypical names. Along with this preference for realistic, everyday scenes—which, according to Nietzsche, is the product of an Apollinian consciousness caught up in the lies of a phenomenal world—new Attic comedy was characterized by a gradual expulsion from its plot of the chorus, whose function was now reduced to that of interlude between the different episodes. With the chorus disappeared the musical element in the play and thus, for Nietzsche, the Dionysian scene that had given Greek drama its tragic joy in the first place. For it is, indeed, in the choral dance that the audience is allowed to forget the conflict accompanying the *principium individuationis,* and to transform this principle of evil—symbolized by the destruction of the hero—into a joyous celebration of oneness with the world. In his absorption with the Dionysian dance of the chorus, the spectator experiences what Schlegel had already described in his reflections on Aristophanes's comedies: a sublime indulgence in the highest form of life—that of man among (wo)men.

In his early reflections on aesthetics, Joyce articulates a similar view on tragedy and comedy, both of which he believes to come together in the pleasures of control that art affords the viewer: "a comedy (a work of comic art) which does not urge us to seek anything beyond itself excites in us the feeling of joy . . . and even tragic art may be said to participate in the nature of comic art so far as the possession of a work of tragic art (a tragedy) excites in us the feeling of joy."[6] In contrast to tragedy, which deals with the feelings of sorrow resulting from the privation of something good, comedy celebrates the satisfaction that accompanies the possession of art.

Countering tragedy's loss with the pleasures of art, comedy emerges in an aesthetic sublimation of the threats of life. With comedy we move from the terror of privation (absence) to the joy of presence, which is, in a manner of speaking, a sublime turn from character to the play itself. Identification with the characters' conflicts—along with the pity and fear that this brings about—gives way to an awareness of that identification. By installing a distance between ourselves and the tragic hero, we allow ourselves a particular place, a focus or frame, from whence the horrifying events can be recognized as what they are: an event of art.

The young Joyce's generalization of comedy is to be understood in the light of his search for an objective art form. Comedy occurs when the tragic artist purges us from fear and terror. What remains is a pleasant sense of being at a play. *Comedy* is the term used to designate the pleasure evoked in us by drama, that of being among an audience—here and now with all the others. Interestingly, then, Joyce's early definition of comic joy is, for all its Aristotelian overtones, close to the romantic view on art as the transformation of the individual—Nietzsche's pain of individuation—into a larger structure of production, which Schlegel redefined as a return to (of) life through art.

Comedy in this sense accords with what so many theoreticians have claimed before: it redeems the tragic strife of individuation by putting it into a larger context, which is that of life. The joy of comedy emerges when the work of art contains the whole world within its boundaries. Paradoxically, with this contradictory definition of art-as-life, the necessity also arises that the comic work never achieves the unity that it promises. This frustration of expectation makes up the difference between joy (Comedy) and laughter (comedy). We laugh when our sense of regain is unmasked as an illusion. Moreover, seen from the vantage point of tragedy, our laughter is duplicitous, manifesting pain and pleasure alike.

At the end of his analytic of the sublime, Kant describes humor as "the talent of being able voluntarily to put oneself into a certain mental disposition, in which everything is judged quite differently from the ordinary method (reversed, in fact)," but which is still "in accordance with certain rational principles."[7] Humor shares with the sublime its power of mutation or reversal of mental attitude. But while the sublime emerges when the limits of the imagination become the occasion for the presentation of the ideas of reason, humor's jolting between two opposites elicits a conflict that may at first enliven the presentment but ultimately dissipates into nothing. The effect, for Kant, is laughter that arises when great (mental) expectations are frustrated: when the unexpected reversal of values does not add up to a major moment of insight. Only the body seems to profit from the occasion, at least insofar as the convulsions provoked by laughter initiate a physical feeling of health. Sublime joy may constitute a renewed sense of unification, in laughter the unity is limited to a physical release of tension.

One century later, Freud will explain that the pleasure of a joke comes with the release of an inhibitory energy, which is unutilizable and hence capable of discharge.[8] We laugh when we perceive somebody (a child, for instance) transgresses a certain barrier through a movement that, when compared to the movement that we would make in a similar situation, seems exaggerated and inexpedient. We imaginatively imitate the excessive movement of the other, while comparing the expenditure thus generated to the energy we would need under similar circumstances. When the difference between the two expenditures is too big, our increased expenditure in order to understand it is checked immediately and declared superfluous. If not used elsewhere (e.g., as moral criticism), the excess of energy is discharged in laughter. Besides this comic of movement, Freud also distinguishes the comic of situation and the comic of expectation. The latter occurs when rather than being disappointed, we laugh at a promise not fulfilled.

While with sublime joy Kant recuperates the transcendent surplus of presentation as the negative sign of (the idea of) the thing-in-itself, his reflections on laughter betray a certain unease about the possibility that the conflict within presentation might not indicate anything beyond phenomenality at all. Schlegel's position is exactly that there is nothing beyond the inadequacy of the phenomenon except an excessive force of (ideal) presentation. The sublime as the signal that there might be nothing beyond the failure of the presentation but the necessity of this failure—an inner conflict through which the presentation becomes all the more unlike itself—is what is known as "grotesque discord." The grotesque is a form of comedy that is presented under the cloak of the ugly and works by combining the most diverse elements—such as the human and the animal, as in the satyr—into a deformed whole. Exceeding ordinary divisions, the grotesque offends all commonsensical expectations and is, therefore, according to Baudelaire the comic form that is closest to the natural, naive joy of the child.[9]

"From the sublime to the ridiculous is but a step," Napoleon is supposed to have said when a near-victory turned into a disastrous defeat. These famous words also capture the disillusionment romantics like Schlegel must have felt by the end of the eighteenth century, when the ideals of the French Revolution were violently shattered, first by Robespierre and later by Napoleon himself. If comedy is the art in which ideality counters its limits in reality—the high faces the low—then surely it is as a comedian that one can confront the absurdity of heroism in a degenerated world with exceptional impunity. Here Nietzsche's eternal return becomes grotesque iteration, a mode of quantity without quality, rhetorical excess. In Aristophanes, Schlegel is fascinated by the wit with which the dramatist counters the Greek audience with the falseness of its ideals. This indulgence in ridicule is what, according to Hegel,[10] separates a polemic like Schlegel from a true philosopher: while the former destroys serious things without retaining anything to believe in, the latter mocks stupid things in order to recuperate what is valuable. The former is engaged in the ridiculous, the latter in the truly comic. The former stands among small inferior things, whereas the latter stands above them.

Hegel's critique is, of course, to be read in the light of his rejection of Schlegel's irony (discussed at length in my introduction), which we remember was first and foremost an attack on Schlegel's refusal to take philosophy (as the science leading to objective truth) seriously. However, as I have argued in the first part of this study, Schlegel's skepticism toward the absolute is anything but a nihilistic play with illusions: it is his way of addressing the "details" on which man has continued to erect his self-assuring, all-encompassing systems—destabilizing particulars that have been relegated to the margins as absence, uncertainty, the minuscule difference between beauty and its realization but that, when viewed from close-by, can have an immensely critical impact.

The Comic Novel

An unmistakable yearning for realism marks Joyce's preference for Ibsen's tragicomic plays. For all its interest in Dionysus and Wagner—that Nietzschean musical dramatist par excellence—Joyce's essay "Drama and Life," from which I quoted above, triumphantly proclaims that Greek drama and its Shakespearean counterpart have had their day. As arbitrarily as Greek drama once emerged from improvisation, the historical conditions of its setting were institutionalized and handed down as universal codes of laws that in Shakespeare's time were replaced by a new set of prescriptions. If drama is to be restored to its primary function as a *living* performance, then, as we have seen, it must let "real life" on the stage. Rather than rattling the daggers and goblets or pouring the blood of unfortunate heroes, Joyce seeks to put on stage the conflicts of everyday life in a world pervaded by such repetitiveness that artistic doubling cannot but be the most natural, even dreariest, part of it: "Still I think out of the dreary sameness of existence, a measure of dramatic life may be drawn."[11] Too much of a realist, Joyce realizes that the residue of art left in a society deprived of its aesthetic receptivity (the rabblement) is going to have to address the parochial commonplace.

To circle back to *Exiles*: the play carries the seeds of a comic view on the tragic necessity of deprivation. As long as Richard refuses to accept the practical implications of Joyce's theory on drama and experiences the duplicity of his condition as a threat or a betrayal by his environment, life befalls him in the guise of tragedy and hence terror. Not until he is willing to reconsider the limits of his position as the threshold from which to enter a communal, albeit base, world does comedy become a serious alternative. Joyce's notes to the play formulate this as follows: "Richard has fallen from a higher world and is indignant when he discovers baseness in men and women. Robert has risen from a lower world and so far is he from indignation that it surprises him that men and women are not baser and more ignoble."[12] Richard's pathos, like Stephen's, consists of his incapacity to relinquish heroism in the face of a conflict that could alternatively be experienced as bathos. This explains the difference not only between Richard and Robert but also between *Exiles* and *Ulysses* and more significantly: between Stephen and Bloom. While the former is too much of a serious romantic to see the world other than as *in conflict with* himself, the latter is comic and down-to-earth enough to experience that division not against but *with* other people. Having abandoned the false posture of heroism, Bloom accepts dramatic conflict as the hallmark of life; this is why he can find comfort in the idea that Molly's betrayal is only one in an infinite series.

In temporal terms—the switch from spatial drama to temporal narrative serves its purpose—we can reformulate the contrast in *Ulysses* as follows: Stephen experiences his historical position as a tragic nightmare from which he tries to awake; Bloom realizes that Stephen's greatest enemy is the farcical arrogance involved in his desire to escape from the nets of history and presents its absurdity by imagining what this post-historical awakening must, literally, be like:

> The resurrection and the life. Once you are dead you are dead. That last day idea. Knocking them all up out of their graves. Come forth, Lazarus! And he came fifth and lost the job. Get up! Last day! Then every fellow mousing around for his liver and his lights and the rest of his traps. Find damn all of himself that morning.[13]

As the modern resurrection of Odysseus, Bloom is, of course, well equipped to know what is involved in Stephen's typically modernist wish to transcend history in a lasting present moment. For one thing, it has to start with a return to the Greeks, whose world evolved in unalterable natural cycles and whose literature, therefore, could concentrate on presenting things that were already there. In this timeless universe, no difference existed between past and present. Hence, the hero did not really "know" how certain events were affecting him until he had lived them through till the very end. For instance, only when the Delphic oracle coincided with Oedipus's whole life did the hero realize the horror of his deeds. And seeing it, he blinded himself. *With that knowledge of the past, the tragic hero could never be the same again*. Nor could he simply act in the here and now again. Herein lies Hamlet's and Stephen's suffering. Their obsessive remembrance of the past—haunting them like a parental ghost—imbues their lives with fear and paralysis. If Stephen wants to leave history behind, he will have to learn to forget, unlearn the past (including the Greeks) and live only in the present, not however as a lasting (Greek) moment, but with the risk of losing the present forever. Released from the repository of memory, his existence will emerge out of, and evolve toward, nothingness. Within this space of improvisation, in which life is cut loose from the historical context that endows it with an inner necessity, a realm is opened up where relations are accidental and hence fragile. To "be oneself" here amounts not to an affirmation of identity but rather to the merry uncertainty that the bits and pieces—the liver and our lights and the rest of our traps—will add up to our own selves that morning.

This joy of the bull in the china shop is what Stephen indulges in during his drinking bouts in the "Oxen" and "Circe" episodes, not unexpectedly the most dramatic chapters in *Ulysses*. The "Circe" episode, in particular, offers a splendid example of how the belligerent destruction of time, although it momentarily enables Stephen to numb the pain of remembrance (cast out his mother's ghost from the stage), does not afford him the heroic victory longed for. The scene in question starts with this Dionysian dance of the hours, allegory of "time running out":

> (*From a corner the morning hours run out, goldhaired, slimsandalled, in girlish blue, waspwaisted, with innocent hands. Nimbly they dance, twirling their skipping ropes. The hours of noon follow in amber gold. Laughing, linked, high haircombs flashing, they catch the sun in mocking mirrors, lifting their arms.*)[14]

Having mockingly reflected the sun—how else could time reflect its own marker but in passing (and) mockery—the hours' dance becomes increasingly twisted and turned:

> (*The morning and noon hours waltz in their places, turning, advancing to each other, shaping their curves, bowing visavis. Cavaliers behind them arch and suspend their arms, with hands descending to, touching, rising from their shoulders.*)[15]

As time develops, both time in and of the play, the hours become more visibly grotesque: they assume masks, wear veils, and in their disappearance turn into self-exhibiting prostitutes and bracelets weaving a colorful arabesque. Time and stage are now one: "(*Arabesquing wearily they weave a pattern on the floor, weaving, unweaving, curtseying, twirling, simply swirling.*)"[16] With time weaving its own setting—both in the sense of stage and production—things can only change quickly: characters swirl each other around "in a mosaic of movements," words literally and figuratively run into each other, "(*Closeclutched swift swifter with glareblareflare . . .*),"[17] and inevitably the dance turns into a dance of death. As is to be expected, Stephen, stopped dead, confronts his dead mother in flesh, only to expel this figure from the past with a Wagnerian gesture of nothingness:

> STEPHEN
> *Nothung!*

> (*He lifts his ashplant high with both hands and smashes the chandelier. Time's livid final flame leaps and, in the following darkness, ruin of all space, shattered glass and toppling masonry.*)[18]

If by the end of the chapter, however, it is Stephen who receives the violent blows, it is because at the other side of the apocalypse, his "feast of reason," with its attendant faith in heroism, no longer holds. Whereas in the scene just quoted Stephen could still imitate a Wagnerian hero, in the final pages of the episode he becomes the protagonist in a burlesque Punch and Judy show. The Lord of Reason loses his mask to his comic counterpart, the Revel of Fools, because in this post-historical era truth no longer reigns. Here the laws of the spirit are subdued by the unruly powers of the flesh. All the good reasons for which the heroes of the past once started their battles—religion, nationality, love (Cissy Caffrey: "They're going to fight. For me!"), honor, and money—are now unmasked as a cacophony of banal misunderstandings. Finally, in an excessively real evocation of what the young Joyce, discussing Ibsen, once described as the "great conflict which is almost independent of the conflicting actors," Stephen is made to feel the redundance of his existence. With one blow of the fist, his spirited interventions are smashed to pieces, while from the "rest of his traps" we hear the débris of history mockingly whisper Yeats's heroic poem. For who goes with Fergus now that he no longer rules the brazen cars, nor the shadows of the wood, the dim sea, the dishevelled wandering stars? It is Leopold Bloom, Joyce's Everyman, who provides the answer:

> STEPHEN
> (*murmurs*)
> . . . . shadows . . . the woods
> . . . white breast . . . dim sea
>
> (*He stretches out his arms, sighs again and curls his body. Bloom, holding the hat and ashplant, stands erect. A dog barks in the distance. Bloom tightens and loosens his grip on the ashplant. He looks down on Stephen's face and form.*)
>
> BLOOM
> (*communes with the night*) Face reminds me of his poor mother.[19]

It is hardly surprising that in this anti-climactic moment, when the relation between the poet and his language is dramatically re-appraised, the figure of Stephen's mother emerges. Joyce's search for the reconfiguration of opposites aims at interrogating fixed categories, not only at the level of periods (classicism versus romanticism) or genres (tragedy versus comedy), but also at the level of gender.

If at the height of Stephen's mock-heroic conflict with his surroundings, the boy is visited by his mother, it is because throughout *Ulysses* she has pursued him as the frightening "mother of all things," the preeminent patriarchal figure of finitude. However, here where the artist, nearly unconscious, has given up his self-aggrandizing ego, she can shed her purely negative function and signal a variable social bond among herself, Stephen, and Leopold in an imaginative communion with the night. Having unmasked whatever heroic will was left as a ridiculous farce, the book can now send its two voyagers back to the mother's home: tired, bored, witless, the epitome of the commonplace.

Ulysses, it has often been said,[20] combines the high and the low in an immensely comical work. What the characters in this novel have in common with each other, what makes them Everyman, is the ground for a comic detachment at the most intimate part of themselves: the human body. The sublime joy that Nietzsche could still reclaim from the sameness of the eternal return, the cyclical movement of nature, is here brought back to its human dimensions: a supple rhythm of daily actions, sensations, and reflections that seem to go on and on. Purged of its idealism, the joy of repetition appears as the boredom of the habitual, the indifference of a larger structure evolving "almost independent" from us. In this tedious state of normal existence, we are not offered a unique position from which we can recognize the individual objects, let alone view the whole. All we get to see is that everything comes and goes in a massively varied flux of forms and styles. If nothing "breaks into" consciousness—as it befits the truly sublime—it is because subject and object are still merged in the affective and sensual immediacy of the body: at once the most typical and private of human existence. Thus, reduced to its worldliness, the sublime designates its own excess. And what is more, this surplus of physicality in *Ulysses* becomes the lowest state in which a man like Bloom can connect with his surroundings. Consider his trip to the jakes: "He went out through the backdoor into the garden: stood to listen towards the next garden. No sound. Perhaps hanging clothes out to dry. The maid was in the garden. Fine morning . . . The hens in the next garden: their droppings are very good top dressing."[21]

Not surprisingly, this commonality of daily expulsion delivers Joyce the material with which to incorporate (and eject) our reading in the motions of Bloom's bowels: "Quietly he read, restraining himself, the first column and, yielding but resisting, began the second. Midway, his last resistance yielding, he allowed his bowels to ease themselves quietly as he read, reading still patiently that slight constipation of yesterday quite gone."[22] Such doubling of the reading process derives its comic effect from the fact that far from elevating the act of reading to a philosophical level—as self-reflexive novels for Schlegel still do—it exposes us to be engaged in the most human, banal act of incorporating and expelling some food for thought. At the height of our identification with the text, we feel stripped from all our intellectual pretensions. In this sense, comedy's propensity toward realism at once draws us close to and eliminates us from the page or stage. Yielding, we resist. Joyce's "slow elaborate patience of the art of satisfaction"—which Dedalus found in "Menander perhaps"—holds up the mirror to our lowest parts in order to refertilize a sterile literary form and give ease and pleasure where there has traditionally been instruction, and obstruction. Needless to say, where the restraint of the spirit yields an excess of the body; where excrement is seized upon to create new realities; where bowels and wombs are inquisitively penetrated to see what new modes of artistic conception they can produce; where cattle and hens function as top dressings for readers; in short, where the body generates and is generated by art, we are in for some serious reconsiderations of biological nature. If Joyce projects himself as the modern champion of the body, then by the same token he fabricates new modes of entering it and drawing out what ordinarily remains inside. By thus defamiliarizing the most intimate parts of ourselves, by removing traditional boundaries between content and form—spirit and matter—he shows the body to be a fluctuating category that yields or resists, flows or stiffens, according to who is cultivating it. This means that the movements of Joyce's bodies are not simply "natural" but rather, as we saw above, movements of reading. What we tend to think of as private spheres are, in reality, the objects of public interventions. Opening up the human body to his penetrating eye, putting the body at the center of his work, Joyce also dissolves it and reveals the political stakes involved in our attempt to delineate its boundaries. In this exposure (and explosion) of the individual body as a social—common—body, Joyce's comic art becomes a serious political practice, which we will further examine in the next chapter. As we will see, Joyce's interest in the "sublime" passages between the individual body and its surroundings focuses on this threshold experience in an Irish maternity hospital. The reason is simply that in a male-dominated society like Mina Purefoy's, the private part that is publicly the most constrained is the mother's womb.

NINE

Medicine, Midwifery, and the Making of Childbirth: Horne's "Sublime Porte" in *Ulysses*

As argued above, the notion of truth as strife is what lies at the core of the young Joyce's theory on drama. In practice, this amounts to a work of art no longer visibly controlled by the subjectivity (dramatist) with which we normally associate it. Hence, a certain degree of arbitrariness governs the development of drama. This impersonality permeating the actions of the players Joyce explains in terms of drama's concern with underlying social laws. However, insofar as these (objective) structures of communion are being generated in the movement of the play, they have not yet gained the universality traditionally accorded to them. Nor do they subsume the part under the whole in a harmonious fashion. In truth, these social laws are actualized in the performance of the conflict of passions between, and within, characters as well as between dramatist and audience.

The strife of passions portrayed by Joyce greatly differs according to which works, which audience, but also which characters we are considering. Stephen's inner conflict, I have argued, still carries many youthful, romantic overtones, while Bloom's "equanimity" suggests the kind of loss of great ideals that we find with older men. The former's passions are, in all their intensity, still dialectical. The latter's are what I would call "materialistic" in the sense of down-to-earth or commonplace. To the extent that Stephen's emotions are in perpetual conflict—for instance, he sees women as either virgins or whores—he is constantly seeking, but never finding, a place to come to rest. Bloom, on the contrary, seems to have gained a certain degree of peace in his reconciliation with the inconsistencies of the world: beyond loathing and desire, he feels love (for Molly and Milly), pity (for Mrs. Purefoy), also arousal, peckishness, bloatedness, sometimes sadness, yet mostly satisfaction.

The sublime, then, as a concept denoting passions, affects, or impulses is much more pertinent to Joyce's *Ulysses* as "animal instinct applied to the mind," than is the traditional approach to the sublime in terms of reason or imagination. One of the main theorists to reconsider this category from a psychological (psychoanalytic) perspective is, of course, Julia Kristeva. Reading Joyce with Kristeva has the further advantage that, in the development from her earlier to her later works, she offers us a transition from a negative to a more positive sublime that allows us to explain the differences between Stephen Dedalus and Leopold Bloom. But far from interpreting *Ulysses* simply by means of Kristeva's theoretical models, this chapter aims to go much beyond her "universal" readings and consider the maternal sublime in the "Oxen of the Sun" episode in its particular, nineteenth-century context: not as a timeless struggle between sons and mothers but as a typically nineteenth-century conflict between surgeons and midwives. Placed in a context as enlightened as Horne's obstetrical department ("Send us bright one, light one, Horhorn"), Kristeva's poetic *chora* as the "sublime incubator" of the word disrupts man's objective-scientific logos and shows it to be motivated by culturally specific aspirations.

What Kant considered to be the victory of reason over the senses—the sublime as a mode of distancing what is closest to us—in this chapter is revealed to be a way of medically silencing the female body. I will argue that the laws installed by the Victorian fathers keep mothers and midwives in the background of the medical theater for only one purpose—to control the (re)production of their race—but that this process of regulating their own births is self-defeating because it deprives them of their natural origins. Upon displacing the mother's womb, the medical patriarchy is confronted with the indeterminacy of its scientific intervention. It is by highlighting the tensions between the objective and the subjective views, science and art, nature and culture that Joyce construes a hybrid body at the intersection of differing and contradictory conceptions: Mrs. Purefoy, whose three days' labor is as much the talk of the town as it is the focus of scientific speculation. An object of the collective imagination, her labor pains become the resource for the construction of a social-medical reality at the same time that they reduce the (scientific) community to a struggle for life. Thus it is that Mina Purefoy's delayed birth concurrently secures and disrupts the unifying "link between nations and generations." Furthermore, as the midway between unity and difference, self and other, the mother is also the female midwife who alone can deliver others by virtue of having been a mother herself. In her hands, science becomes entangled with the world.

Kristeva's Maternal Sublime

From her earliest works, Kristeva has focused her attention on recuperating the repressed maternal body from what Lacan had described as the symbolic construction of the speaking subject. The decomposition of the symbolic order, governed by the Law of the Father, amounts to the fragmentation of the traditional subject conceived as an autonomous being, in favor of what Kristeva calls the subject-in-process. This is the subject as it emerges from a more primordial texture (genotext) in which the words of the speaker occur in a physical bondage to the maternal other.[1] Kristeva locates this "semiotic" order in the phase of primary narcissism, the moment prior to the mirror stage, when, according to Lacan, the subject first perceives itself as a unified *Gestalt* in an image exterior to itself: the face of the mother. In Kristeva's "transition" into the mirror phase, by contrast, the mother appears, not as an image with which to identify, but as an underlying movement destroying the social order while pointing toward a new, more physical form of organization: the *chora*, or that membrane in the womb in which the child is conceived. A divided space, that is, within which the speaking subject comes into being and which lets itself be heard only by the letter, as the material receptacle of language: as sounds, rhythms, and gestures. To return to our discussion of Joyce's dramatic form, we could say that the *chora* is what we are made to feel or hear, but not yet see, when Joyce's "lawlessness" produces its own inner structure at the very limit of the logically conceivable.

In her book *Powers of Horror*, Julia Kristeva defines the preobjectal relation between the child and its mother in terms of the "abject."[2] The abject is the maternal body from which the subject first separates itself in the phase that precedes the mirror stage as the first step toward the constitution of identity in the symbolic order. Prior to the advent of the father, Kristeva says, the child feels the presence of the father through the mother's desires, which now function as "signs of something else." At that moment the mother's presence is mobilized, and a first break takes place between the child and its object of love. This thetic break precedes Freud's constitution of the unconscious through the child's repression of its love for its mother. Prior to the Freudian division between the conscious and the unconscious—prior to the gap that alienates the subject from itself and allows it to enter the symbolic—there is a stage of multiple and repetitive division or repression: the abject, the prohibited maternal body from which the subject is *in the process of* separating itself. The abject is the maternal body from which the subject is not yet distinguished, but from which it cannot cease to differentiate itself if it wants to identify with the Name of the Father and enter language. Since the abject is not yet separate from the subject, it is not yet an object. Kristeva calls it an affect, the violence of a revolt against the maternal body as the latter, in turn, is constituted by the desires for the father. The violence of that confrontation fills the "I" with disgust and loathing. And it is in these negative feelings that the maternal body manifests itself in its difference. Incapable of being contained by language, by the repression enacted in language (the linguistic sign as the articulation of an absent object), the maternal shatters the walls of repression and lets itself be felt as that which always exceeds the subject.

In this pre-oedipal, narcissistic stage, the subject experiences the ambiguity of the Law of the Father: the maternal is established as that space from which the subject sets itself back in an act of self-positing. Negative limits are drawn, in other words, between the subject and what it exceeds. Constituting itself by those limits, the subject at once withdraws from and engages in excess, or perversion. "The abject is perverse because it neither gives up nor assumes a prohibition."[3] And a little further: "The writer, fascinated by the abject, imagines its logic, projects himself into it, introjects it, and as a consequence perverts language—style and content."[4] The logic of the maternal is pre-verbal in the sense that it designates the *material* signifying process in excess of the structures of the sign as this is based on an absent object. Its logic is that of excessive presence as well as depletion: while it subverts (depletes) the paternal sign, it also doubles (exceeds) it into a mock figure. With the maternal we retreat from signification into figuration or rhetoric. Here the word is less an instance of giving meaning than a mode of actively producing effect. The identity of the child is made to arise from the gestures of language: we could say that it is being given a face (or mask) to wear. In Joyce's terms: the father's "word is made into flesh," into a body at once corporeal and social (a relation to others), objective and subjective, free and limited. This body is what signals identity by revealing it to be a common condition of the human species. The subject is, in other words, revealed in its bond—in *Ulysses* a "navelcord"—to its surroundings.

Whereas in *Powers of Horror* Kristeva's sublime is constituted by the joyful horror that the subject feels toward the maternal object, in "Joyce 'the Gracehoper' or the Return of Orpheus"[5] she introduces a more positive moment in the exchange by focusing on the love between father and son—an amorous fusion that she describes as a mixture of Christian *agape*, the love that the son receives from above, and Greek *Eros*, the violent and destructive love toward the father's body. As in *Tales of Love*, Kristeva's focus on Joyce's obsession with the theme of the Eucharist aims at reinterpreting the dual link between the son (Stephen Dedalus) and the mother (May Dedalus) as pointing toward a third moment: the love of the father as the condition of possibility of the thetic rupture. What motivates the passage through the mirror phase is now no longer the joyful expulsion of the maternal body, as Kristeva had argued previously. Neither is it the symbolic law of a threatening father, as Lacan had said. Instead, Kristeva finds the motif in the child's "intrapsychic identification" with the *imaginary* paternal object of the mother's love—a process that she describes as a transference of the body "to the place of an Other who causes me to become One with him: body and soul."[6] The Eucharist replaces the *chora* as the metaphor for this illusory but necessary empathy with the other: a transubstantiation between father and son that Kristeva sees as destructive (we are invited to eat Christ's body) as well as unifying and that she explicitly goes on to call metaphorical rather than metonymical insofar as she believes the movement of displacement to synthesize into "an osmosis not only symbolic but real, between creator and created, father and son, loved and beloved. That one may therefore see a reabsorption of homosexuality is but secondary with regard to the most astounding result of this operation: namely, style."[7] The imaginary space of identification with the pre-oedipal father, whose unstable appearance entails the maternal body's life, allows the son-artist to project an identity in style. Characteristic of Joyce's style, is, of course, his liquidation of style, "halting at no one identity,"[8] precisely because he knows them all, both mothers and fathers. But are things that simple?

Given the claim Kristeva makes that the image of the preoedipal father is unstable and androgynous, her fixation on only one of Joyce's progenitors, Shakespeare (why not Ibsen?), is remarkable to say the least. It is equally astonishing that in support of her argument that Joyce managed to integrate the maternal and paternal into his work, she refers to the "Oxen of the Sun" episode, not to discuss the theme of gestation, but to locate the intervention of the androgynous father, who, in her view, made the parody of styles possible: Shakespeare's beardless face, "simultaneously sublime and impotent."[9] Kristeva here misses the point of the episode. If "Oxen of the Sun" imitates the growth of the fetus in the maternal womb as Joyce claimed, then this stylistic principle, I would suggest, is occasioned not by the intervention of an effeminate Shakespeare but by the discharge of a mother: Mrs. Purefoy, fiercely struggling to deliver the son (Stephen, but also the chapter), whose imaginary identification with the father (Bloom, Joyce) presupposes the violent dispossession of her (pro)creative powers. Rather than staging a mystical unity between father and son, Joyce's chapter shows this divine transubstantiation to be based on a painful conflict between mother and fetus, carrier and content. If the mother delivers the style, it is because she does not possess her content. Thus it is that the "Oxen" episode tells a story much more disconcerting than Kristeva claims. Having lost its meaning, the mother's birth here becomes a sham. On the one hand, this leads to what Stephen grimly observes in the passage quoted below, namely, that the son may never be born at all. In this sense, Mrs. Purefoy's extended pregnancy radically depletes the symbolic unity of father and son into "a ritual theater—a carnivalized liturgy."[10] On the other hand, however, this subversion of the son's birth entails an exasperating labor on the part of the mother, who in turn is being threatened by death. If the Black Mass in the "Circe" episode—"On the altarstone Mrs Mina Purefoy, goddess of unreason, lies, naked, fettered, a chalice resting on her swollen belly"[11]—makes anything clear at all, it is the fact that this "carnivalized liturgy" is borne out on a woman's body. What the later Kristeva, in her insistence on man's capacity for love and identification, seems to prefer to repress (or sublimate) is the violence that the son's "sublime but impotent" birth into the divine Word does to the mother's body. Associating birth mainly with the carnivalesque identity of the male offspring rather than with the mother's labor or sacrifice,[12] Kristeva's position is uncannily close to the drunken joy with which the medical students in "Oxen of the Sun" parody the Eucharist while silencing Mrs. Purefoy's cries: "About that present time young Stephen filled all cups that stood empty . . . Now drink we, quod he, of this mazer and quaff ye this mead which is not indeed parcel of my body but my soul's bodiment" (320.277–83). Bloom, perhaps a better example of Kristeva's new womanly man than is Shakespeare, at least has a more sympathetic ear for the fact that the mother "had been in such pain through no fault of hers" (333.884).

In what follows I will demonstrate that Kristeva is right in foregrounding the intervention of the father in "Oxen of the Sun," not however as a loving act as she claims, but as an act of appropriation. Here fathers intervene for the sole purpose of becoming the progenitors of their race. In "Scylla and Charybdis" Stephen admits as much:

> When [Shakespeare] . . . wrote *Hamlet* he was not the father of his own son merely but, being no more a son, he was and felt himself the father of all his race, the father of his own grandfather, the father of his unborn grandson who, by the same token, never was born, for nature, as Mr Magee understands her, abhors perfection. (171.865–71)

In his typically bawdy manner, Buck Mulligan adds the literal implications of Stephen's esoteric remarks: "Himself his own father, Sonmulligan told himself. Wait. I am big with child. I have an unborn child in my brain. Pallas Athena! A play! The play's the thing! Let me parturiate! He clasped his paunchbrow with both birthaiding hands" (171.875–78). In this carnivalesque mimicry, the medical student anticipates the linguistic capitalization of childbirth that I find to be the central theme of "Oxen of the Sun." What his little play illustrates is that in a male-dominated environment childbirth is not so much woman's "natural" domain (as Schlegel could still claim) as the effect of man's preoccupation with his self-imagery. The son's identification with an imaginary father leads him to monopolize the act of procreation and redefine it for his own purposes: childbirth becomes an act of substitution of a mother by her son, who turns her womb into a word or play "that shall never pass away," at least not as long as men continue to consider themselves the progenitors of their race. The universality of Stephen's definition—"In woman's womb word is made flesh but in the spirit of the maker all flesh that passes becomes the word that shall not pass away. This is the postcreation" (320.292–94)—depends upon its not being accessible to everyone: women for instance must be excluded if childbirth is going to be men's way of "always meeting ourselves."

The "Oxen of the Sun" episode is Joyce's major contribution to an interrogation of what precisely childbirth means: "an apostolic succession, from only begetter to only begotten" (170.838–39) or a site of contestation between women and men? An act of love by an imaginary father or the "virile potency of the old bucko that could still knock another child out of her" (334.892–93)? A natural event supervised by a doctor (artist) or the mechanical reproduction of his views? As could be expected, the answers to these questions will have to take into account Joyce's self-critical pastiche of style in this chapter. Given that, according to Joyce's scheme, the central "art" of the episode is medicine, nothing short of a surgical analysis of form is called for. Our ultimate aim, then, will be to regard the emergence of style in the light of man's (medical) dispossession of the maternal body: what kind of art can he reproduce out of the usurpation of his—female—model?

Mina Purefoy's Liminal Experiences in Horne's "Sublime Porte"

For all its apparent incoherence, "Oxen of the Sun" is possibly one of the most structured episodes in *Ulysses*. Besides the correspondence to the Linati scheme—organ: womb, art: medicine, color: white, symbol: mothers, technique: embryonic development—and the allusion to the Homeric model (the slaughter of the sacred cattle), there are Joyce's parody of English literary history, the link to previous parts of the book, the references to faunal evolution, to the development of the medical profession in Ireland, to the history of biology and anatomy. Not to mention the chapter's biblical citations. These structures, then, are the "devices" aiding the birth of the chapter. Alternatively, they can be regarded as the layers of technique that we have to traverse in order to reach the core of the episode: Bloom meets Stephen in the maternity hospital. In the latter case, Joyce's indication that the chapter contains the nine-month development of the fetus must be seen as an attempt to "naturalize" what is first and foremost a technically construed encounter between father and son. To be more precise, the pervasive embryological vocabulary in this chapter serves the dual function of giving Joyce's structuring devices a natural look, while at the same time revealing what we consider the "natural" growth of the fetus to be couched in a series of metaphors: sperm (Bloom) meets ovum (nurse Callan), fertilized egg (Bloom) enters womb (the waiting room), embryo (Stephen) emerges, and so forth. By thus transforming the narrative development of the novel into an allegory of fetal development, Joyce emphasizes the extent to which linguistic structures can shape such a supposedly natural experience as a woman's pregnancy. While *condensing* her nine months of pregnancy into a one night encounter between father and son, the chapter, simultaneously, *extends* Mina Purefoy's time to incorporate more than two thousand years of literary history. This double movement of concentration and expansion is also emblematized by the comparison that Joyce sets up between the students' can of sardines and the fetus in the womb's amniotic fluid: "And there was a vat of silver that was moved by craft to open in the which lay strange fishes withouten heads . . . in an oily water brought there from Portugal . . ." (317.149–53). While the can of sardines can be said to *contain* two months of foetal development (when the embryo "has a notochord rather than a vertebral spinal column"[13]), its oil, imported from Portugal, carries connotations of geographical *expansion*. Partly inside and partly beyond their material container, the sardines symbolize the mechanism of metaphorical configuration accompanying the birth of the child. Like the fetus, they are a product of an evolution that is as natural as it is artificial: they are fish out of water.

The womb as space of man's imaginary self-conception which in Kristeva's earlier work still has a natural appearance—that of the *chorion*—in Joyce's chapter accrues all the technical connotations that childbirth in 1904 already has: the womb becomes a silver can to be opened by craft. Having studied medicine for one year,[14] Joyce was undoubtedly aware of the controversies that existed in the medical world over the question whose craft was needed here and to what extent intervention was called for: could one rely on the manual labor of the midwives, or did one use technical devices such as forceps (can openers, so to speak) and chloroform.[15] In *Ulysses* the debate is introduced as follows:

> A couch by midwives attended with wholesome food reposeful, cleanest swaddles as though forthbringing were now done

> and by wise foresight set: but to this no less of what drugs there is need and surgical implements which are pertaining to her case not omitting aspect of all very distracting spectacles in various latitudes by our terrestial orb offered together with images, divine and human . . . (315.61–67)

This passage comes from the opening of the chapter and occurs at the end of a series of paragraphs in honor of the Celts' concern for childbearing women. Since "nature, as Mr Magee understands her, abhors perfection," thc health of a race depends upon its medical intervention in childbirth, the biological source of racial continuation: "therefore a plan was by them adopted . . . whereby maternity was so far from all accident possibility removed" (315.41–46). Among the chief legacies of the Irish health care system are its maternity hospitals, established in the eighteenth century, at a time when Thomas Malthus publishes his controversial *Essay on the Principles of Population* in England. What Irish eugenics and Malthus's economics have in common is the emphasis they place on the maternal body as the locus from which to generate a healthy society. Having placed woman's body at the center, both then go on to develop a system of regulation that has to purge the mother's physical nature from its possible negative effects.[16] Malthus's famous postulate that "food is necessary to the existence of man" and that, if population growth is not curtailed, starvation will follow, is echoed in Joyce's repetitive association of sex and food throughout the chapter. "Malthusianists," a Joycean term, may well have installed the "couch by midwives attended with wholesome food reposeful, cleanest swaddles as though forthbringing were now done and by wise foresight set." Just as in Homer's *Odyssey* the crime against fertility (the killing of the Sun God's oxen) is motivated by the fear of starvation, so population control in early-twentieth-century Ireland is carried out with the Great Famine in mind.[17] Given these political and economic considerations, Mary Lowe-Evans can argue—and I follow her lead—that Joyce's thematization of the "crime against fecundity" in this chapter entails not simply a condemnation of contraception (often heard in Joyce criticism) but more generally a critique of the reproductive doctrines that have governed women's sexual lives in Ireland for several centuries: Aristotle's theory of the soul; the Catholic idea that "woman should bring forth in pain" (318.208–9); medieval superstitions about pregnancy; social Darwinism (exemplified by Mulligan's national fertilizing farm); the "Socratic discussion" between eighteenth- and nineteenth-century physiologists, embryologists, and gynaecologists concerning women's reproductive biology:

> Must we accept the view of Empedocles of Trinacria that the right ovary (the postmenstrual period, assert others) is responsible for the birth of males or are the too long neglected spermatozoa or nemasperms the differentiating factors or is it, as most embryologists incline to opine, such as Culpepper, Spallanzani, Blumenbach, Lusk, Hertwig, Leopold and Valenti, a mixture of both? (341.1231–36)

Does woman conceive through orgasm as Blumenbach argued, or does fertilization occur through the sperm's penetration of the egg as Hertwig discovered in 1876? By situating Mina Purefoy's labor within the context of these scientific debates over the status of conception, Joyce shows the operation of the womb to be discursive rather than natural. The effect of a technical and textual intervention, the mother's body becomes the place for delivering scientific as well as economic, racial, religious, and social truths, all of which are based on a purely biological definition of femininity. Even the medical students' defense of contraception and abortion is couched in a vocabulary that explicitly reaffirms the female body as a natural territory governed by men and their instruments:

> Maledicity! he [Bannon] exclaimed in anguish. Would to God that foresight had but remembered me to take my cloak along! I could weep to think of it. Then, though it had poured seven showers, we were neither of us a penny the worse. But beshrew me, he cried, clapping hand to his forehead, tomorrow will be a new day and, thousand thunders, I know of a *marchand de capotes*, Monsieur Poyntz, from whom I can have for a *livre* as snug a cloak of the French fashion as ever kept a lady from wetting. (331.771–78)

Rather than being a mere euphemism for contraception, as has been suggested by various Joyce critics,[18] Bannon's "cloak" (*capote*) serves to shield his girl friend from regeneration (through rain or semen) at the same time that it reaffirms the traditional association between femininity and fecundity. Clothed by metaphors of nature—showers, thunders—Bannon's story about the forgotten condom reinscribes the procreative function of female sexuality that it apparently resists. If his "cloak" simultaneously hides and reveals anything at all, it is not the preservative for which it serves as a metaphor but the fact that in his mind woman is still associated with earth, birth, fertility, regeneration. While figuratively (i.e., read as a condom) his "cloak" may protect Milly Bloom from motherhood, taken literally (i.e., as a device against the rain) it reinscribes old stereotypes: man protects woman from her own fertility. He is the medical man monitoring the procreative being that she is. Condoms, like the "drugs" and the "surgical implements" cited before, belong to that part of technology whose function it is to differentiate between scientific men and natural women. It is in this light also that we have to read Lynch's story about the "umbrellas" (diaphragms) that his Kitty refuses to wear: "My dear Kitty told me today that she would dance in a deluge before ever she would starve in such an ark of salvation" (331.787–88). Reminiscent of what Bannon called Milly's "artless disorder" (331.759), Kitty personifies the natural wildness of female sexuality that must be protected against itself.

Given this association between femininity and corporality, it is not surprising that in "Oxen of the Sun" Mrs. Purefoy's actual delivery is in the hands of two nurses, Miss Callan and Miss Quigley, whose physical labor is hidden by the students' theoretical debates in the foreground. This division between foreground and background, presence and absence, theory and practice, reflects the power relations prevalent in the Victorian world. While men make sense, women make children. Men are associated with meaning, science, and technology, women with matter, maternity, and nature. Men are the subjects, women the objects of medical regulation. As Mary Poovey and others have illustrated,[19] even the medical profession was organized around this opposition: manual labor was considered fit mainly for midwives and general practitioners, technical intervention belonged to surgeons and physicians. In *A Portrait* this gender-related distinction between "poor and rich practices" is introduced in the following way:

> He [Stephen] heard the students talking among themselves. They spoke of two friends who had passed the final medical examination, of the chances of getting places on ocean liners, of poor and rich practices.
>
> —That's all a bubble. An Irish country practice is better.
>
> —Hynes was two years in Liverpool and he says the same. A frightful hole he said it was. Nothing but midwifery cases. Half a crown cases.

—Do you mean to say it is better to have a job here in the country than in a rich city like that? I know a fellow . . .
—Hynes has no brains. He got through by stewing, pure stewing.[20]

Traditionally, female midwives assisted in the birth of the child without, however, using surgical instruments.[21] Not allowed to go beyond a "natural" delivery, they had to call for medical assistance by men in cases where drugs or instruments were needed: for miscarriages, dismemberment of the baby, extraction, or cesarian section. Since female midwives were considered to possess practical knowledge—knowledge derived from the experience of being a mother—the increasing emphasis placed on scientific training and technical assistance in the seventeenth- and eighteenth-century medical profession worked to exclude them from the prestigious position they still had in the Middle Ages.[22] Since women had no access to a formal training, midwifery gradually came into the hands of men. By the nineteenth century, female midwives had largely been displaced by male obstetricians—except in the country and poorer urban areas—and what was originally considered a natural experience among women became a(n) (inferior) medical event among men.

As said, in "Oxen of the Sun" this sexual division of labor governs the arrival of Mina Purefoy's son. While the physical work takes place upstairs, the definition of that event is staged downstairs. Here Purefoy's swollen belly is emptied of its (material) content by those professionally certified to name it: "a birth without pangs, a body without blemish, a belly without bigness" (321.310–11). However—and this will be the focus of the rest of this chapter—this transition from womb to word, meant to verbally contain the physical reproduction of the body-in-labor and deprive the mother of her autonomous procreative powers, is itself subject to the conflict of views that characterizes man's articulation of the female body as either sexual or maternal. This problematic passage from flesh to self-contradictory word is embodied by nurse Callan as she enters the boys' waiting room to ask Dixon for medical assistance at the afterbirth (post-creation). While the "masculine" Costello calls her a "monstrous fine bit of cowflesh . . . Have you a way with them?" (332.807–8), the more effeminate Dixon reprimandingly responds: "I am positive when I say that if need were I could produce a cloud of witnesses to the excellence of her noble exercitations which, so far from being a byword, should be a glorious incentive in the human breast. I cannot away with them" (332.826–29). Rather than "having" a way with Callan, as Costello suggests, Dixon cannot "do" (?) away with her. She is the figure that brings him into the world and transforms his objective science into a subjective relatedness to others. Through her interference, he is literally and figuratively "moved" in the sense that she offers him an "incentive in the human breast" as well as an incentive to go upstairs. Combining sympathy with science, modesty with severity, upstairs with downstairs, nurse Callan's appearance questions the boundaries that separate men from women and that have, more specifically, excluded women from the medical profession for several years. What her entrance downstairs makes clear is the prejudices and material conditions under which men have "objectively" fixed the borders between sexes and professions: while to Costello she is nothing but flesh, to Dixon she is only a human heart. Shifting in accordance with the masculine voice articulating her, this female figure is alternatively whore and virgin. She is, I would argue, an unstable—for rhetorical—category confronting man's logical order with the artifice of its boundaries, in such a way that Bloom concludes that what unites the students over and against the female sex is not the universality of reason but a fictive bond "that discursiveness which seemed the only bond of union among tempers so divergent" (335.954–55).

With nurse Callan's entrance into the waiting room there irrupts a conflict of views that destabilizes the patriarchal bond in Horne's maternity hospital: Dixon leaves, while "some were for ejecting the low soaker [Costello] without more ado" (332.836–37). The medical theater as the symbol of civilization turns into a bestial struggle for life. While Costello degenerates into "a cropeared creature of a misshapen gibbosity" (333.854–55), the mark of the surgeon's pliers on his head reminds Bloom "of that missing link of creation's chain desiderated by the late ingenious Mr Darwin" (333.858–59). The missing link that Darwin installed in his *Descent of Man* was the process of evolution whereby man had lifted himself from his bestial origins, not according to some God-given plan, but according to a natural process of elimination. "The survival of the fittest" is what Herbert Spencer would later call this principle behind man's superiority vis-à-vis the lower animals. It is a struggle for existence that at once links the human species to, and differentiates it from, the rest of nature. What the marks of the forceps on Costello's brains tell Bloom is that man's process of civilization consists of an increasingly refined struggle for survival.

Man's evolution is one in which a bestial conflict is increasingly carried out by technological means. A condensed version of this process occurs during childbirth: what is supposed to be a natural struggle between mother and child is carried out as a conflict between midwives and doctors—the former settling the dispute by hands, the latter by pliers and drugs. To say that the bestial Costello carries the marks of the surgeon's pliers is to emphasize the extent to which nature and culture, for all their apparent differences, have become indistinguishable in Horne's hospital. Nurse Callan, I would argue, embodies this missing link between the two realms. Her interruption of the boys' assembly establishes the differences between them—Costello is the animal, Dixon the human—while reinscribing a less secure bond between them: man's intellect is not something universal, but the product of a struggle for power as well as a tool that has helped those who have taken possession of it to legitimate their violent subjugation of the others. Bloom is made to recognize this as he observes "that the mere acquisition of academic titles should suffice to transform in a pinch of time these votaries of levity into exemplary practitioners of an art which most men anywise eminent have esteemed the noblest" (334.899–902).

With this confusion of nature and culture, the possibility arises that man was never simply naturally born. "I was too, made not begotten" Stephen already realized, "By them, the man with my voice and my eyes and a ghostwoman with ashes on her breath" (32.45–47). The ghostwoman is as much Stephen's dying mother as it is one of those terrifying Sisters of Fate who

> lugged [him] squealing into life. Creation from nothing. What has she in the bag? A misbirth with a trailing navelcord, hushed in ruddy wool. The cords of all link back, strandentwining cable of all flesh. That is why mystic monks. Will you be as gods? Gaze in your *omphalos*. Hello! Kinch here. Put me on to Edenville. Aleph, alpha: nought, nought, one. (32.35–40)

The two midwives that Stephen once saw on the beach fulfill the same function as nurse Callan in the hospital: they raise doubts about the way men have defined the natural bonds in the world. For to the extent that the "navelcord," which is supposed to link the fetus to the mother, here serves to relate man back to himself ("Gaze in your *omphalos*"), it appears less as woman's natural than as man's self-reflexive bond. What is more, calling Eden—symbol of man's lost origins—Stephen connects to a woman who, since she too was, in McGee's words, "restricted and constricted by the patriarchal code,"[23] "had no navel" either. What else then does Stephen see in the midwife's "trailing navelcord" if not the possibility that "as no man knows the ubicity of his tumulus nor to what processes we shall thereby be ushered nor whether to Tophet or to Edenville in the like way is all hidden when we would backward see from what region of remoteness the whatness of our whoness hath fetched his whenceness" (323.396–400). Confronted with the artifice of childbirth as well as with the discursive-technical constitution of motherhood, Stephen is made to realize that there is no such thing as a natural origin and, hence, also no clear-cut end. Evolutions, such as pregnancies, are man-made. At best, they are a matter of style.

Midwives are the midways between nature and culture. The rite of passage between inside and outside, womb and word, that they bring about during birth, stages a double movement of unification and separation: on the one hand, they "put asunder" the woman and child that "God [read: man] has joined"; on the other, they introduce a variety of prejudices and cultural practices into what man considers to be a natural event: their manual delivery, for one, is a sign of their professional inferiority. Cutting the umbilical cord with the only tool they are allowed—the scissors—they establish a multitude of missing links with the surrounding world. What emerges from the midwife's double gestures is a contradictory view on childbirth, as both natural and scientific, corporeal and technical. Instead of a given, a place of origins, childbirth becomes a problem to turn on and return to in labyrinthine circles of text. In "Oxen of the Sun," Mina Purefoy's birth is endlessly delayed precisely because it generates this excess of texts from which it is to derive its ultimate meaning or content.

Not surprisingly, therefore, the afterbirth, which we remember is in the hands of Dixon, becomes the occasion for introducing new means of containment which recall "the ceremonial usage of the Sublime Porte" (335.942–43)—according to Gifford,[24] a reference to the medieval Courts of Justice which, in the Near East, supervised the legitimacy of the sultan's offspring. Bound to reproduce paternity's legal fictions rather than arbitrary or even missing links, the maternal body must once and for all be legalized by "the secretary of state for domestic affairs and the members of the privy council" (335.947–48). As for the medical students, what better way to preside over the postcreation than by defining it as an event fraught with dangers to such an extent that medical supervision is at all times necessary:

> Every phase of the situation was successively eviscerated: the prenatal repugnance of uterine brothers, the Caesarian section, posthumity with respect to the father and, that rarer form, with respect to the mother, the fatricidal case known as the Childs Murder and rendered memorable by the impassioned plea of Mr Advocate Bushe which secured the acquittal of the wrongfully accused, the rights of primogeniture and king's bounty touching twins and triplets, miscarriages and infanticides . . . the benefits of anesthesia or twilight sleep, the prolongation of labour pains in advanced gravidancy by reason of pressure on the vein . . . the recorded instances of multiseminal, twikindled and monstrous births conceived during the catamenic period or of consanguineous parents . . . (335.955–75)

As the "eviscerated" afterbirth becomes increasingly verbal, reality gives way to ghostly fantasies, science to superstition, and Purefoy's heir to Bloom's fleeting visions of little Rudy and Stephen. The afterbirth that was to guarantee the students an occasion for renewed self-creation dissipates into a flux of hallucinations not far removed from the kind of underworld that we are about to enter in the "Circe" episode. If Stephen had hoped that the passage from womb into word would yield him a posterity that "shall not pass away," then the reproduction of twilight phantoms, ghosts of beasts, zodiacal hosts, a myriad metamorphoses of symbol, cannot but reaffirm its passing nature. As Maud Ellmann says: "ghosts are the visions which arise when words have failed to purge the agony of loss."[25] If anything, then, the rhetorical displacement of Purefoy's body offers Stephen the means with which to express his fears about her self-reproductive labor, fears that his verbal representations should have alleviated but that they cannot but intensify exactly because once they have been exteriorized they are always beyond the reach of what is inside: "Yet a chance word will call them [evil memories] forth suddenly and they will rise up to confront him in the most various circumstances, a vision or a dream . . . shrouded in the piteous vesture of the past, silent, remote, reproachful" (344.1348–55).

No sooner is Mina's happy *accouchement* an occasion for installing the presence of the father (the Universal Husband) than "a chance word"—"thou good and faithful *servant*" (344.1343, emphasis added)—calls forth Stephen's "non *serviam*" (his refusal to pray) at his mother's deathbed. The rhetoric induced by the mother's verbal(ly emptied) body disrupts the arrival of the Name of the Father, only to deliver "the piteous vesture of the past," his dead mother. Silently but authoritatively, the ghostly words of the afterbirth confront him with the massive weight of the past, when "[s]ilently, in a dream she [his mother] had come to him after her death, her wasted body within its loose brown graveclothes . . . her breath, that had bent upon him, mute reproachful . . ." (5.102–5). Although the language occasioned by the postcreation may name the identity of the son, Mortimer Edward, in the image of the father, "with the true Purefoy nose" (343.1333), at the same time it reasserts the lack of identity of another heir, Stephen, haunted by the bond to his dying mother: "the son unborn mars beauty" (170.854).

Stephen, whose identity as an artist depends upon the degree to which he can substitute his words for his mother's dying flesh, is here seen to be caught in a continuing act of division between his word and her matter, presence and absence. Born from an ongoing struggle between mother and child, his language is torn by the conflict between life and death. At most, Stephen's language designates its ephemeral origination right there where the reach of his control ends, somewhere in that unattainable zone of splitting known as birth (from the perspective of the son), labor or delivery (from the perspective of Mina Purefoy), death (from the perspective of May Dedalus). Haunting him like a shadow, this scene of expulsion is so much part of him that to express it is already to lose, or expel, it and hence inadvertently reproduce it. This indeterminacy inherent in language is what effectuates the abundance of style in this chapter.

"Oxen of the Sun" is Joyce's contribution to the "lot of nonsense . . . talked about style."[26] His pastiche of the various styles in the history of English literature—those of Malory, Swift, Dickens, Carlyle, and many others—raises questions on two levels. First, is there such a thing as an artist's style? And second, how do we go about systematizing it (in a literary companion, for instance)? Style is traditionally regarded the writer's place of individuation: say, the mark of difference between Dickens and Joyce. A writer's style is his signature, uniquely his own. In this sense, style is incommunicable, for irreducibly singular. And yet, it is also what allows an author to project a recognizable identity in public: reading page 343 of *Ulysses*, for instance, we "recognize" Dickens's style. At that moment, however, we freeze, even conventionalize, what is supposed to be the epitome of creativity. For a style to retain its originality, it must continue to elude both writer and reader, which is to say that an artist's style cannot be known nor represented, least of all by himself. That is why it also, in a manner of speaking, signals the alterity of the work vis-à-vis the creator: the manner in which the work of art is most "objectively" his own. As we have seen, Joyce's characteristic style is the one in which the work assumes the shape of an independent character, known as the dramatic form. But, as I have shown, the concrete appearance of that Joycean dramatic form differs from work to work: it may appear as essay (*Critical Writings*), play (*Exiles*), or unfinished novel (*Stephen Hero*). In *Ulysses*, the form even changes with the chapter, or from line to line. And with each alteration of style, Karen Lawrence has argued, a different (mis)conception of the plot, its characters, and its maker is born.[27]

In the "Oxen" episode, this arbitrariness is likened to the movements of the body in labor: style becomes a mode of origination that involves the painful expulsion of that part of the self that the subject no longer controls. The borders of what is being delivered are themselves open to conflicting interpretations. According to the context, some will want to fix the boundaries objectively (taking the scientific approach), while others will emphasize the importance of empathy (the perspectivists). Joyce's view is that however we go about defining style (the artist's offspring)—whether we look for generalities or particularities—we are always involved in adding our own signature to the marks gathered. This reproduction with a difference is called parody, pastiche,[28] or in Hugh Kenner's words, the modern regeneration of a "past writing in word-museums."[29] Objectivity as well as subjectivity are modes of re-ordering the world, in a variety of borrowed styles. Bearing in mind Joyce's essays on drama, where he defined reality as based on the structures of feeling of a community, we might say that style is where our sense of reality and our sense of ourselves meet.[30]

In "Oxen of the Sun" Joyce traces the literal origins of man's imaginary and symbolic self-conception. He recuperates, so to speak, the maternal flesh from the paternal word by illustrating that man's production of art and science, his favorite realms, is made possible through the subjugation of women to the plight of childbearer on the one hand, through the displacement of her labor by his creative activities on the other. The word known to all men—childbirth—is here placed in its cultural context, such that it loses its natural connotations and acquires the meaning it deserves: that of the medium through which men bring about the world as they conceive it. By embedding Purefoy's birth within a parody of the history of the English language, from its nationalist beginnings in Celtic texts to the melting pot variation in true American style, Joyce evokes the textual layers childbirth has grotesquely accumulated over time according to the contexts in which it is used: politics, religion, economics, obstetrics, aesthetics. Mimicking an etymology of sorts is Joyce's way of confronting the scientific (universal) definition of childbirth with the cultural forces that have (re)shaped its (literal and figural) content to such an extent that profuse shape (style) has itself become the content.

In an early essay, "Study of Languages," the young Joyce describes this historical method remarkably well: "in comparing the speech of to-day with that of years ago, we have a useful illustration of the effect of external influences on the very words of a race."[31] Only by combining Mina Purefoy's pregnancy with a parody of English literary history can the writer evoke the influence that the "underlying social laws" and "conflict of passions" (to use the terms from his essays on drama) exert on the significance of such supposedly neutral terms as *birth*, of course, but also *sons*, *mothers*, *navelcord*, or *Eucharist*. In that same youthful essay, Joyce even goes one step further by explicitly stating that science, be it natural or literary science, cannot be moral until it combines its search for objective truth with the "most natural aspect of man, namely, as a living being, and regard him as an infinitely small actor, playing a most uninteresting part in the drama of worlds."[32] Reading the latter quote in the light of the previous citation leads us to conclude that in his earliest reflections on art and science, Joyce was already emphasizing the need to integrate the two disciplines for the sake of a more critical insight into the workings of both. Only when science is seen as a historical discourse; only when it makes room for an analysis of (its) style and language, including the etymology of (its) words, does its entanglement with the world become visible and can objectivity make room for morality.[33] In "Oxen of the Sun" Joyce practices obstetrics with a heart, thereby assuming the role of a female midwife, who, as argued, combines sympathy and science, experience and knowledge, body and mind. Rather than teaching us how "to bring thoughts into the world," as Socrates's mother did, Joyce thus brings the whole historical world back into thought. If Joycean midwifery cuts several traditional bonds (e.g., between woman and nature), it is only to reinscribe a multitude of missing ones: between nature and culture, science and art, present and past, language and its daily surroundings. What initiates the style of *Ulysses* can, then, hardly be called (with Kristeva) the sublime intervention of an impotent father, be he imaginary or real. As soon as Joyce's intertwining hands start to deliver a text, the birth of truth is delayed such that its painful genealogy—the mother's perpetuating labor—may become visible in a profusion of form, or style.

TEN

In the Wake of Criticism

An Earwicked Exchange of Letters

In his *Ideology of the Aesthetic* Terry Eagleton articulates an insightful critique of the category of the aesthetic as this has dominated Western philosophy since the Enlightenment.[1] Arising at the time art gains its autonomy from political and religious institutions by getting involved in the economic processes of bourgeois capitalism, aestheticism is a powerful instrument in the hands of the bourgeoisie. Free artistic self-development, accepting no other law than the one the artwork sets itself, confirms the possessive individualism of the autonomous bourgeois subject as it is trying to appropriate the absolutist power of the ruling aristocracy. Just as eighteenth-century aestheticism (Baumgarten, Kant) brings into harmony the universal law of reason with the particularities of sensuous experience, so the social order of the middle classes is installed by virtue of the successful integration of the abstract law of individual freedom with the private pleasures of the particular subject. "The ultimate binding force of the bourgeois social order, in contrast to the coercive apparatus of absolutism, will be habits, pieties, sentiments and affections. And this is equivalent to saying that power in such an order has become *aestheticized*."[2] Not coercion but consensus is the basis on which the law of (economic) independence can effectively regulate its subordinates while offering them the illusions of freedom and self-determination. For power to obtain the uncompromising subservience of the individual, a new subjectivity must be invented—in terms of sympathy, collectivity, free harmonious unity—that will give the subject's subjugation to the social order a "natural" and spontaneous look.

While such aesthetic unification of the particular and the whole serves to hide the operations of political hegemony, it also provides us with an exceptionally powerful challenge to such mystification. If Enlightenment aesthetics begins with the colonization of the body, this insertion of the physical into the discourse of reason also constitutes the very limits of its idealism. "To lend fresh significance to bodily pleasures and drives, however, if only for the purpose of colonizing them more efficiently, is always to risk foregrounding and intensifying them beyond one's control."[3] It is this contradiction of the aesthetic that Eagleton explores in a variety of thinkers. In the case of Kant, for instance, the feelings of the beautiful and the sublime are the occasion for experiencing the possibility of an accord between nature and man on the one hand, the limits of such a relation on the other. Kantian judgment of beauty holds out the promise that the thing-in-itself might not be totally indifferent to man's aspirations, be it that such consolation in the end confirms not so much the agreement between the subject and the object as the pleasurable indeterminacy of the imagination vis-à-vis the understanding. The freewheeling of our faculties is what we have in common with the purposive purposelessness of nature. In the sublime, by contrast, we encounter the negative implications of such a harmony between spirit and nature: at home in nature, we threaten to lose our uniqueness as human beings. The subject is made to painfully feel its limitation and is filled with a yearning for totality. Luckily, this immense desire only momentarily paralyzes the subject. No sooner does the subject feel decentered than it comfortably identifies with the threatening power and sets out on an immensely creative—capitalist—enterprise that cannot but prove that the infinite is securely lodged inside the subject. Eagleton concludes: "Morality is 'aestheticized' in the sublime as feeling, but as a feeling which, since it denigrates the sensory, is also 'anti-aesthetic.'"[4]

How can the aesthetic, as the extension of reason to the realm of the senses, contribute to the liberation of the particular without reinscribing it within the dominant ideology of bourgeois individualism? For Eagleton, the answer lies in a dialectical approach to aestheticism that redeems its attention to the body and to nature in order to challenge, rather than mystify, bourgeois ideology. His solution implies, among other things, a definition of the particular, not as the exemplification of a universal, bourgeois subject, but as "a material implication with others." Eagleton's individual body will be non-identical and self-transgressive insofar as it raises larger questions of reason, justice, and equality: whose pleasures are being neglected, which desires should be realized, and so on. For him universality needs to be reinscribed for one purpose only: to guarantee that the *particularity of every single citizen* may be realized.

What one learns from Eagleton's study of the ideological workings of the category of the aesthetic is that in order not to fall prey to the mystifications of power in the writings of Kant, Fichte, Hegel, Heidegger, and many others, one should pay close attention to the historically determined details of the universal that they define. For all his theorizing on the underlying material-historical processes, however, Eagleton remains remarkably oblivious of them. Instead, he limits himself to a taxonomy of the aesthetic on the basis of (somewhat simplified) philosophical texts alone. One may rightfully wonder whether his own lack of interest in historical and textual details does not risk universalizing the aesthetic that he seeks to limit.

Although Eagleton acknowledges that it is only at the risk of a serious simplification that one equates Enlightenment aestheticism with either particularism or universalism, his own approach tends to confuse one particular—Marxist—way of comprehending the world with the world itself. As a result, everything becomes exchangeable: Heidegger, Hegel, but also Joyce—all of them have, in their opposition to the universal through a particularization of identity, subverted the kind of bourgeois expectations that on another level they affirmed. Thus, Eagleton can claim that Joyce's irreverent recycling of old masterpieces in *Ulysses* and especially *Finnegans Wake* "marks the historic point at which capital begins to penetrate into the very structures of the symbolic order itself, reorganizing this sacrosanct terrain in accordance with its own degraded, emancipatory logic."[5] But invoking Joyce's texts as the moment in which the process of commodification enters modern art is to leave intact the conceptual hegemony of exchange (one word for one referent or meaning) that I believe Joyce is discarding. Rather than interpreting Joyce's art as encompassing the principles of bourgeois economy, one should, as Margot Norris has also noted, consider it as the *staging* of that economy.[6] The difference is not simply that in the latter case Joyce is aware of, and hence above, bourgeois ideology. Norris's portrait of Joyce-the-intended-socialist governing over Joyce-the-paradoxical-aesthete is difficult to accept, especially when we consider that her aim is nothing less than to unravel the politics *of* (not beyond) his art. What my emphasis on the performative nature of Joyce's art does imply, however, is that the artist "uses" the principle of economic exchange on which his autonomy depends for all it is worth: his is an acknowledgment of debt that enables him not to overcome capitalism but to reproduce it in a gesture of dispense. This makes Joyce into "aboleshqvik,"[7] a Bolshevik who abolishes quick the marketplace as the "murketplots" (368.09), the murky plots.

As Mark Osteen has recently illustrated,[8] Joyce used to spend freely the money that he borrowed from his brother and friends, because by thus perversely accumulating a sense of privation he could convince himself that he sacrificed material prosperity to produce artistic currency. Hence, it was the artist, not his benefactors, who proved to be able to give without getting much in return. Not he, but the others were in debt. If, as Stephen says in *Ulysses*, "[a] merchant . . . is one who buys cheap and sells dear,"[9] then Joyce's exchange with his creditors was based on a perversion of that mechanism: they bought dear the art that he claimed to have given for free. Through such a self-proclaimed generous gift, Joyce could buy his freedom from debt—and he did it cheaply. Art became Joyce's (Irish?) mode of simultaneously touching the English (Weaver, for instance) for a quid, while misappropriating what in *Ulysses* is called their proudest boast: "*I paid my way.*"[10] Thus it is that Joyce recognized his debts to his benefactors, friends, but also readers and literary predecessors, only to reinscribe that bond with and in his art. To quote from Osteen's book:

> To Harriet Shaw Weaver he presented copy number one of *Ulysses* . . . the manuscript of *Portrait* . . . and an autograph manuscript of *Finnegans Wake* . . . Upon completing the latter book he wrote to her: "with reference to a commission given to me some time ago by your good self I have pleasure in informing you that the order in question has now been duly executed as per instructions . . . I have therefore this day delivered the goods and trust that the same will be found satisfactory" . . . His books are his currency, remittances to his most patient and sympathetic patrons and readers.[11]

We know that Joyce's exchange of letters with Harriet Shaw Weaver (and with Sylvia or Stanislaus or Eugène or Nora, for that matter) manipulated the gift of writing for the sole purpose of owning more: money, of course, but also gratitude, recognition, love, even dirty underwear. In this respect, the artist's author-ity was derived from his being an *auctor*: according to Rabaté,

> the one who augments, adds to: he has clearly enlarged our notion of literary totality, a notion which, it might be recalled, is never too far from that of the monstrous. A writer who pretends to disposses himself of his traditional prerogatives in order to leave the burden of debt and sin to his reader . . . [comes] back like a bogeyman to scare critics and readers.[12]

The economy of Joyce's letters, and of his literature, functions along the give-and-take model that we analyzed in *Exiles* and that, more specifically, implies a generosity on the part of the artist (Richard) toward an audience (Bertha and Robert) with the intention of possessing and hence alienating it completely: indeed, what is freely given (Bertha) cannot be taken away (by Robert). However—and this adds an important modification to the discussion so far—this duplicity of the Joycean gift, which disposes only to retain, raises doubts as to the nature of artistic mastery. *Exiles*, I have argued, also questions the extent to which an author, who wants to be "all in all," can still be said to be anybody at all. That this desire for complete power not only over his work (its preparation and publication) but also over his readers, and predecessors, that this immense desire left Joyce with an enterprise which daunted his own imagination, can be witnessed from his letters to Miss Weaver.[13] Repeatedly he expresses his fear of losing control over his notes and over the various drafts of *Finnegans Wake*: "I am overwhelmed by works and worries,"[14] "I have invented a whole system of my own—a great deal of it very childish—by which I keep my brains from falling about,"[15] "I am sorry my cyclopeyed face has that worried look. Really I have got some rest and a good deal of sea air. But it is true that I have been thinking and thinking how and how and how can I and can it—all about the fusion of two parts of the book,"[16] "Do you not like anything I am writing. Either the end of part I (Δ) is something or I am an imbecile in my judgment of language. I am rather discouraged about this as in such a vast and difficult enterprise I need encouragement."[17]

Hence the question emerges: what kind of a *rapport* exists between the artist and his reader, if the former's capacity to freely give is based on the coerced participation of the latter? Does this not imply a conflation of power and its representation/reception that may easily lead to disempowerment on both sides? Can we still speak of an "exchange" between author and reader when the patronage of both is the effect of the uncontrollable nature of the text?

For Joyce to *stage* an exchange of sorts in *Finnegans Wake* is to give full credit to his readers with a gift that neither (traditional) donor nor (traditional) recipient can appropriate. In this excessiveness or expenditure, he not only augments but also limits the role of reader and writer alike such that their interaction—or diffraction—encompasses the crisscrossing movement of the text. In the chapter to follow, I will argue that this motion can best be described as the dissipation of the text's smallest unit, the *point* of encounter between writer and reader, into ALP's (Δ) tea-stain, along the *crossing* (X) lines of Mamalujo (the four interpreters). However, before engaging into a detailed analysis of section 1.5, let me first briefly anticipate how I think Joyce is minimally tying together his text and then point out some of the implications of my reading for the concept of the (monstrous?) sublime.

In one of those remarkably self-reflexive (and therefore oft-cited) passages, the *Wake* suggests to its readers the hermeneutical craft that alone can crack its code: "(Stoop) if you are abcedminded, to this claybook, what curios of signs (please stoop), in this allaphbed! Can you rede (since We and Thou had it out already) its world? It is the *same told of all*" (18.17–20, emphasis added). That the world of Joyce's alphabet is the "same told of all" may imply that it is the same as that which has been told by all ("since we and Thou had it out already"), or about all. Or that it tells itself the same about all, over and over again. Its *sameness* thus concerns the text's relation to itself, the text tells the same as itself, as well as to other texts: the text tells the same as what others have told. This confusion is not insignificant because it already captures—prior to saying anything at all—what the sentence stands for. And what the whole of the *Wake*—prior to saying anything at all—stands for. For Joyce's text tells the same—the same as itself, the same as others—and can thus hardly claim a point of originality.

To the extent that its sameness is that of all, it is also that which it shares with all: its sameness is what relates it to all others, others who in turn are characterized by the same sameness relating them to all. Thus it is that what the *Wake* shares with all others—what is the same in the *Wake*—is the relatedness to others itself: the *Wake* is the *same*-as-*others*, it is the metaphorical "as"-

structure of similarity (to be the same as), in which the same is already (as) other. Because the sameness of the *Wake* is thus a sharing with others, one could say that its point of identity (or what is the same, its point of sameness) is a cluster of relations to others; relations, however, that, Joyce once said, do not add up to "ordinary connections": "In writing of the night, I really could not, I felt I could not, use words *in their ordinary connections*."[18] For to the extent that the *Wake*'s *rapport* to all is shared by all, its relations are always plural, or punctual. Conversely, here in the punctuality or sameness of relations all relations interconnect; it is their point of connection.

Emblematic of this endlessly plural intersection is the shifting identity of, to name only one, HCE as *H*ere *C*omes *E*verybody—also Humphrey Chimpden Earwicker, God, Adam, Finn Mac Cool, Abraham, Cromwell, Jarl van Hoother, Wellington, Napoleon, Gladstone, Shakespeare, Caesar, and Joyce: "An imposing everybody he always indeed looked, constantly the *same as* and *equal to himself* and magnificently well worthy of any and all such universalisation" (32.19–22, emphasis added). Insofar as HCE is the same *as* himself, he is separated from himself by a (metaphoric) relation to himself. In that structure of *equality to* himself, HCE is already different—signaled by the fact that his identity is constituted by *three* letters of the alphabet, that is, ultimately three letters that are the same for all: Hush! Caution! Echoland; How Charmingly Exquisite; Happinest Childher Everwere.[19] It is a plurality that the sameness-as-himself aims to overcome but that cannot but affirm his relation to all the others (eventually, all the other letters of the alphabet). Living at the rupture between himself and the world, *H*e be-*C*omes *E*verybody, well worthy of such "universalisation." HCE is the part for the whole only insofar as the whole lies fragmented in the equality of the part to itself: "When a part so ptee does duty for the holos we soon grow to use of an allforabit" (18.36–19.2).

Because of its minimal or punctual structure of coherence, Joyce's growing text, rather than simply capitalizing on the reader and becoming monstrous as Rabaté suggests, also hesitantly situates us: at once somewhere and everywhere. The *Wake*'s infinite repetition, through concentration, of a totality of languages and histories and cultures ("The untireties of livesliving being the one substrance of a streamsbecoming. Totalled in toldteld and teldtold in tittletell tattle," 597.7–9), may cross the threshold of comprehension and momentarily baffle us, at the same time it constitutes the minimal degree/point/space of intersection between writer and reader (self and other) without which his text—any text, for that matter—would not be a text to begin with. Totality totaled in its being told draws out the past and the future that writer and reader share (hence it is already repeated as toldteld, and crosswise, teldtold) and that thus make our reading, albeit liminally, possible. Contained within a minimum of structure, whose effect is an infinite series of structures, Joyce's totality achieves what everybody in particular but nobody in general, not even the author, has imagined before. If for Schlegel the common denominator of writer and reader was the *address*, the *Wake*'s "comedy nominator" (283.07), I will argue, is the literalization of the *directing of words* in a fourfold direction.[20] Here in the crossing of two lines (x, +), of writing and reading, words double, triple, quadruple an infinite number of times.

Thus, the *Wake* is unique in the way it repeats everything that has already been and will be said or written in order to gather the field of literature covered so far and unearth or hatch its basic skeleton. As a consequence, we readers, poised as we are at this extremity, cannot but remark ("remarx") the limits. If there is a remnant of the sublime here, as Klaus Reichert claims,[21] it lies shattered in our endless reiteration and exhaustion of the Joycean themes, structures, letters, archives, and notebooks that the artist himself could hardly fit into his work. And yet they are what makes up that work and our reading. The romantic sublime as the paradoxical presentation of what in art lies beyond art—this infinitely perfectible and historical event of art, at once singular and universal—has reached its completion at the Wakean curve of space and time.[22]

This is the theme of the fable of the Ondt (space) and the Gracehoper (time), when the latter says to the former: "Your genus its worldwide, your spacest sublime! / But, Holy Saltmartin, why can't you beat time?" (419.7–8) The Ondt/Shaun, deaf but economical and therefore rich, may have "volumes immense" (419.5), "andt, and andt" (418.9), "meat soveal behind" (419.4), however he cannot, for all his Ondtship, do away with time. By contrast, the Gracehoper/Shem loves to waste time and thus money (he is not on the Ondt's socialist "social list"), and lives in a world at first full of fun and "joicity" (414.23) later of "chronic's despair" (417.35–36). His is an "in risible universe" (419.3): made invisible and risible by time, not exactly risen to the sublime heights of the Ondt's heavenly "spacest." Although contraries, space and time are divided by only a minimal difference. As the Gracehoper tells the Ondt: "the *prize* of your save is the *price* of my spend" (418.21, emphasis added). What separates gain from loss is as minuscule as the difference between Z and C, which is as much a minimal matter of space—the difference between two written letters—as of time: in speech, the difference lies in sonority and in the length of (talking about displacement) the preceding vowel. Together the Ondt and the Gracehoper are doubles who while adding onto each other also subtract and eventually develop into a mutual need: "An extense must impull, an elapse must elopes" (418.33), "We are Wastenot with Want" (418.30).

It is interesting to note that, in this passage, the *Wake*'s return to the sublime occurs in a context that Eagleton will many years later philosophically describe as "a material implication with others." What Joyce's fable tells us is that a world governed by the economic principles of checks and balances produces two kinds of art. The first gladly acknowledges its degraded, material status because it offers opportunities for joyfully debunking universal values (including the pound) as "everlistings" (414.28). This is the Joycean economic gesture, seeing everything as only one in a series: also capitalism is regarded serially and hence not seriously. "Not one pickopeck of muscowmoney" (416.17–18) is left when the Gracehoper's spendthrift has consumed itself and encounters its opposite: the restraint of the bourgeois modernist aesthete. One might argue that the Gracehoper thus embodies a non-Marxist kind of material historicism: the insect understands that precisely in its *possibility* of reproduction (and, yes, there is a lot of "insectual" sex going on), "the" system hardly exists, let alone assumes a singular, capitalist identity. Therefore, it is not worth saving. Unless one adheres to the labor of the ant, of course, who only works in order to negate time: rather than Gracehoper's "schoppinhour" (414.33), he puts "schelling in kopfers" (416.4).

The Ondt's neo-romantic stance is the second mode of art possible in a capitalist world, and it is, not suprisingly, based on an idealization of reality: seated "upon his dhrone" (417.11) "before his comfortumble phullupsuppy" (417.14–15)—"(for he was a conformed aceticist and aristotaller)" (417.16)—the philosopher, he could be Eglinton as much as Eagleton, is surrounded by a halo of "Hosana cigals" (417.12–13) and angelic prostitutes. Excluding time and history from his heavenly abode, he condemns the Gracehoper to be "Artalone the Weeps" (418.1): Lord Ardilaun, full of lice, producing art along the weeps or tears. The Ondt (alias "windhame" [415.29], Wyndham Lewis?[23]) exemplifies the bourgeois aesthete/philosopher proclaiming his freedom from materiality and the masses with a snobbery made possible by the very exclusion of the masses from Havana cigars and high-blown philosophy. Retreating from reality in the name of high art and philosophy, the Ondt's dependence on gold, sex, and food becomes all the more visible.

It is precisely in the Ondt's rejection of the wasted Gracehoper that time, the big waste, reasserts itself. In one of those strokes of "genus," Joyce couples this inevitable passing (historicity) of the Ondt's sublime to a vision of the future that even Adorno would have to affirm. The fable ends "[i]n the name of the former [space] and of the latter [time] and of their holocaust. Allmen" (419.9–10). Since the annihilation of time leads to a totalitarian oppression of the other (and here one thinks of the awe-inspiring architecture of the Nazis), sublime space must be approached historically. This means that it becomes questionable—why can't you beat time?—and, more joycefully, the occasion for thundering laughter.

In *Finnegans Wake*, Joyce completes the search that he started when, as a boy, he was trying to articulate some minimal, non-contingent universal structure in human nature. His early essays on art and life articulate this primary element in a definition of drama that, self-consciously if you wish, addresses the community in which the definition comes about. There the laws of human nature are described as the strife of passions that art in general, and drama in particular, has as its theme and founding structure. Although historically variable, these passions are communal and hence transcend the idiosyncrasy of the private feelings of the individual. If drama is the object of Joyce's attention, it is because it visibly plays out, and singularizes, the conflict of tempers that is constant in art, in human nature, and in society as a whole. Ibsen's drama, for example, not only tells us something about conflicting passions between men and women but also performs and appears as the affective conflict between the artist and the audience that constitutes the essence of drama in the first place. Not only does the young Joyce, then, define reality—the constant in human nature—as a conflict of emotions that ties us into the community (like a law), he is also aware that this reality assumes a visible form in the irreconcilability of play and audience, which, as said, makes possible the dramatic art form. It is precisely this creative tension brought about by the dramatist between the play and the communal reality it immediately effectuates that Stephen Dedalus in *Stephen Hero* describes as the "veritably sublime process of [the artist's] nature" but that Joyce rewrites as the impersonality of his creation. For the latter art makes visible the unarticulated rules of his community. Indeed, it has been my contention that Joyce's theory and practice of the dramatic form offer us an intrinsically political view of art, albeit a view radically *constrained* by his concern for achieving an adequate form in which his "theory" could be instantiated in front of a reader. Moreover, the community of men and women that Joyce addresses from the very beginning is first and foremost an affective one, and hence defiant of rational interpretation. Thus, Joyce (and Stephen with him) repeatedly emphasizes the need to *satisfy* the audience. Politics is going to take place at the level of taste, certainly, but also by staging within the text the very contingency of such an enterprise: the multitude of aesthetic responses that comes from an inherently varying audience.

And what better place in which to locate this indeterminacy than the human body, better still: the gendered female body, object of conflictual affection par excellence. It is here that the limits of Joyce's political stance become blatantly visible: for, as I have argued, while some feminists insist on describing Joyce as a patriarchal sexist, others continue to applaud him as the proto-champion of women's rights. If I myself have chosen to highlight some fragments of the feminine sublime in Joyce's oeuvre, it is because, prompted by my own passion for theory, I wanted to resist the irreducible tensions in his work and reproduce that minimal tie between form and content, art and its reception, art and its effects without which the artist could not even begin to address me.

Of course, there are always limits to our reading, and it is in *Finnegans Wake* that they are most clearly felt. In the end, the *Wake*'s (egg)burst of meaning carries the concept of the sublime beyond itself. And it would become "sublimer" (551.35) were it not for the laughter resounding from it. Indeed, what is not seen in Joyce—the disappearance of the sublime—*can* be heard in multiple peals of laughter, in the abundant presence of the Joycean pun. Thus, the passage "from the sublime to the ridiculous" (445.27) in the *Wake*, a passage that the fable of the Ondt and the Gracehoper described as the movement of space in time, goes by way of the ear. As Joyce tried to explain in a letter to Weaver:

> For instance Shaun, after a long absurd and rather incestuous Lenten lecture to Izzy, his sister, takes leave of her "with a half a glance of Irish frisky from under the shag of his parallel brows." These are the words the reader will see but not those he will hear. He also alludes to Shem as my "soamheis" brother; he means Siamese.[24]

In order to track the smallest difference (in romanticism, the beyond of art) out of which Joyce's writing chuckles itself, the reader must cease to read, or better still: she needs to *hear* differently what she is *reading*. This implies decoding not so much Joyce's authoritarian voice, as its necessary drifting, which is a movement toward reception: the voice *as it is heard*.[25] From this perspective, the sliding between different words characteristic of the Joycean pun or portmanteau takes place in a conflictual transition from eye to ear. Where the eye tends to look at face value, the ear hears more figuratively if you wish: it captures the multiple minimal (homophonic) threads between different sounds.[26] Hearing more than what is said, the listening reader "overhears" the Joycean text, which in turn becomes "hearsay," an echo of rumors: "The gossiple so delivered in epistolear" (38.23) by "Shun the Punman" (93.13).

Like the feeling of the sublime, laughter is the affect emerging from the perception of conflict. Only now the bodily sensations cannot be respectfully viewed, and thus repressed, from a distance. In fact, laughter in the *Wake* arises in the discrepancy between the eye and the ear, which designates the moment when we joyfully *hear* the connection between the lexical element just *read* and various other sounds. In the burst of laughter that accompanies our ear-wicked "insight" (the Dutch *wikken* means "to judge"), we momentarily gather various threads between what we read on the horizontal axis of contiguity (Jacobson's metonymic axis) and what we hear on the vertical axis of similarity (the metaphoric axis). Laughter, then, affirms not simply our superiority over the text but, rather, the fact that the *Wake*'s minimal structure is a sensual one: it tentatively but intimately positions us vis-à-vis the book by way of the different senses. This is what we have in common with angels (vertical connection) and insects (horizontal connection) alike.

In what follows, I will tease out this sensual pleasure of Joyce's jokes by focusing on ALP's mamafesto (chapter 1.5) and, more particularly, on the tea-stain with which she *affectionately* signs her letter to her children: Shem, who copies it; Shaun, who delivers it; Issy-Maggy, who occasions it, both as addressee and as seductress of HCE.[27] If it is true that Joyce liked Budgen's comparison between the sense of absolute pitch in music and that of tea-tasting,[28] then the tea-stain might well be considered as the visual mark of the disjunction between what we see or read on the one hand and what we hear or taste on the other. In the stain, the text ends—or consumes—the traditional acts of writing and reading as these are based on sight, or insight. In the stain of writing, Joyce's model author—ALP but also Shem/James who writes at his mother's dictation—scrapes away, criticizes, the text as she writes. Writer and critic, mother and sons, I will argue, are minimally related in this all too literal but tasteful *end* of the text. Furthermore, and perhaps most significantly: the stain is characterized by a T- or X-shape, at once a point and the crossing of relations.

ALP's Teatimestained Terminal

But let us now align ourselves with chapter 1.5, where Anna Livia Plurabelle's "mamafesto" lies under the scrutinizing eye of an unidentifiable critic, who could be me or you or the whole world for that matter, but whom I will call "for the space of the time being" (109.22) Shaun, the postman. Maybe not that inappropriately because it seems that we are dealing with a manuscript that by and large looks like a letter:[29]

> Dear whom it proceded to mention Maggy well & allathome's health well only the hate turned the mild on *the van* Houtens and the general's elections with a *lovely* face of some born gentleman with a beautiful present of wedding cakes for dear thankyou Chriesty and with grand funferall of poor Father Michael don't forget unto life's & Muggy well how are you Maggy & hopes soon to hear well & must now close it with fondest to the twoinns with four crosskisses for holy paul holey corner holipoli whollyisland pee ess from (locust may eat all but this sign shall they never) affectionate largelooking tache of tch. The stain, and that a teastain (the overcautelousness of the masterbilker here, as usual, signing the page away . . . (111.10–21)

Signing the page away with four crosskisses and a tea-stain, the masterbilder—is it ALP or the dead Finn?—completes her correspondence to Maggy in the very act of consuming it: by crossing out and staining the affectionate kisses with which she signs her name. The cross and stain are the fourfold moments in which addressor and addressee meet in a point that literally and figuratively ends the correspondence it establishes. Here at the end of the letter, when the page is signed *away* in a forwarding gesture of delivery, the cross-stain establishes a relation between the writer and the reader by undoing it in a cross (+, x), which is the mark of two intersecting lines as well as the symbol of the Four Old Men in the *Wake*.[30]

The letter, "selfpenned to one's other" (489.33–34), is staged in its consumption. Hence the references to the milk, the cocoa and the cake, all of which function much as the tea-stain does, namely, as modes of "relating" the letter and its outside; that is, not simply the reader, but the writer's surroundings—the *salon* or the inn ("Yours very truthful. Add dapple inn" [113.17–18], also "at Dublin")—in which the writing first took place. With ALP's letter we are back at the gossipy atmosphere of the afternoon tea, in which the story about Humphrey Chimpden Earwicker's voyeurism was first made public, and which the previous chapters had already evoked at length. Through the stain, this circulation of gossip that makes up the context and pre-text of the letter is transposed to the inside of the text in a gesture usually described as self-production. What else is this tea-drop, then, but the mark of the reality of the text as this results from an inscription of its *circumstances*: a case of *circumlocution*, that is, through which the outside, perhaps all the gossip of Dublin, makes up the stereotyped inside of the message.[31] We might call it Joyce's hermeneutics of the epistolary commonplace (also common place or marketplace), "as usual" signing the page away: the preemptive *circumscription* of meaning in the public consumption of language.[32]

This idea of meaning erased in "the vulgarity of speech" (Stephen's epiphany) or social consumption of language is Joyce's twentieth-century version of the romantic hermeneutic circle. For Schlegel, we remember, the act of reading—an interaction that concerns the text and its interpreter and that ultimately yields meaning—aims at the reconstruction of the whole, or the original context, in which the writing first took place. Since that context (Lucinde) is negatively reflected in the text's fragmentariness, to reconstruct the whole implies that we read the text *as fragments*. However, since to thus derive the original context from the work's incompletion amounts to the completion of what necessarily remains provisional, the hermeneutic enterprise alters or destroys as it proceeds. Its progression—also the growth of the text—results in its suspension. The path of the critic, is, in other words, paved with halts and falls, but it is in those ironic twists and turns that the infinity of the ideal is guaranteed.

In ALP's letter, the hermeneutic circle as the interpretive

interaction between text and (social) context subversively returns in the form of a tea-stain. Accordingly, to read this stain implies that we further develop it, for instance by adding a few more drops or cups in a *Finnegans Wake* discussion group. In imitation of the Jena Circle of the romantics, this kind of collective reading activity is the best response to Joyce's novel: for in such a milieu of coffee, tea, or lukewarm beer, Joyce's fusion of text and context in an act of consumption is adequately realized.[33] It is a public practice for which Joyce himself provided the theoretical model when, in the *Wake*, dead Finnegan is revived through the smell of a whiskey-stain (24.15). And yet, one should not take Joyce seriously and naively be convinced that the perfect Joyce critic is (s)he who revives the body of the text with a liquor-stain (in Ireland) or a cup of tea (in England), or (s)he who "distills" the meaning from the page by sprinkling it with "seedy ejaculations" (183.23) (in imitation of HCE's transgression in Phoenix Park) and a "jotty young watermark" (112.32) (imitating the girls urinating in the Park). For such a perverse coincidence of text and context—although admittedly as insignificant as ALP's tea-stain—would not only blur the distinctions between private and public but also confuse the pleasures in the park outside (the sexual ones) with those of the drawing room inside (the textual ones). For our own academic purposes, it is more important that we attempt to reconstruct ALP's peculiar correspondence and the end or outside thereof, without falling back into mere gossip or the rituals of tea-tasting (tea-sthetic). I will, then, consider the issue from a more theoretical perspective, one that accounts for the incorporation of writing and its ordinary connections in terms of Joyce's attempt to conflate language and its *end or outside*, that is, ultimately its irreducible remnant. "[L]et us see all there may remain to be seen" (113.32–33). What is left is a signature in Derrida's sense: "the pure reproducibility of a pure event."[34]

The letter—which, as said, needs to be read in accordance with its outside—makes it impossible to distinguish the interior content from the exterior form. This confusion of inside and outside explains the *Wake*'s numerous associations between a "Boston letter" (a pun on the Boston Tea Party?) and the dungheap in which it was preserved and finally found by a hen. Chapter 1.5 reintroduces this subplot on page 110.22—"About that original hen . . . a cold fowl behaviourising strangely on that fatal midden or chip factory or comicalbottomed copsjute (dump for short)"—and most concretely as follows:

> The bird in the case was Belinda of the Dorans, a more than quinquegintarian (Terziis prize with Serni medal, Cheepalizzy's Hane Exposition) and what she was scratching at the hour of klokking twelve looked for all this zogzag world like a goodish-sized sheet of letterpaper originating by transhipt from Boston (Mass.) of the last of the first to Dear . . . (111.5–10)

Then follows the letter to Maggy that was quoted earlier in my discussion. It seems that this (remainder of a) personal correspondence could only have been preserved in a public dump because the latter was already present inside the document in the form of ALP's tea-stain (the locus of public consumption). The dunghill, in other words, is nothing more than the preservation or incubation of the letter itself or, rather, of the end of that letter. The forwarding movement of the tea-stained signature—previously described as a gesture of completion—has lit(t)eralized into an enveloping wasteland. What relates the inside and the outside, the letter and the litter, could now be redefined as a self-consuming historical development through which the correspondence is preserved in its "[h]eated residence" (111.33) in the dump; a sedimentation, which as we know, constituted the stereotyped writing in the first place.

That in the *Wake* the establishment of correspondence is an act of composition-as-decomposition has so far been illustrated in spatial terms: as the tea-stained transgression of the borders between inside and outside, text and context, the private and the public. One can now reconsider it in historical terms and, more particularly, in the light of the *Wake*'s obsessive reconstruction of the Adamic Fall. Indeed, in Joyce's lapsarian paradise there are no longer any clear-cut spatiotemporal distinctions. The *Wake* is the site where everything has already taken place or, better still, where everything is actively *falling* into place. That the *Wake* stages a return to the Adamic Fall implies that it resurrects not only the origin of history (the *point* of origin), but also the whole of human history as the history (the *relating*) of that Fall. Hence, first of all, Joyce's endless variations on the same theme: Adam's Fall from paradise, Finnegan's fall from the ladder, HCE's sexual crime in the park, Parnell's political fall. Hence also the excessive allusions to historical events—the French Revolution, the American Civil War, Irish and Roman history—that Joyce has woven into the legends of his hero's fall.[35] Humpty Dumpty, Finn, HCE, Caesar . . . theirs is a literal and moral fall that in its continuous movement downward relates the course of history: a course, however, that is itself nothing but the reiteration of its point of origin. Thus, Fin-no-more is also Fin-again. *La Fin*, the end as the beginning of a historical "vicus of recirculation" (03.02).

If the course of history is also a collecting of origins, then surely the hen who first picked ALP's correspondence from the dump is the historicist or archeologist par excellence: "the farther back we manage to wiggle the more we need the loan of a lens to see as much as the hen saw. Tip" (112.01–2). And what she retrieves from beneath the garbage is nothing short of a new mode of literature: "No, assuredly, they are not justified, those gloompourers who grouse that letters have never been quite their old selves again since that weird weekday in bleak Janiveer (yet how palmy date in a waste's oasis!) when to the shock of both, Biddy Doran looked at literature" (112.23–27). As this parody of literary criticism suggests, Biddy Doran's culling coincides with the act of "looking at literature," which is a mode of reading as much as of writing (summoning of a document). It is a "shocking" resuscitation of writing-as-reading, hardly to be dissociated from ALP's tea-stained writing gathering its own ends. Biddy Doran's picking resembles the letter's "proteiform graph" (107.08) in that it emphasizes the fragmentation constituting the literary document. What the two women have in common is the extent to which they are creatively gathering the old bits and pieces, thereby showing the parts to be residing in expansive contexts. This process of relating, in which each single element is an incorporation of a whole mass of material surrounding it, reinterprets the concept of representation as a mode of instant consumption. The dynamic transference between the fragmented signs thus installs a semiotic order that punctures any stable structure. ALP's narrative relates the breakdown of the concept of "narration." Its movement arrests any linear direction and instead releases a polymorphous correspondence that puts to an end any ordering of parts into a whole.

What remains is the trajectory of the "travelling inkhorn" (118.23) as it moves from one letter-character to the next and, in this "interpretation of any phrase in the whole" (117.36–118.01) blurs the spaces in between. For Joyce, this narrative "de-structuring," as should be clear by now, destroys the neatness of identifications and transforms the text into a series of tea-stained signatures. Writing as interpretation or as the apprehension of wholeness in time halts as it proceeds, "our social something bowls along bumpily, experiencing a jolting series of prearranged disappointments, down the long lane of (it's as semper as oxhousehumper!) generations, more generations and still more generations" (107.32–35). This "prearranged" jolting interaction between writing and interpretation characterizing ALP's "sexmosaic of nymphosis" (107.13–14) marks the moments in which the singular alphabetic letter draws into itself the surrounding ("circumstantiating," 109.14) letters that make up the epistolary document and, beyond that, the whole of the *Wake*. The plural whole—outlined by the movement of the hand—becomes visible in the part at the very moment the latter blots out its concrete shape in a dance of figures that shake their identity as they appear, "jerking to and fro, flinging phrases here, there, or returns inhibited, with some half-halted suggestion" (121.06–7). The *Wake* thus captures the rhythm of writing as it passes by or ends, suspended in "the space of the time being." Here language acquires the force of theoretical (or voyeuristic) interpretation to arrest the text in a minimal gesture: "interrupted by visit of seer to scribe or of scribe to site" (108.03–4).

Such a confusion of "scribe" and "seer" embraces a mode of graphic visibility beyond that of the traditional text. The visibility that here takes place is one that belongs to the radical outside of writing: to Joyce's invisible night. It implies, in other words, a break with or distance from the traditional concept of language. Indeed, only through the destruction of human speech, and only by violently bringing our literary tradition to its completion, can language bring about this—feminine—outside: "Who in his heart doubts either that the facts of feminine clothiering are there all the time or that the feminine fiction, stranger than the facts, is there also at the same time . . ." (109.30–33). Joyce's task is, therefore, a double one: his writing is to accomplish the end of language and, by doing so, bring about a new kind of invisible discourse. Moreover, posited at the end of tradition and of time, Joyce re-writes the concept not only of "writing" but also of the "end" of that writing. His is an ending that ends all ending in a traditional sense and that can affirm itself only through a return to what has been abolished. This end-less and therefore incomplete return is what can be defined as language's tendency toward the outside, which, since it is invisible is of course as much space as it is time. This confusion of time and space in the outside of language explains the text's reference to the chaos of the arabesque—which is the spatial presentation of time: "The end? Say it with missiles then and thus arabesque the page" (115.02–3).

Thus it is that what the *Wake*'s arabesque reveals is the incompletion of its return to tradition: the moment the return is completed (its "dropped final" achieved), its initial—that to which it (re)turns—is "illuminated," in a double sense, with a blinding fullness of "coloured ribbons" and "confused drapery":[36] "the touching reminiscence of an incompletet trail or dropped final; a round thousand whirligig glorioles, prefaced by (alas!) now illegible airy plumeflights, all tiberiously ambiembellishing the initials majuscule of Earwicker" (119.13–17). Because the fulfillment of Joyce's return to origins also constitutes its end, Joyce's language disintegrates into a plurality of (re)turns as soon as it emerges and functions simultaneously as a mode of writing and as a form of *illumination* that decorates—signs or scrapes away—the text. Hence Shaun's insistence on the graphic quality of ALP's hieroglyphic signifiers insinuating themselves into their own void while folding and turning in the sliding motion of a serpent: "the innocent exhibitionism of those frank yet capricious underlinings: that strange exotic serpentine, since so properly banished from our scripture . . ." (121.19–21). Witness also Shaun's pictorial description of the confusion between the different letters of the alphabet: "the pees with their caps awry are quite as often as not taken for kews with their tails in their or are quite as often as not taken for pews with their tails in their mouths . . ." (119.35–120.01). With its tail in its mouth, Joyce's writing is caught in its Viconian "ricorso"; his is a writing that turns as it returns and that, more specifically, arises—in a punctual but rhythmic fashion—from the disruption of this return.

If Shaun's interpretation of ALP's document lingers with such emphasis on the decorative quality of her writing it is because the exteriority of her signifier also constitutes its invisibility, that is, its "banishment from our scripture." Since his search is for visible "word, letter, penstroke, paperspace is a perfect signature of its own" (115.07–8), Shaun is caught in a double bind: he wants to describe the identity of the single letter by locating the "paperspace" that surrounds it and that separates it from the other letters. However, to locate the contours of that "paperspace" he needs to read the blankness of the page against the "penstrokes" marking (or staining) its shape. But the "penstrokes" can be identified only by locating the "paperspace." Because of this undecidability between the page and the blots of ink, the materiality of ALP's language is invisible in its extreme visibility. Shaun's quest for a signature (his attempt at "seeing") is essentially a search for the space (the whiteness of the page) that is being stained in its appearance. It is a quest for the space of writing refracted (scraped away) by the text that gives this space a colorful form. To see this surplus of colors the way Shaun does implies—precisely—a vision of the excess of writing: "the toomuchness, the fartoomanyness of all those fourlegged ems: and why spell dear god with a big thick dhee (why, O why, O why?)" (122.36–123.02).

But there is yet a more striking way in which ALP's document stages its own excess, one that was already touched upon in the previous chapter when we described Joyce's language as the conflation of the horizontal axis of reading and the vertical axis of hearing:

> One cannot help noticing that rather more than half of the lines run north-south in the Nemzes and Bukarahast directions while the others go west-east in search from Maliziies with Bulgarad for, tiny tot though it looks when schtschupnistling alongside other incunabula, it has its cardinal points for all that. These ruled barriers along which the traced words, run, march, halt, walk, stumble at doubtful points, stumble up again in comparative safety seem to have been drawn first of all in a pretty checker with lampblack and blackthorn. Such crossing is antechristian of course, but the use of the homeborn shillelagh as an aid to calligraphy shows a distinct advance from savagery to barbarism. (114.02–13)

The lines of the text, Shaun tells us, run from north to south, and from west to east, in the form of a "pretty checker" characterized by a series of "cardinal" points. These points, which mark the intersection between the vertical and horizontal discourses, are the moments in which the two texts are held together in their opposition. The lines that run toward or between these points are, therefore, paths tracing their own vanishing point. The points are "cardinal" exactly because they represent the instants at which the line disappears in its (opposite) course; or, if you wish, they are the moments at which the lines are *visibly* running their course. To be sure, mobility and immobility, line and point need to be thought together in this graphic dispersal of ALP's tea-stain or T-stain. The checkerboard can, indeed, be viewed as a multiplication of T-forms running into each other along vertical and horizontal lines. From this perspective, the minimal structure of the board or page is the T-stained signature spreading in vertical and horizontal directions, in such a way that what first appeared as a formless blot now gives rise to a carefully structured text. What the "pretty checker" reveals is the rhythmic recurrence of its T-shaped disfigurations, its continuity of discontinuity through which the flow of the lines takes on the appearance of a "ruled barrier."

Given the fact that ALP's writing runs in four directions, every inscription of the text needs to be read as a cardinal point drawing together four-dimensional discourses, be they written, read, spoken, or heard. This implies that the movement forward and backward between the (hypothetical) letter a and b1 on the horizontal axis is mediated or interrupted by a movement upward and downward between a and b2 on the vertical axis. It is this folding or intertwining of the metaphoric and metonymic movements within the single inscription that transforms the writing process—as passage from a to b—into a repetitive act of judgment. Writing and criticism are one because at every point of ALP's text the writer selects one direction while discarding it in favor of the others. Writing in this way sets into play a motion of deletion, editing, or *crossing out*. Similarly, we could say that reading ALP's "cruciform postscript" implies that one is forced to choose one direction while leaving behind the others. The progression of the reader, like that of the writer, leaves behind a trail of crossed out T- or +-shaped lines. Thus moving along a path of crosses—and here I remind you of ALP's "travelling inkhorn" writing out a series of stains—writing and reading negate the linearity of their enterprise and instead straddle the four-dimensional spatiotemporal distance between the course left behind and the one to be followed.

Now there is a way in which the progress of ALP's writing as this movement along a path of crosses parodies the magnificent illuminations of the "Tunc" page in the *Book of Kells*.[37] It has, of course, often been argued that the references to the chaos of ALP's arabesque ironize the language of Sir Edward Sullivan's description of the *Book of Kells*.[38] The text itself witnesses its indebtedness to the Irish manuscript when during Shaun's discussion of the closing of the letter (the crosses and the stain) references are made to the "Tunc" page: "the cruciform postscript from which three *basia* or shorter and smaller *oscula* have been carefully scraped away, plainly inspiring the tenebrous *Tunc* page of the *Book of Kells*" (122.20–23). Joyce's parody however goes much beyond these "halfhalted suggestions" that many Joyce critics have seized upon: what ALP's document and the "Tunc" page have in common is the T-shape of their illuminated writing; a T-shape that derives from the initial or cardinal T in *Tea*—in ALP's case—or in *Tunc* and

Then in the case of the *Book of Kells*. But there is more, for the text of the "Tunc" page deals with that other most famous of disfiguring T-shapes: Christ's cross. According to Campbell,[39] the page is devoted to the words: "Tunc XPI cum eo duos latrones" [Then were there two thieves crucified with him (Matt. 27:38)]. The beautiful T-decorations or T-stains of the *Book of Kells*—and of ALP's document—are therefore more than simply a reproduction of the letter T. They become instead the "illumination" of the Christian sacrifice evoked by the text of the "Tunc" page. In its intricate maze of colors and forms the text *inscribes* the suffering (the cross) that the "Tunc" page *describes*.[40] Thus, in the arabesque of ALP's checkerboard lies hidden a vision of the sacrificial nature—and of the sacrifice or end—of the artistic enterprise. Here, in the crossing of four movements, the writer-reader is made to carry his or her "cross," which is also that of the monk (or cardinal) in the case of the *Book of Kells*. What the crossing of ALP's cruciform script denotes is the hardship (the cross) of artistry, shared (let us say "joined" or "crossed") by both the creator and his or her public. We can say of the crucifix-form of the T-page—also the crossed out signature of ALP, or AL~~P~~—that it unites writer and reader in their communal "way of the cross." In imitation of Christ's Way of the Cross toward Calvary Mount—the biblical version of Ireland's Howth Head covered by Finn's dead body—the path of the writer-reader is marked by halts and falls. These halts are what was previously defined as the "cardinal" points making visible the disappearance of the path (or line) in its course. They are, in other words, markers of the death or the end of the sentence (also Christ's death sentence). In the context of the Catholic ritual of the Way of the Cross, the halts or stations are the moments at which priest and worshippers stop to reflect upon Christ's death in the form of a dialogue. Thus, to proceed from one station to the next is to halt at every one of them and anticipate the death to come.

Or in the words of the "Tunc" page, on the cross—+T+hen, at that moment of death—were there two thieves crucified with him: the man crucified is of course HCE-ALP-Joyce-the monk-Christ, all martyr figures. The two thieves are the two soldiers catching HCE in the act of voyeurism; the soldiers in their turn are guilty of obscenely observing HCE. They are also two readers—you and I—guilty of reading Joyce's transgressive work; guilty of reading the *Book of Kells* and its reference to the Holy Book; guilty also of looking at, maybe worshiping, a naked figure on the Cross.

From what has been said so far, we can conclude that what unites ALP's letter and the "Tunc" page is also what unites writer and reader: the laborious sacrificial nature of the text. Here art becomes a mode of Christian sacrifice for both artist and critic. The reason is that the illuminations scrape away what has been written, so that what is left is a text caught between visibility and invisibility, between the visual and the aural. Moreover, not only is the text a cross *for* writer and reader, it is itself the cross *as* "seer" and "scribe," the two being intertwined in Joyce's language: the juncture of literature and criticism called staining, signing away, or simply, the end of writing.

We can now return to the beginning of this chapter: ALP's signature-cross points up the moment when writer and reader unite, or when the writer becomes her own patient critic. The cross is the point of encounter between two discourses, each of which runs in a double direction. Because of this continuous interplay between literature and criticism ALP crosses out not simply *what* she creates, but the fact *that* she writes. The cross, in other words, destroys even as it writes.

To be sure, this conflict between creator and critic at the heart of ALP's writing style also inflicted Joyce's own project. Joyce's "cross" was just this obsessive desire to control the criticism of his work, not only through a relentless drive toward revision and perfection, but also through a compulsive devouring, even staging, of the reviews concerning his work (see chapter 6). Seen in this light, the stylistic distortions of Joyce's text are first of all the expression of the man's need to determine the course of Joyce scholarship. Precisely by incorporating the reader's critical view within the smallest unit of the text (the "cardinal" point), Joyce's work has alienated as well as haunted so many readers.

Not surprisingly, therefore, Shaun eventually turns to the discussion of the holes that a certain professor ("Brotfressor Prenderguest") has pierced into the page: "to=introdùce a notion of time [ùpon à plane (?) sù" fàç' e'] by pùnct!ingh oles (sic) in iSpace?! Deeply religious by nature and position, and warmly attached to Thee . . ." (124.10-13). Seated at his breakfast table while trying to decipher ALP's document, the professor-critic (Gabler?) has stabbed his fork into the page in an attempt to create a notion of time in space. A peculiar research style, indeed, even if we consider that the performance was charged with significance for the one who is willing to read: "These paper wounds, four in type, were gradually and correctly understood to mean stop, please stop, do please stop, and

O do please stop respectively" (124.03–5). The holes as representative of the professor's call for more time or less space (text) confront us with the gravity of the man's disposition. For it is ironic that, in an attempt to stop the text and give himself a substantial amount of time, the critic furthers the fragmentation of the text. By puncturing the page, the professor literally removes or "edits" unwanted portions of the text while re-inserting the "doubtful points" (or holes) that were undoubtedly the cause of his impatience. It follows that by offering himself some more time (loopholes) for interpretation, the unfriendly critic continues the text in an act of destruction. Suspicious as we may be of the man's love for literature, we cannot deny the fact that by thus editing the page, he literally accomplishes ("ends") Joyce's search for the representation of the outside in the inside. The holes in the document are as far as Joyce would have gone in representing a vision of the outside. ALP, at least, refrained from such elliptical gestures, be it that she shared Brotfressor's taste for coffee and bread, or was it tea and cake. What both have in common is the extent to which they write as they read or eat. What separates them is the detachment with which ALP regarded (or destroyed) her writing as a piece of cake, or her cup of tea. Not so the professor. His forking of four holes (double bi-furcation, the Four Old Men) are clearly signs of angry attachment. His is a mode of criticism in an act of total commitment to the text: in an act of re-writing.

The professor, as we could have expected, is Joyce's "ideal reader suffering from an ideal insomnia" (120.13–14). His early "morning edition" erases the text and writes over it in a way similar to Joyce's arabesque. It also echoes Schlegel's deliberate fragmentation as the presentation of the theory and history of art. We have come a long way since the absent Lucinde first destroyed Julius's writing and confronted him with a critical view of the whole. What unites Schlegel and Joyce is also what separates them: the development of the fragment to the point of its completion, a moment in which lies obliterated any vestige of "wholeness" and hence of the fragment (which is a part of the whole). It is in the continuation of a process that never really developed beyond its origin—remember Julius's repetitive beginnings—that Joyce has been able to perfect and even end the ruse of writing in its material inscription. With the *Wake* we are at once at the end and at a new beginning of the romantic fragment as synthesis of art and criticism. Perhaps we can now begin to understand Schlegel's insistence that the history of literature cannot be completed because "[o]nce the end has been reached, it should start again from the beginning."[41] It took Joyce's wit to literalize this romantic infinity in the form of a writing that turns as it returns. In this Viconian *ricorso*, Joyce conflates art and its destruction, while writing out the idea, or theory, of literature as such.

CONCLUSION

Friedrich Schlegel's aesthetics of the fragment has claimed our attention because it reformulates the Kantian sublime—as the presentation of the ideas of (moral) reason in the defeat of the imagination—in art-historical terms, that is, as the presentation of the history of beauty in which artistic representation shows itself *as itself* (i.e., as non-mimetic). The sublime as the ongoing (re)production of beauty, and of the idea of beauty, opens up the truth about art, unmasks it so to speak. Ironizing art in the very process of presenting its ideality, Schlegel's sublime "turn" constitutes an important step toward the kind of demystification of beauty and sublimity that we saw Eagleton demand. In my analysis of the sublime, I have emphasized its duplicity as what at once constitutes art's truth and its destruction. While this antithetical movement opens up art to its other—reality—it is not simply a matter of reducing the world to a shimmering reflection of the artist's inspiration. On the contrary, although romantic art, according to Schlegel, stages a return to nature (long lost since the Greeks), this development is suspended in the infinite growth of the genre of all genres: the anti-mimetic novel.

It would be hard to claim that when Schlegel wrote down his flash of insight about the future novel containing all genres in its generality, he had *Finnegans Wake* in mind. How could he, since the completion of the idea of the novel, as he conceived of it, also staged its destruction. And yet Joyce's totalizing Anti-Novel seems to sum it all up. If I have insisted on raising the question of the fragment and of the sublime in my discussion of the *Wake* and Joyce's oeuvre in general—and it *is* a question: "why can't you beat time?"—it is because Joyce as little as Schlegel can escape the tradition of representation that he has inherited, and which is nothing other than representation as a tradition: as what has been formed over and over again and in that repetition presents itself not only as itself but also as what is already different. This minimal difference between art and its concretization out of which, according to Schlegel, the history of the novel spins itself, is what I have called the (fragment of the) sublime.

Of course, by the time Joyce is writing the *Wake*, the question of the sublime as the presentation of representation in and for itself has been exhausted: only raised once more by Mallarmé, who absolutely emptied it.[1] According to Lyotard, this arrival of the sublime as the presentation of the unpresentable *without nostalgia*, opens up within modern art the condition of postmodernity.[2] Without wanting to add fuel to the debate on the postmodern, let me just point out that Lyotard's failure to define the sublime as anything other than what escapes presentation (what he calls the fact that something happens or not—the phrase, the color, the paint) does little justice to the *particular* conflicts involved in the occurrence of what he elsewhere more generally calls "the differend."[3] By definition unpresentable, Lyotard's (sublime) "differend" cannot distinguish, for instance, between the impossibility of talking about one's experience in Dachau on the one hand and the impossibility of getting started on the *Wake* on the other. By homogenizing the silence of the Jew, the Greek, and the Irishman under the rubric of "the" unpresentable, Lyotard can neither hear nor see the many different ways in which victims but also artists have over the years (not) presented the inadequacy of existing language games. That we give a particular face to the indeterminacy of the linkage between the old and the new does not have to lead to fascism. On the contrary, calling it by its many names might do less harm than mystifying it as the "Is it happening?" of art. In this study, I have tried to undo that reification of the sublime through a careful analysis of what it looks like when it does happen: which conflicts are involved, between whom, and in whose interest are they kept silent?

Thinking the sublime as the limits of art within art itself has offered me a model with which to begin to understand the *Wake*, but also to raise questions about the status of the model itself. For centuries, artists have worked within a particular frame of reference, which although historically variable has seldom really been allowed to change: the artist is male, and his model is ordinarily female and supernatural. Woman as the source of inspiration looms large in man's world of art. Obviously, her all-pervasive presence as a muse is a sign of her absence in reality. Thus, the female nature of the artistic model is the symptom of woman's marginal position in a man's world: while man is the eloquent producer, woman is the silent recipient or instigator. Situated at the margins of man's symbolic order, she offers him his origin and end. Her function is to deliver, from the outside, the very shape or frame of man's thought: like Socrates's mother, she teaches her sons how to bring thoughts into the world.

However, since this female model is necessarily absent—it belongs to the essence of the model to precede what she outlines—she also threatens her sons' creation with evanescence. By definition a threatening "mother of all things," the muse at once destroys what she makes possible. No sooner has the maternal (re)productive womb been appropriated than it becomes a cause for fear and further control.

For both Schlegel and Joyce, this untested matrix underlying man's birth as an artist needs to be recognized for what it is: the means with which men have for centuries established their authoritative position as the makers of the world (and of women in particular). This is, then, the paradox inherent in the artist's stance: on the one hand, the (absent) female model is the projection of the creator and indicates his authority over the world; on the other hand, it is what is supposed to make his artistry, and the shaping of the model, possible in the first place. Moreover, viewed within the tradition of Western art, the female muse becomes a stereotype and, consequently, clearly not a point of origin (or novelty) for the artist. Thus historicized, the model—Lucinde, May Dedalus, Irene, Bertha, Mina Purefoy, ALP—serves less to tie together the artist's work than to gather the different models in history and, indeed, history as the model itself. As a result, the model is what inscribes the historical event of its appropriation by the artist: its being transplanted into a different context that is equally a repetition of what came before.

At the same time that the model structures the work, it overflows its borders and lays bare the underlying laws: what the young Joyce called the strife of passions as the universal structure of human nature. Although constitutive of a system of conventions, these laws are affective and conflictual—they designate the conflict between the sexes, for instance—and hence subject to change. The sublime space of presentation opened up by the model is where individual and community, pathos and ethos, art and its social context, praxis and theory meet in their opposition. That in *Ulysses* and especially *Finnegans Wake,* Joyce's models (his sources, schemes, notes) have proliferated to such an extent that they make it impossible to begin to distinguish between model and work (interestingly, Joyce's early works also begin to function as models for his later writings) is a logical consequence of the fact that in his early writing his models already do not simply fit in but literally threaten to overtake what they are being made into. Out of this primordial strife between model and work of art is born Joyce's belabored style gesturing the "dramatic cohesion" of his earlier but above all later works, and of his oeuvre as a whole.

Given the profusion of style and technique with which *Ulysses* and *Finnegans Wake* put into practice, rather than conceptualize, the basic structure of literature, my attempt to draw out the philosophical implications of the Joycean enterprise may seem to some somewhat reductive. Here I would like to call to mind, however, that it is precisely in our most (presumably) basic approach to Joyce—one that purports to derive its legitimacy from its intimacy with the basic stuff alone, namely, the texts and preferably the notes and manuscripts as well—precisely in such a back-to-basics philosophy that we call on the law of the text. The irony is not only that a legitimation by means of such a vastly polymorphous principle is far from authoritative, but also that it is in a sense based "upon the *certitude* of the void." For, as we know, the law of the Joycean text commands us to begin to read elsewhere—Homer, Tristan and Isolde, the Bible, Shakespeare, but also less authoritative works: the Dublin newspapers, nursery rhymes, children's games, obituaries. It is not enough simply to insist that Joyce did or did not do theory. Neither can it suffice to prove that philosophers do not read Joyce. Rather, we must examine what it is in Joyce's works that allows us to define his oeuvre not as philosophy but as literature. What is this law of the literary text that radical philologists, inadvertently to be sure, call upon to save Joyce from the abuses of the latest fad in literary criticism? What are the unarticulated rules, neither scientifically objective nor simply subjective, that enable us to identify the *Wake* first as a novel, then as a radicalization of the novel, and finally as a textualization of everything Joyce could lay his hands on? And how does Joyce's rewriting of the genre of the novel as the genre of literature in general (is it still literature?) offer us a pretext (a model) for returning to his notebooks, look up their cited sources, and confirm, with the authority of a Joyce Institute, what was already in the *Wake*? My book has traced a possible path along which we could begin to formulate an answer to these complex questions. But the ultimate question—whether literature begins in a conflict of interests between addressor and addressee—is up to the reader to decide.

Notes

Introduction

1. *Letters of James Joyce*, ed. Stuart Gilbert, vol. 1 (1959; New York: Viking, 1966) 204–5. Emphasis added.

2. A good example of the way Joyce criticism has started to reflect on itself is offered by Janet Egleson Dunleavy, ed., *Re-Viewing Classics of Joyce Criticism* (Urbana: U of Illinois P, 1991). Geert Lernout's *The French Joyce* (Ann Arbor: U of Michigan P, 1990) offers a good survey of the reception of Joyce in France. Alan Roughley too has been involved in reconstructing a history of Joyce studies as it reflects various schools of criticism: *James Joyce and Critical Theory: An Introduction* (New York: Harvester Wheatsheaf, 1991).

3. Klaus Reichert's "Von den Rändern her oder Sortes Wakeianae" provides a fine introduction to the manner in which the *Wake* re-thinks the traditional fragment: Lucien Dällenbach and Christiaan L. Hart Nibbrig, eds., *Fragment und Totalität* (Frankfurt am Main: Suhrkamp, 1984) 294–307. See also his "Fragment and Totality" in *New Alliances in Joyce Studies: "When It's Aped to Foul a Delfian,"* ed. Bonnie Kime Scott (Newark: U of Delaware P; London: Associated UP, 1988) 86–90.

4. Joyce wrote two essays on Mangan: one in 1902 and the other in 1907, collected in *The Critical Writings of James Joyce*, ed. Ellsworth Mason and Richard Ellmann (London: Viking, 1959) 73–83, 175–86. The complete collection is henceforth cited as *Critical Writings*.

5. Bernard Bosanquet, *A History of Aesthetic* (London: Swann Sonnenschein; New York: Macmillan, 1892).

6. Jacques Aubert, *The Aesthetics of James Joyce,* rev. ed. (Baltimore: Johns Hopkins UP, 1992). F. C. McGrath has also identified Hegel as the source of Stephen's aesthetics in *A Portrait of the Artist as a Young Man*: "Laughing in His Sleeve: The Sources of Stephen's Aesthetics," *James Joyce Quarterly* 23 (1986): 259–75.

7. Joyce cited in Aubert 9.

8. O. A. Silverman has collected Joyce's notes called "epiphanies" housed in the Poetry Room at the State University of New York at Buffalo: James Joyce, *Epiphanies,* ed. O. A. Silverman (Lockwood Memorial Library, University of Buffalo, 1956). For an interpretation of Joyce's oeuvre in the light of his theory of epiphanies, see Irene Hendry, "Joyce's Epiphanies," *James Joyce: Two Decades of Criticism,* ed. Seon Givens, new ed. (1948; New York: Vanguard P, 1963) 27–46. And more important: Hélène Cixous, *The Exile of James Joyce,* trans. Sally A. J. Purcell (New York: David Lewis, 1972).

9. *Critical Writings* 41. Emphasis added.

10. [G. W. F.] Hegel, *Introductory Lectures on Aesthetics,* trans. Bernard Bosanquet, ed. and introd. Michael Inwood (1886; Harmondsworth: Penguin, 1993) 83. I have used Bosanquet's translation of Hegel's introductory lectures, rather than Knox's, because it was the one available when Joyce was writing.

11. Bosanquet 347.

12. On Hegel's reception of *Lucinde,* see Ernst-Ullrich Pinkert, "Hegels *Lucinde*-Kritik—und ihre Aktualisierung in der Auseinandersetzung der Junghegelianer mit Romantik und Jungem Deutschland," *Text & Kontext* 9 (1981): 343–80; Philippe Lacoue-Labarthe, "L'imprésentable," *Poétique* 21 (1975): 53–95; Ernst Behler, "Friedrich Schlegel und Hegel," *Hegel-Studien,* ed. Friedhelm Nicolin and Otto Pöggeler, vol. 2 (Bonn: Bouvier, 1963) 203–50.

13. My translation is based on Georg Wilhelm Friedrich Hegel, *Vorlesungen über Rechtsphilosophie: 1818–1831,* ed. Karl-Heinz Ilting, vol. 4 (Stuttgart: Frommann-Holzboog, 1974) 436–37.

14. Hegel as cited in Pinkert 362.

15. Hegel, *Introductory Lectures on Aesthetics* 72.

16. Schlegel in *Philosophie der Sprache* as cited by Hans Eichner, *Friedrich Schlegel,* Twayne's World Authors Ser. 98 (New York: Twayne, 1970) 135.

17. The most exhaustive reflections on the issue are collected in the essay *Über das Studium der griechischen Poesie* (1795–97), which has been republished in Friedrich Schlegel, *Studien des klassischen Altertums*, ed. Ernst Behler, vol. 1 of *Kritische Friedrich-Schlegel-Ausgabe*, 35 vols. (München: Ferdinand Schöningh; Zürich: Thomas, 1958–). Henceforth the edition will be cited as *KFSA*.

18. *Critical Writings* 73–74.

19. *Critical Writings* 81.

20. *Critical Writings* 75.

21. *Critical Writings* 78.

22. *Critical Writings* 82.

23. Thomas Weiskel, *The Romantic Sublime: Studies in the Structure and Psychology of Transcendence* (Baltimore: Johns Hopkins UP, 1976) 42.

24. Weiskel 56.

25. Hugh J. Silverman and Gary E. Aylesworth have adopted the theme of the "textual sublime" to gather a series of essays that reflect on the differences between works of criticism, concerned with the particularity of the text, and philosophy, involved in generalities: *The Textual Sublime: Deconstruction and Its Differences*, Contemporary Studies in Philosophy and Literature 1 (Albany: State U of New York P, 1990). In Silverman's introduction, deconstruction is identified as the theory or practice in which the textual sublime, as the marker of otherness in the text, is played out in all its alternatives: concerned with both literature and philosophy (the beyond), deconstruction makes the text into much more than what it literally says without appropriating this surplus philosophically. Because of this "purposiveness without purpose," the readings of Derrida and de Man bring out the differences of the text as explicitly textual—differences that Silverman's volume describes as operating "between philosophy and literature, theory and criticism, reading and text, translation and original, but also between the Derridean and de Manian versions of deconstruction, between deconstruction and alternative critical practices" (xiii). Needless to say that in this book on deconstruction and all its differences, the concept of the sublime is itself marginalized and made to designate an alterity so vast and varied that the purpose of the title—I must admit—eludes me.

26. In its pragmatist character, Schlegel's rhetorical sublime comes close to Longinus's *Peri Hypsous* (*On Sublimity*) (first century). The first theoretician to extensively deal with the sublime, Longinus defines it in terms of "great writing." The sublime is the elevated diction with which

such varied authors as Demosthenes, Plato, or Sappho seek to transport their audience and bring about a unity with the speaker. Inspired by great visions and passions, these speakers resort to figural language, noble diction, and lofty composition to convey the frenzy of their feelings in an effective manner. Longinus's view that figurative diction finds its origins not in the drive to imitate nature—as Aristotle would have it—but in the intensity of the speaker's feelings, together with his emphasis on the sublime as a mode of persuading the listener, was to have a great impact on a pre-romantic like Vico (who in turn inspired Joyce) and on Schlegel. A good discussion of Longinus's rhetorical strategies can be found in Neil Hertz, *The End of the Line: Essays on Psychoanalysis and the Sublime* (New York: Columbia UP, 1985).

27. Andreas Huyssen, *After the Great Divide: Modernism, Mass Culture, Postmodernism* (Bloomington: Indiana UP, 1986) 215.

28. Winfried Menninghaus has brought together Schlegel's reflections on the role of woman in the development of a philosophy of art ("Über die weiblichen Charakteren in den griechischen Dichtern" [1794], "Über die Diotima" [1795], *Lucinde* [1799], "Brief über die Philosophie: An Dorothea" [1799]) in Friedrich Schlegel, *Theorie der Weiblichkeit* (Frankfurt am Main: Insel, 1983). Several critics have interpreted Schlegel's work from a feminist perspective: M. Kay Flavell, "Women and Individualism: A Re-examination of Schlegel's *Lucinde* and Gutzkow's *Wally die Zweiflerin*," *Modern Language Review* 70 (1975): 550–66; Sigrid Lange, "Zum Beispiel: *Lucinde*. Das 'Ewigweibliche' im Horizont der bürgerlichen Emanzipation," *Weimarer Beiträge* 33.4 (1987): 616–31; Sigrid Weigel, "Wider die romantische Mode: Zur ästhetischen Funktion des Weiblichen in Friedrich Schlegels *Lucinde*," *Die verborgene Frau: Sechs Beiträge zu einer feministischen Literaturwissenschaft*, with contributions by Inge Stephan and Sigrid Weigel, Literatur im historischen Prozeß 6 (Berlin: Argument, 1983) 67–82; Kurt Lühti, *Feminismus und Romantik: Sprache, Gesellschaft, Symbole, Religion* (Wien: Hermann Böhlaus, 1985) 81–104; Renate Kühn, "Der Leser—die Frauen: Resultate einer pragmatischen Lektüre von Friedrich Schlegels *Gespräch über die Poesie*," *Jahrbuch der deutschen Schillergesellschaft* 30 (1986): 306–38.

29. *Critical Writings* 21.

30. *Critical Writings* 18.

31. Patricia Yaeger, "Toward a Female Sublime," *Gender and Theory: Dialogues on Feminist Criticism*, ed. Linda Kauffman (Oxford: Blackwell, 1989) 205.

32. Yaeger 209.

33. Anne K. Mellor, *Romanticism & Gender* (New York: Routledge, 1993) 101.

34. Rob Wilson, *American Sublime: The Genealogy of a Poetic Genre* (Madison: U of Wisconsin P, 1991) 30.

35. See Edelman's response to Yaeger's article: "At Risk in the Sublime: the Politics of Gender and Theory," Kauffman 213–24.

36. Margot Norris, *Joyce's Web: The Social Unraveling of Modernism*, Literary Modernism Series (Austin: U of Texas P, 1992).

37. Norris 6.

38. Norris 31.

39. Norris 141.

40. To my knowledge, only one article mentions Joyce's indebtedness to Schlegel: Robert Scholes and Marlena G. Corcoran, "The Aesthetic Theory and the Critical Writings," *A Companion to Joyce Studies*, ed. Zack Bowen and James F. Carens (Westport, CT: Greenwood P, 1984) 689–705. The critics point out (but do not discuss) the influence of Hegel, Schelling, and Schlegel on Stephen's theory of the different genres. However, their comments—especially those concerning Schlegel's poetics of genre—remain superficial. They conclude: "Joyce's reading in the German philosophers, and his debt to them, is still *terra incognita* for students of his work. But his whole discussion of the three forms of literature is as steeped in the language of German *Ästhetik* as his earlier discussion of beauty is in the language of Shelley and Aquinas" (693). I will discuss this interrelation between Schlegel's and Stephen's genres later on.

41. Of Schlegel's early works, only *Lucinde* was (partly) translated into English and collected in Kuno Francke's *German Classics Series*, published in New York in 1913. Of the later works, several lectures and essays were translated and edited by H. G. Bohn in London around the 1850s. Of Schlegel's works translated into English, his *Geschichte der alten und neuen Literatur* (1815) seems to have received the widest attention in British magazines (e.g., *Athenaeum*) around the middle of the nineteenth century. See Bayard Quincy Morgan and A. R. Hohlfeld, eds., *German Literature in British Magazines 1750–1860* (Madison: U of Wisconsin P, 1949) 106–7. Besides its bibliographical information, the book offers a good introduction to a growing British and American interest in Anglo-German relations at the turn of the century.

Chapter 1

An earlier version of this chapter appeared as "Friedrich Schlegel's Practice of Literary Theory," *The Germanic Review* 69.1 (1994): 28–35.

1. Schlegel's *Gespräch über die Poesie* (here abbreviated as *GP*), *Kritische Fragmente* (*KF*), *Athenäum Fragmente* (*AF*), and *Ideen* (*I*) have been

collected in Friedrich Schlegel, *Charakteristiken und Kritiken I (1796–1801)*, ed. Hans Eichner, vol. 2 of *KFSA*. Henceforth I will provide both Schlegel's German text and its English translation in an attempt to convey the rhetorical subtleties of the original, which tend to get lost in translation.

2. Rodolphe Gasché has argued this point from a Kantian perspective, in his introduction to the new edition of Peter Firchow's translation of Schlegel's fragments: Rodolphe Gasché, "Ideality in Fragmentation," *Philosophical Fragments*, by Friedrich Schlegel, trans. Peter Firchow (Minneapolis: U of Minnesota P, 1991) vii–xxxii.

3. For a discussion of the role of irony in Schlegel's work, see Steven E. Alford, *Irony and the Logic of the Romantic Imagination*, American University Studies, Comparative Literature 13 (New York: Peter Lang, 1984); Beda Alleman, *Ironie und Dichtung: F. Schlegel, Novalis, Solger, Kierkegaard, Thomas Mann, Musil* (Pfullingen: Neske, 1956); Ingrid Strohschneider-Kohrs, *Die romantische Ironie in Theorie und Gestaltung* (Tübingen: Max Niemeyer, 1977); Anne K. Mellor's introductory chapter, "The Paradigm of Romantic Irony," in *English Romantic Irony* (Cambridge: Harvard UP, 1980) 3–30 and her article "On Romantic Irony, Symbolism and Allegory," *Criticism* 21 (1979): 217–29. For an overview and re-interpretation of the "schools" of subjective or objective irony in early Schlegel criticism, see Raymond Immerwahr, "The Subjectivity or Objectivity of Friedrich Schlegel's Poetic Irony," *The Germanic Review* 26 (1951): 173–91.

4. *AF* 116, *KFSA* 2:182–83.

5. The English translation of the fragments and the ideas is taken from Friedrich Schlegel, *Philosophical Fragments*, trans. Peter Firchow (1991). In the future, reference to the fragment and idea will be followed by: Firchow (1991) and then the page number. In this case: *AF* 116, Firchow (1991) 31–32.

6. For an excellent discussion of the romantic concept of the "Absolute Genre" or "Literature as Absolute," see Philippe Lacoue-Labarthe and Jean-Luc Nancy, *The Literary Absolute: The Theory of Literature in German Romanticism*, trans. Philip Barnard and Cheryl Lester, Intersections: Philosophy and Critical Theory (Albany: State U of New York P, 1988). And Manfred Frank's fine essay "The Infinite Text" in *Glyph: Textual Studies* 7 (1980), *The Strasbourg Colloquium: Genre. A Selection of Papers*, ed. Samuel Weber: 70–101.

7. See Hans Eichner, "Friedrich Schlegel's Theory of Romantic Poetry," *PMLA* 71 (1956): 1018–41. See also Ernst Behler, *German Romantic Literary Theory* (Cambridge: Cambridge UP, 1993) 24–33. Behler's book offers a splendid introduction to the main themes in early German romantic theory.

8. Literary note 602 in Friedrich Schlegel, *Literarische Notizen 1797–1801, Literary Notebooks*, ed. Hans Eichner (Frankfurt: Ullstein Materialien, 1980) 78. Future references to Schlegel's *Literary Notebooks* will be abbreviated as *LN* followed by the number of the note.

9. *AF* 22, *KFSA* 2:169.

10. *AF* 22, Firchow (1991) 21.

11. Peter Szondi describes this reflexive movement as follows: "The existence of the world and of oneself becomes more and more one of mere appearance, and reflection becomes even emptier," in "Friedrich Schlegel and Romantic Irony, with Some Remarks on Tieck's Comedies," *On Textual Understanding and Other Essays*, trans. Harvey Mendelsohn, foreword by Michael Hays, Theory and History of Literature 15 (Minneapolis: U of Minnesota P, 1986) 63. For a re-interpretation of Schlegel's concept of art criticism as a concept of reflexivity see Walter Benjamin, *Der Begriff der Kunstkritik in der deutschen Romantik*, vol 1.1 of *Gesammelte Schriften*, ed. Rolf Tiedemann and Hermann Schweppenhäuser (Frankfurt am Main: Suhrkamp, 1974). Winfried Menninghaus has convincingly illustrated the misinterpretation characterizing Benjamin's appropriation of Schlegel's romantic philosophy in *Unendliche Verdopplung: Die frühromantische Grundlegung der Kunsttheorie im Begriff absoluter Selbstreflexion* (Frankfurt am Main: Suhrkamp, 1987). For a discussion of the concept of historical change pervading Schlegel's and Benjamin's thinking, see Marcus Bullock, *Romanticism and Marxism: The Philosophical Development of Literary Theory and Literary History in Walter Benjamin and Friedrich Schlegel*, American University Studies, Germanic Languages and Literature 51 (New York: Peter Lang, 1987).

12. For a discussion of the history of the notion of intellectal intuition from Kant via Fichte to Schelling, see Moltke S. Gram, "Intellectual Intuition: The Continuity Thesis," *Journal of the History of Ideas* 42.2 (1981): 287–304. See also Manfred Frank's essay "Intellektuale Anschauung: Drei Stellungnahmen zu einem Deutungsversuch von Selbstbewußtsein: Kant, Fichte, Hölderlin/Novalis," *Die Aktualität der Frühromantik*, ed. Ernst Behler and Jochen Hörisch (Paderborn: Ferdinand Schöningh, 1987) 96–126; and John Neubauer, "Intellektuelle, intellektuale und ästhetische Anschauung: Zur Entstehung der romantischen Kunstauffassung," *Deutsche Vierteljahrsschrift für Literaturwissenschaft und Geistesgeschichte* 46 (1972): 294–319.

13. *AF* 76, *KFSA* 2:176.

14. *AF* 76, Firchow (1991) 27.

15. *I* 8, *KFSA* 2:257.

16. *I* 8, Firchow (1991) 95.

17. *GP*, "Brief über den Roman," *KFSA* 2:337.

18. References to the English translation of *GP* are from Friedrich Schlegel, *Dialogue on Poetry and Literary Aphorisms*, trans. Ernst Behler and Roman Struc (University Park: Pennsylvania State UP, 1968), 51–117 (henceforth cited as *DP*). This citation is taken from *DP*, "Letter about the Novel" 102–3.

Chapter 2

1. This point has been dealt with in depth in a book which contains one of the most thorough discussions of Kant's category of the sublime that I have read so far: Renée van de Vall, *Een subliem gevoel van plaats: Een filosofische interpretatie van het werk van Barnett Newman* (Groningen: Historische Uitgeverij, 1994). Unfortunately it is only available in Dutch. See also Suzanne Guerlac, "The Sublime in Theory," *MLN* 106 (1991): 895–909.

2. Dietrich Mathy, "Zur frühromantischen Selbstaufhebung des Erhabenen im Schönen," *Das Erhabene: Zwischen Grenzerfahrung und Größenwahn*, ed. Christine Pries (Weinheim: VCH, Acta Humaniora, 1989) 143–60. Two more essays on Schlegel's theory of the sublime (and the ugly) are included in Helmut Schanze's collection *Friedrich Schlegel und die Kunsttheorie seiner Zeit* (Darmstadt: Wissenschaftliche Buchgesellschaft, 1985): Franz Norbert Mennemeier, "Unendliche Fortschreitung und absolutes Gesetz: Das Schöne und das Häßliche in der Kunstauffassung des jungen F. Schlegel" (pp. 342–69) and Günter Oesterle, "Friedrich Schlegels Entwurf einer Theorie des ästhetisch Häßlichen: Ein Reflexions- und Veränderungsversuch moderner Kunst" (pp. 397–451).

3. *AF* 108, *KFSA* 2:181.

4. *AF* 108, Firchow (1991) 30.

5. *Über das Studium der griechischen Poesie* (henceforth cited as *Studium*), *KFSA* 1:313. My emphasis.

6. Bosanquet 301.

7. *Studium, KFSA* 1:314.

8. "Up to now everyone has managed to find in the ancients what he needed or wished for: especially himself" (*AF* 151, Firchow [1991] 37).

9. Bosanquet 301.

10. *GP*, "Epochen der Dichtkunst," *KFSA* 2:292–93.

11. *DP*, "Epochs of Literature" 62–63.

12. *Studium, KFSA* 1:247–48.

13. Tragedy is about the conflict between laws and values, personified by the struggle between two characters (e.g., Creon vs. Antigone). The conflict does not take place within one person, for this would imply a recognition of the contingency of the law that one embodies.

14. *Critical Writings* 45.

15. *LN* 106.

16. *LN* 1699.

17. "Vom ästhetischen Werte der griechischen Komödie," *KFSA* 1:19–33. Henceforth the essay is cited as "Komödie."

18. "Komödie," *KFSA* 1:22–23.

19. *LN* 237.

20. M. M. Bakhtin, *The Dialogic Imagination: Four Essays,* ed. Michael Holquist, trans. Caryl Emerson and Michael Holquist, University of Texas Press Slavic Series 1 (Austin: U of Texas P, 1981) 23.

21. "Komödie," *KFSA* 1:24.

22. From *Geschichte der europäischen Literatur,* in *Wissenschaft der europäischen Literatur,* ed. Ernst Behler, *KFSA* 11:88.

23. "Komödie," *KFSA* 1:26–27.

Chapter 3

1. "Über die weiblichen Charaktere in den griechischen Dichtern" (henceforth cited as "weiblichen Charaktere"), *KFSA* 1:45–69.

2. "Über die Diotima," *KFSA* 1:70–115.

3. "weiblichen Charaktere," *KFSA* 1:64–65.

4. "weiblichen Charaktere," *KFSA* 1:67.

5. "Über die Philosophie: An Dorothea" (henceforth cited as "An Dorothea"), *KFSA* 8:41–62.

6. "An Dorothea," *KFSA* 8:45.

7. "An Dorothea," *KFSA* 8:42.

8. Mellor, *Romanticism & Gender* 5, 6.

CHAPTER 4

1. All references to *Lucinde* are from Friedrich Schlegel, *Dichtungen*, ed. Hans Eichner, *KFSA* 5:3–82.

2. For a survey of the book's critical reception in Germany, see Ernst Behler, "Friedrich Schlegel: *Lucinde* (1799)," *Romane und Erzählungen der deutschen Romantik: Neue Interpretationen*, ed. Paul Michael Lützeler (Stuttgart: Philipp Reclam jun., 1981) 98–124; Gisela Dischner, *Friedrich Schlegels* Lucinde *und Materialien zu einer Theorie des Müßiggangs* (Hildesheim: Gerstenberg, 1980) 131–76; Hans Eichner's introduction to *Lucinde* in *KFSA* 5:xlvi–lv.

3. In "Neues vom Dichter der *Lucinde*: Mitteilungen aus Friedrich Schlegels jüngst entdecktem handschriftlichen Nachlaß," Josef Körner reads the novel as a philosophical-poetical work, as a *Naturarabeske*, rather than as a naive reflection of the love relationship between Friedrich Schlegel and Dorothea Veit. The critic argues that Schlegel first conceived the plan for his novel in 1794, three years before he met his future wife. If there is any link between the novel's origin and Schlegel's private life, then Körner believes, it is ironically to be situated in Schlegel's love for Caroline, his brother's wife. The essay has been published in Schanze's collection *Friedrich Schlegel und die Kunsttheorie seiner Zeit* 7–33.

4. Simonetta Sanna has written on *Lucinde* as a love novel and an aesthetic novel. The most interesting point of her discussion is the relation she establishes between Lucinde as beloved, Lucinde as reader and *Lucinde* the novel. Her analysis remains, however, descriptive and misses the theoretical thrust that holds Schlegel's Lucinde as character, critic, and novel together: "Schlegels *Lucinde* oder der ästhetische Roman," *Deutsche Vierteljahrsschrift für Literaturwissenschaft und Geistesgeschichte* 61.3 (1987): 457–79. Gary J. Handwerk has thought through the ethical implications of this intersubjective mode of irony in Schlegel (Novalis, Wordsworth, Lacan, and Beckett) in his superb *Irony and Ethics in Narrative: From Schlegel to Lacan* (New Haven: Yale UP, 1985). His discussion of *Lucinde*, however, is preliminary and incorrectly concludes that "the novel remains at the level of dialogic irony, what Schlegel himself calls an irony of form alone, which he hoped in a continuation to bring over into the content" (62). As my own discussion illustrates, one cannot maintain such a naive separation of content and form.

5. *Lucinde*, *KFSA* 5:63. Henceforth references to the German and English text will be added in brackets.

6. The English translation of *Lucinde* is from *Friedrich Schlegel's* Lucinde *and the Fragments*, trans. Peter Firchow (Minneapolis: U of Minnesota P, 1971) 41–140. Where I have found his translations inadequate, I have provided my own. This quotation is taken from p. 106.

7. *LN* 1471 "Die Liebe ist die intellektuelle Anschauung des Lebens.- Er sieht in ihr die Schönheit der Welt—sie in ihm die Unendlichkeit des Menschen.-" [Love is the intellectual view on life.- He sees in her the beauty of the world—she in him the infinity of man (my translation)].

8. On *Lucinde* as a celebration of ideal love, see Sara Friedrichsmeyer, *The Androgyne in Early German Romanticism: Friedrich Schlegel, Novalis and the Metaphysics of Love,* Stanford German Studies 18 (New York: Peter Lang, 1983); Paul Kluckhohn, *Die Auffassung der Liebe in der Literatur des 18. Jahrhunderts und in der deutschen Romantik* (Tübingen: Max Niemeyer, 1966); Ernst Behler, "Friedrich Schlegels Theorie der Universalpoesie," Schanze, *Friedrich Schlegel und die Kunsttheorie seiner Zeit* 228–33.

9. I say "near-Hegelian" because the synthesis is only preliminary, as indicated by the fact that at the closing of the "Apprenticeship," that is, at the moment the love (synthesis) between Julius and Lucinde is established, the text falls back into an I-You dialogue.

10. For a re-interpretation of Schlegel's hermeneutics in the light of poststructuralist theory, see, in Behler and Hörisch's *Aktualität der Frühromantik,* Ernst Behler, "Friedrich Schlegels Theorie des Verstehens: Hermeneutik oder Dekonstruktion?" (141–60) and Hans-Georg Gadamer's "Frühromantik, Hermeneutik, Dekonstruktivismus" (251–60). Gadamer's essay has been translated as "Hermeneutics and Logocentrism" in Diane P. Michelfelder and Richard E. Palmer, eds., *Dialogue and Deconstruction: The Gadamer-Derrida Encounter* (Albany: State U of New York P, 1989) 114–25. It is not surprising that in his defense against Derrida's attack on hermeneutic "logocentrism," Gadamer aligns himself with the dialogism of the early romantics and with the act of *Verstehen* or *Selbstverständnis* central to it. In the essay mentioned above, he acknowledges to be close to Schlegel's concept of the "work." Like Schlegel he sees the meaning of the work arise in the dialogue not only between text and reader but also between the text and the unspoken question that precedes it (and which I will later define as the question of *Gattung*): "Yet it remains correct that every assertion must be understood as the answer to a question, if it is to be understood at all. The same goes for an assertion made by a work of art" (124).

11. This questioning of origins runs counter to Cornelia Hotz-Steinmeyer's reading of *Lucinde* in *Friedrich Schlegels* Lucinde *als "neue Mythologie": Geschichtsphilosophischer Versuch einer Rückgewinnung gesellschaftlicher Totalität durch das Individuum* (Frankfurt am Main: Peter Lang, 1981). While the critic notices the circularity at the heart of the novel, she does not problematize the narrative development—let alone the "autobiography"—that arises from it. Instead she insists that Julius "first had to find the center of his life, his love for Lucinde, before he could pre-

sent himself in a uniform cohesion . . . Only this center of love made it possible for him to recognize himself and the meaning of his life. Until this moment, he was not able to see his life as a meaningful, homogeneous whole and grasp it in the form of the novel" (my translation of p. 39).

12. For a detailed discussion of Schlegel's view of the arabesque as literary, philosophical, and artistic concept, see Karl Konrad Polheim, *Die Arabeske: Ansichten und Ideen aus Friedrich Schlegels Poetik* (München: Ferdinand Schöningh, 1966). In a remarkable analysis of Schlegel's "Brief über den Roman" Raymond Immerwahr relates the letter's multilayered structure and shifting tone of irony to its untenable distinction between the *Roman* in a romantic age (e.g., *Arabeske, Groteske*) and the *Roman* in a non-romantic age (e.g., *Bekentnisse, Briefsammlungen, Selbstgeschichte*), between the novel as *Erzählform* and as *Lektüre*. Immerwahr concludes that in its ironic elaboration of its "serious" center-piece on the theory of the novel, the *Brief* resembles a Renaissance painting "which shows a solemn portrait, surrounded by a double or multiple arabesque frame" (my translation). "Die symbolische Form des 'Briefes über den Roman,'" *Zeitschrift für deutsche Philologie* 88 (1969): 60. Hans Eichner points out a similar deliberate structuring of arabesques around *Lucinde*'s centerpiece in his introduction to the German text (*KFSA* 5:xlv) and in *Friedrich Schlegel* 89. However, he does not think through its theoretical implications. See also Günter Oesterle, "Arabeske und Roman: Eine poetikgeschichtliche Rekonstruktion von Friedrich Schlegels 'Brief uber den Roman,'" *Studien zur Ästhetik und Literaturgeschichte der Kunstperiode*, ed. Dirk Grathoff, Gießener Arbeiten zur neueren deutschen Literatur und Literaturwissenschaft 1 (Frankfurt am Main: Peter Lang, 1985) 233–92. For a discussion of the development from the enlightened to the romantic arabesque, see Günter Oesterle, "'Vorbegriffe zu einer Theorie der Ornamente': Kontroverse Formprobleme zwischen Aufklärung, Klassizismus und Romantik am Beispiel der Arabeske," *Ideal und Wirklichkeit der bildenden Kunst im späten 18. Jahrhundert*, ed. Herbert Beck, Peter C. Bol, and Eva Maek-Gérard, Frankfurter Forschungen zur Kunst 11 (Berlin: Mann, 1984) 119–39.

13. *GP*, "Brief über den Roman," *KFSA* 2:338.

14. *DP*, "Letter about the Novel" 104.

15. *GP*, "Brief über den Roman," *KFSA* 2:337.

16. *DP*, "Letter about the Novel" 103.

17. "Was ist denn nun dieses Sentimentale? Das was uns anspricht, wo das Gefühl herrscht, und zwar nicht ein sinnliches, sondern das geistige. Die Quelle und Seele aller dieser Regungen ist die Liebe, und der Geist der Liebe muß in der romantischen Poesie überall unsichtbar sichtbar schweben . . . für den wahren Dichter ist alles dieses, so innig es auch seine Seele umschließen mag, nur Hindeutung auf das Höhere,

Unendliche, Hieroglyphe der Einen ewigen Liebe und der heiligen Lebensfülle der bildenden Natur. Nur die Fantasie kann das Rätsel dieser Liebe fassen und als Rätsel darstellen; und dieses Rätselhafte ist die Quelle von dem Fantastischen in der Form aller poetischen Darstellung" (*GP*, "Brief über den Roman," *KFSA* 2:333–34). [What then is this sentimental? It is that which appeals to us, where feeling prevails, and to be sure not a sensual but a spiritual feeling. The source and soul of all these emotions is love, and the spirit of love must hover everywhere invisibly visible in romantic poetry . . . for the true poet all this—no matter how intensely it embraces his soul—is only a hint at something higher, the infinite, a hieroglyph of the one eternal love and the sacred fullness of life of creative nature. Only the imagination can grasp the mystery of this love and present it as a mystery; and this mysterious quality is the source of the fantastic in the form of all poetic representation (*DP*, "Letter about the Novel" 99–100).]

18. For Paul de Man's interpretation of Schlegel's parabasis in terms of the relation between irony and allegory, see his "The Rhetoric of Temporality," *Interpretation: Theory and Practice*, ed. Charles S. Singleton (Baltimore: Johns Hopkins UP, 1969) 173–209. For a discussion of the difference between Schlegel and de Man, see Mellor, "On Romantic Irony, Symbolism and Allegory" 217–29.

19. *LN* 395.

20. *LN* 852.

21. *LN* 461.

22. *GP*, "Rede über die Mythologie," *KFSA* 2:319.

23. *DP*, "Talk on Mythology" 86.

24. The phrase is from Maurice Blanchot, "The Athenäum," trans. Deborah Esch and Ian Balfour, *Studies in Romanticism* 23 (1984): 166. Blanchot's most likely source is Schlegel's *Idee* 69, *KFSA* 2:263: "Ironie ist klares Bewußtsein der ewigen Agilität, des unendlich vollen Chaos."

25. I am thinking of Walter Benjamin's view of *Ursprung* as "an eddy in the stream of becoming, and in its current it swallows the material involved in the process of genesis" in *The Origin of German Tragic Drama*, trans. John Osborne (London: NLB, 1977) 45. Compare, in this respect, Benjamin's "Angel of History": "His face is turned toward the past . . . a storm is blowing from Paradise . . . This storm irresistibly propels him into the future to which his back is turned . . . This storm is what we call progress" (*Illuminations*, ed. Hannah Arendt, trans. Harry Zohn [1968; New York: Schocken Books, 1969] 257–58). And Schlegel's *AF* 80, *KFSA* 2:176: "Der Historiker ist ein rückwärts gekehrter Prophet" [The historian is a prophet facing backwards (*AF* 80, Firchow [1991] 27)]. The same stance character-

izes the appearance of Søren Kierkegaard's ironist: "That which shall come is hidden from him, concealed behind his back, but the actuality he hostilely opposes is the one he shall destroy. Toward this he directs his consuming gaze . . ." (*The Concept of Irony with Constant Reference to Socrates*, trans. Lee M. Capel [Bloomington: Indiana UP, 1965] 278).

26. "Der dramatische Zusammenhang der Geschichte macht den Roman im Gegenteil noch keineswegs zum Ganzen, zum Werk, wenn er es nicht durch die Beziehung der ganzen Komposition auf eine höhere Einheit, als jene Einheit des Buchstabens, über die er sich oft wegsetzt und wegsetzen darf, durch das Band der Ideen, durch einen geistigen Zentralpunkt wird" (*GP*, "Brief über den Roman," *KFSA* 2:336) [On the contrary, the dramatic context of the story does not make the novel a whole, a work, if the whole composition is not related to a higher unity than that of the letter which it often does and should disregard; but it becomes a work through the bond of ideas, through a spiritual central point (*DP*, "Letter about the Novel" 101)].

27. "Die Romane sind die Sokratischen Dialoge unserer Zeit. In diese liberale Form hat sich die Lebensweisheit vor der Schulweisheit gefluchtet" (*KF* 26, *KFSA* 2:149) [Novels are the Socratic dialogues of our time. And this free form has become the refuge of common sense in its flight from pedantry (*KF* 26, Firchow [1991] 3)]. In spite of Schlegel's constant reference to Socrates (*KF* 42, 108, 125; *AF* 104, 160, 295), Kierkegaard insists on a radical disjunction between the Greek philosopher concentrating his ironic powers on a particular object on the one hand and Schlegel directing his irony not against the object but against the whole of existence on the other. Seen in this light, *Lucinde* becomes an "obscene" celebration of poetry's victory over the historical world, which Kierkegaard cannot but reject in favor of a religious reconciliation with the world (*Concept of Irony* 315). For a more detailed discussion of the reasons behind Kierkegaard's misreading of Schlegel, see Hans Dierkes, "Friedrich Schlegels *Lucinde*, Schleiermacher und Kierkegaard," *Deutsche Vierteljahrsschrift für Literaturwissenschaft und Geistesgeschichte* 57.3 (1983): 431–49. Donald Barthelme's "Kierkegaard Unfair to Schlegel" fictionalizes the confrontation between the two philosophers in the form of a Socratic dialogue that consciously tries to read the point of divergence around which the disagreement revolves: the essence of irony as divergence. *City Life* (New York: Farrar, 1968) 83–93.

28. Schlegel often refers to Petrarch, Boccaccio, and Cervantes as prime exemplars of the poetic wit and genius that he views as essential to the romantic novel. See his *GP*, "Epochen der Dichtkunst," *KFSA* 2:290–303.

29. *KF* 112, *KFSA* 2:161. My emphasis.

30. *KF* 112, Firchow (1991) 112. My emphasis.

31. For the interrelation between dialogue, epistolarity, and autobiography (memoirs), see *AF* 77, *KFSA* 2:176: "Ein Dialog ist eine Kette, oder ein Kranz von Fragmenten. Ein Briefwechsel ist ein Dialog in vergrößertem Maßstabe, und Memorabilien sind ein System von Fragmenten. Es gibt noch keins was in Stoff und Form fragmentarisch, zugleich ganz subjektiv und individuell, und ganz objektiv und wie ein notwendiger Teil im System aller Wissenschaften wäre" [A dialogue is a chain or garland of fragments. An exchange of letters is a dialogue on a larger scale, and memoirs constitute a system of fragments. But as yet no genre exists that is fragmentary both in form and content, simultaneously completely subjective and individual, and completely objective and like a necessary part in a system of all the sciences (*AF* 77, Firchow [1991] 27)].

32. *I* 26, *KFSA* 2:258.

33. *I* 26, Firchow (1991) 96.

34. One is reminded of Roland Barthes, *The Pleasure of the Text*, trans. Richard Miller (New York: Hill and Wang, 1975) 17: "How can we take pleasure in a *reported* pleasure (boredom of all narratives of dreams, of parties)? How can we read criticism? Only one way: since I am here a second-degree reader, I must shift my position: instead of agreeing to be the confidant of this critical pleasure—a sure way to miss it—I can make myself its voyeur: I observe clandestinely the pleasure of others, I enter perversion; the commentary then becomes in my eyes a text, a fiction, a fissured envelope. The writer's perversity (his pleasure in writing is *without function*), the doubled, the trebled, the infinite perversity of the critic and of his reader."

35. *LN* 416.

36. In his introduction to *Lucinde* Hans Eichner briefly mentions the irony at work in Julius's arbitrary choice but fails to recognize its full complexity and instead interprets the involuntary act—and the dithyrambic fantasy that results from it—as a means of introducing "the book's main themes . . . predestination and love death, the need to attenuate and cool love's 'consuming heat' jokingly, but especially the idea that man can only become complete and harmonic by means of love" (my translation of *KFSA* 5:xxxviii). For Schlegel's view on *Willkür* as absolute choice or systematic arbitrariness, see *AF* 116, 121, 385.

37. Maurice Blanchot, *The Writing of the Disaster. L'écriture du désastre*, trans. Ann Smock (Lincoln: U of Nebraska P, 1986): "Fragmentary writing is risk, it would seem: risk itself. It is not based on any theory, nor does it introduce a practice one could define as *interruption*. Interrupted, it goes on. Interrogating itself, it does not co-opt the question but suspends it (without maintaining it) as nonresponse . . . The fragmentary imperative, linked to the disaster. That there is, however, practically nothing disas-

trous in this disaster: this is surely what we must learn to think, without, perhaps, ever knowing it" (59–60).

38. In this chapter I disagree with Patricia Stanley's argument that since Schlegel never completed a full study of the arabesque "we have . . . no labeled equivalent to the 'Phantasie' chapters of *Lucinde* from which to investigate stylistic features of a Schlegel 'Arabeske'" ("Hoffmann's *Phantasiestücke in Callots Manier* in Light of Friedrich Schlegel's Theory of the Arabesque," *German Studies Review* 8.3 [1985]: 402). As my discussion will show, Schlegel's dithyrambic fantasy is thematically and stylistically (the difference is purely ironic) characterized by this lack of "labeled equivalent" or completed design. That is indeed the stylistic feature of this fantasy, that there are no generalized features with which to measure the arabesque quality of the text. Stanley's article remains interesting in its fine ear for the musical qualities of Schlegel's language.

39. The history of the dithyramb may be divided into two parts. Originally (600 B.C.) a choral song to Dionysus, it was first sung by a regular chorus and then made into a subject for composition at the festivals of Dionysus. Famous Athenian poets such as Simonides and Pindar participated in this poetry contest. After 470 B.C. the character of the dithyramb began to change and the music became more important than the words. Other elements of change were the abolition of the strophe-antistrophe alteration characteristic of the choral ode and the development of a pompous language (Cecil Maurice Bowra, "Dithyramb," *The Oxford Classical Dictionary*, 2nd ed.).

40. Winfried Menninghaus has argued that because of its linguistic character, Schlegel's *Geist* could well be considered as a transcendental signifier or as the forerunner of the Saussurian linguistic system in which the meaning of the signs is determined by their position in the system, which, in turn, takes place through the positing of signs (Menninghaus, *Unendliche Verdopplung* 82–84). For other discussions of Schlegel's notion of rhetoric, see David E. Wellbery, "Rhetorik und Literatur: Anmerkungen zur poetologischen Begriffsbildung bei Friedrich Schlegel," *Aktualität der Frühromantik* 161–73; and Helmut Schanze, *Romantik und Aufklärung: Untersuchungen zu Friedrich Schlegel und Novalis*, Erlanger Beiträge zur Sprach-und Kunstwissenschaft 27 (Nürnberg: Hans Carl, 1966) 94–106.

41. *LN* 983.

42. For Schlegel the *Buchstabe* denotes the radical finitude of language which in Greek nature poetry achieved a perfection (a *Gattung*) of its own because the Greeks were the first to create the different literary genres. As a result their poetry was characterized by an immediate interconnectedness but without a unified spirit. Theirs was an "abstract poetry," unified in its natural, organic growth. In the literature that followed, this

abstraction became concretized and the natural perfection lost in a plurality of genres. From now on, the letter was an ideal to be realized: "In den Alten sieht man den vollendeten Buchstaben der ganzen Poesie: in den Neuern ahnet man den werdenden Geist" (*KF 93, KFSA* 2:158) [In the ancients we see the perfected letter of all poetry; in the moderns we see its growing spirit (*KF* 93, Firchow [1991] 11)]. See also Schlegel's early essay *Über das Studium der griechischen Poesie, KFSA* 1:217–367.

43. Julius's broken text can perhaps be described as a *Parodie des Buchstabens* in imitation of that most parodic of all Renaissance masters that Schlegel so admired: Shakespeare (*AF* 253, *KFSA* 2:208).

44. *LN* 620.

45. *LN* 625.

46. *LN* 684.

47. This prefigures what Paul de Man in his controversial essay on the impossibility of confession has described as follows: "The excuse is a ruse which permits exposure in the name of hiding, not unlike Being, in the later Heidegger, reveals itself by hiding. Or, put differently, shame used as excuse permits repression to function as revelation and thus to make pleasure and guilt interchangeable. Guilt is forgiven because it allows for the pleasure of revealing its repression. It follows that repression is in fact an excuse, one speech act among others" ("Excuses [Confessions]," *Allegories of Reading: Figural Language in Rousseau, Nietzsche, Rilke, and Proust* [New Haven: Yale UP, 1979] 286).

48. On criticism as an act of eating, see *KF* 27, *KFSA* 2:149: "Ein Kritiker ist ein Leser, der wiederkäut. Er sollte also mehr als einen Magen haben" [The critic is a reader who ruminates. Therefore he ought to have more than one stomach (*KF* 27, Firchow [1991] 3)].

49. For Schlegel's view on androgyny, see Sara Friedrichsmeyer 109–29. See also Joel Black, "The Aesthetics of Gender: Zeuxis Maidens and the Hermaphroditic Ideal," *New York Literary Forum* 8 & 9 (1981), *Fragments: Incompletion & Discontinuity*, ed. Lawrence D. Kritzman: 189–209.

50. See my discussion of Schlegel's essay "Über Goethes Meister" in Ginette Verstraete, "Friedrich Schlegel's Practice of Literary Theory," *The Germanic Review* 69.1 (1994): 28–35.

Chapter 5

1. Jacques Derrida has raised the interdependence of the feminine gender and the question of genre in "La loi du genre/The Law of Genre," *Glyph: Textual Studies* 7 (1980), *The Strasbourg Colloquium: Genre. A Selection of Papers*, ed. Samuel Weber: 197.

2. *LN* 842.

3. See Lacoue-Labarthe and Nancy's *Literary Absolute* and their "Le dialogue des genres: Textes de Shaftesbury, Hemsterhuis, Schelling," *Poétique* 21 (1975): 148–75. In this article the authors view dialogue as the *Genre* par excellence, that is, as literature in general. The dialogue is above all one between literature (the particular *Darstellung*) and philosophy (the general idea). Whereas literature grants the idea a visible outside, philosophy constitutes the interiorization, the return of art to itself. In this re-turn literature re-produces itself. Implicit to their argument is thus the interrelation of genre and generation, and of verbal and sexual intercourse. Werner Hamacher reads Schlegel's *Transzendentalpoesie* in the light of Fichte's self-positing *Ich* in "Der Satz der Gattung: Friedrich Schlegels poetologische Umsetzung von Fichtes unbedingten Grundsatz," *MLN* 95 (1980): 1155–80. Hamacher emphasizes the fact that to speak about *Gattung* is to speak about the (im)possibility of speaking about *Gattung*. This self-reflexivity of the absolute speech-act is therefore simultaneously an expression of totality and of nothingness, of truth and of fiction, of ground and abyss.

4. That the address or apostrophe (from the Greek *apostrophe*, turning away, escape) is closely linked to Schlegel's parabasis is implicitly witnessed by Jonathan Culler when he writes that "[t]o read apostrophe as sign of a fiction which knows its own fictive nature is to stress its optative character, its impossible imperatives: commands which in their explicit impossibility figure events in and of fiction" ("Apostrophe," *The Pursuit of Signs: Semiotics, Literature, Deconstruction* [Ithaca: Cornell UP, 1981] 146). On the relation between apostrophe and *prosopopeia* (or figuration)—a relation first established by Quintilian—see Paul de Man, *The Rhetoric of Romanticism* (New York: Columbia UP, 1984) 67–81, 239–62; Michael Riffaterre, "Prosopopeia," *Yale French Studies* 69 (1985): 107–23; Barbara Johnson, "Apostrophe, Animation, and Abortion," *Diacritics* 16 (1986): 29–39.

Chapter 6

1. Stuart Gilbert, *James Joyce's* Ulysses: *A Study*, rev. ed. (1930; New York: Vintage Books, 1952) vii.

2. Ian Crump has analyzed these tensions between the young and the mature Joyce in the development of his early writings. He argues that the author's experiment with represented speech and interior monologue in *A Portrait*, needs to be viewed as an attempt to ascribe his youthful opinions (from *Critical Writings*) to his protagonist, whose thoughts are now to be represented from a neuter space (Blanchot), which has neither speaker nor addressee: "the author thus succeeds in breathing 'a proper and intangible life' into this self and in becoming, in the resulting text, as intellectualized—or as impersonalized—to his or her readers as Shakespeare is to his

audiences" (Ian Crump, "Refining Himself out of Existence: The Evolution of Joyce's Aesthetic Theory and the Drafts of *A Portrait*," *Joyce in Context*, ed. Vincent J. Cheng and Timothy Martin [Cambridge: Cambridge UP, 1992] 229).

3. *Critical Writings* 41.

4. See his essay "Royal Hibernian Academy: 'Ecce Homo,'" *Critical Writings* 31–37.

5. For the implications of Joyce's view on his art as gesture, see David Hayman, "Language of/as Gesture in Joyce," *James Joyce: A Collection of Critical Essays*, ed. Mary T. Reynolds (Englewood Cliffs: Prentice Hall, 1993) 37–47.

6. *Critical Writings* 69.

7. *Critical Writings* 42.

8. *Critical Writings* 42.

9. *Letters of James Joyce* 1: 224–25.

10. *Critical Writings* 45.

11. *Critical Writings* 6.

12. *Critical Writings* 45.

13. *Critical Writings* 41.

14. *Critical Writings* 63.

15. John Paul Riquelme has argued that Stephen's definition of the epiphany, based on a conjunction of "vulgarity of speech" and "a memorable phase of the mind itself," introduces a vacillation between realism and symbolism that is characteristic of the development of the boy's character and of Joyce's oeuvre as a whole. His essay is also interesting for its bibliographical references on the topic. "*Stephen Hero*, *Dubliners*, and *A Portrait of the Artist as a Young Man*: Styles of Realism and Fantasy," *The Cambridge Companion to James Joyce*, ed. Derek Attridge (Cambridge: Cambridge UP, 1990) 103–30.

16. *Critical Writings* 63.

17. *Critical Writings* 101.

18. James Joyce, *Stephen Hero*, ed. and introd. Theodore Spencer (New York: New Directions, 1944) 95. Henceforth cited as *Stephen Hero*.

19. *Critical Writings* 101.

20. *Critical Writings* 42–43.

21. *Critical Writings* 49.

22. *Critical Writings* 101.

23. *Critical Writings* 101.

24. *Stephen Hero* 171.

25. Jean-François Lyotard, *The Differend: Phrases in Dispute*, trans. Georges Van Den Abbeele, Theory and History of Literature 46 (Minneapolis: U of Minnesota P, 1988).

26. *Critical Writings* 40.

27. Robert Spoo has recognized "a crisis of the neo-Romantic imagination" in the young Joyce's futile desire to transcend the textualization of the past (literature) in favor of an unmediated access to an underlying unpredictable historical reality (drama) (*James Joyce and the Language of History: Dedalus's Nightmare* [Oxford: Oxford UP, 1994] 152). For a discussion of Joyce's roots in the romanticism of Shelley and Wordsworth, see Robert Scholes, "In Search of James Joyce," *James Joyce Quarterly* 11 (1973): 5–16.

28. *Stephen Hero* 186.

29. *Critical Writings* 43.

30. *Critical Writings* 41.

31. *Critical Writings* 42.

32. There is a long-standing debate about the question whether the Joycean artist's attitude toward his characters is ironic or not. A good introduction to this problem of irony—including the various ways in which it was approached in early Joyce criticism—can be found in Robert S. F. Ryf, *A New Approach to Joyce: The* Portrait of the Artist *as a Guidebook* (Berkeley: U of California P, 1966) 156–70. See also Thomas Connolly, ed., *Joyce's* Portrait: *Criticisms and Critiques* (London: Peter Owen, 1962) and especially the essays by Hugh Kenner ("The *Portrait* in Perspective," 25–60) and Eugene M. Waith ("The Calling of Stephen Dedalus," 114–23). For a stylistic approach to Joyce's irony, see Hugh Kenner, *Joyce's Voices* (Berkeley: U of California P, 1978), and John Paul Riquelme, *Teller and Tale in Joyce's Fiction: Oscillating Perspectives* (Baltimore: Johns Hopkins UP, 1983).

33. *Stephen Hero* 77.

34. This contradiction at the basis of Stephen's authoritative stance, has been well argued in Vicki Mahaffey, *Reauthorizing Joyce* (Cambridge: Cambridge UP, 1988).

35. James Joyce, *Ulysses*, ed. Hans Walter Gabler et al. (New York: Random House, 1986) 31.2–3. Henceforth cited as *Ulysses.*

36. *Ulysses* 41.453–60.

37. *Critical Writings* 74.

38. *Critical Writings* 75.

39. *Stephen Hero* 97.

40. For a discussion of Stephen's misinterpretation of Shelley's romanticism (as neo-Platonic) in *A Portrait,* see Mahaffey 86–96.

41. *Stephen Hero* 36–37.

42. *Ulysses* 170.837–42.

43. James Joyce, *A Portrait of the Artist as a Young Man,* definitive text by Chester G. Anderson and reviewed by Richard Ellmann (New York: Viking, 1964) 208–9.

44. *A Portrait* 211.

45. *Stephen Hero* 175.

CHAPTER 7

1. Ewa Ziarek, "'Circe': Joyce's *Argumentum ad Feminam,*" *James Joyce Quarterly* 30 (1992): 51.

2. An exhaustive list of all contributors to the debate on Joyce and feminism would require a study on its own, the beginnings of which can be found in Alan Roughley's book and Bonnie Kime Scott, *Joyce and Feminism* (Bloomington: Indiana UP; Brighton: Harvester, 1984) as well as Bonnie Kime Scott, *James Joyce* (Brighton: Harvester, 1987). I think we know the most important ones by now: Sandra Gilbert, Susan Gubar, Kate Millet, Marilyn French, Elaine Unkeless, and Suzette Henke have focused on the good old Victorian stereotypes in Joyce's works. Among the more positive—but not less critical—responses are: Shari Benstock, John Bishop, Christel van Boheemen, Sheldon Brivic, Kimberley Devlin, Maud Ellmann, Karen Lawrence, Vicki Mahaffey, Margot Norris, and of course Roughly and Scott, and numerous others. See, for instance, the issue brought out by *Modern Fiction Studies* 35 (1989): *Feminist Readings of Joyce,* ed. Ellen Carol Jones. For a good survey of Molly Bloom's reception by the first generations of male Joyceans, I refer to Kathleen McCormick, "Reproducing Molly Bloom: A Revisionist History of the Reception of 'Penelope,' 1922–1970," *Molly Blooms: A Polylogue on "Penelope" and Cultural Studies,* ed. Richard Pearce (Madison: U of Wisconsin P, 1994) 17–36.

3. Also cited by Ziarek: Alice Jardine, *Gynesis: Configurations of Women and Modernity* (Ithaca: Cornell UP, 1985).

4. *Stephen Hero* 80.

5. *Stephen Hero* 80. In his essay "James Clarence Mangan" the young Joyce says of Blake and Dante: "but the life of the poet is intense . . . taking into its centre the life that surrounds it and flinging it abroad again amid planetary music" (*Critical Writings* 82).

6. Arthur Power, *Conversations with James Joyce*, ed. Clive Hart (London: Millington, 1974) 35.

7. *A Portrait* 209.

8. *Stephen Hero* 210.

9. "A few moments after he [Stephen] found himself on the stage amid the garish gas and the dim scenery, acting before the innumerable faces of the void. It surprised him to see that the play which he had known at rehearsals for a disjointed lifeless thing had suddenly assumed a life of its own. It seemed now to play itself, he and his fellow actors aiding it with their parts. When the curtain fell on the last scene he heard the void filled with applause and, through a rift in the side scene, saw the simple body before which he had acted magically deformed, the void of faces breaking at all points and falling asunder into busy groups" (*A Portrait* 85).

10. *Stephen Hero* 84.

11. *Stephen Hero* 84.

12. *Stephen Hero* 86.

13. *Stephen Hero* 88.

14. *Stephen Hero* 88.

15. *A Portrait* 90.

16. See Maud Ellmann's fine interpretation of this scene in "Disremembering Dedalus: *A Portrait of the Artist as a Young Man*," *Untying the Text: A Post-Structuralist Reader*, ed. Robert Young (Boston: Routledge, 1981) 189–206. Ellmann reads *A Portrait* as a series of moments in which Stephen's name takes on flesh. Those moments are scars out of which oozes the text in the form of a repetitive scarring. The word *Foetus* is one of the instances of scarring, in this case one in which Stephen's name presents the initials of the Name of the Father but eventually leads back to the mother's womb, the horror of namelessness. In the word *Foetus* lies a vision of man's first scar—the navel, "Where, indeed, the body has no definite ending, nor beginning, but branches out in every direction into the

intricate network of its amniotic world. The navel marks the spot at which identity dissolves" (204).

17. *Stephen Hero* 87.

18. *Stephen Hero* 87.

19. *Stephen Hero* 87.

20. *Critical Writings* 54–55.

21. *Critical Writings* 57.

22. *Critical Writings* 64–65.

23. *Critical Writings* 64.

24. *Critical Writings* 67.

25. *Critical Writings* 66.

26. According to John MacNicholas, one of the few successful productions of *Exiles* must have been Pinter's in 1970–71, thanks to the typically Pinteresque style: "'exact phrasing, pregnant pause-composition, pointed stylization of characters into the mythic realm, and emphatic multiplicity of gestural meaning'" ("The Stage History of *Exiles*," *James Joyce Quarterly* 19 [1981]: 17).

27. *Critical Writings* 32.

28. James Joyce, *Exiles: A Play in Three Acts*, introd. Padraic Colum (Harmondsworth: Penguin, 1973) 24. Henceforth references to *Exiles* will be given in the text.

29. Cf. Edward Brandabur, "*Exiles*: A Rough and Tumble between de Sade and Sacher-Masoch," *A Scrupulous Meanness: A Study of Joyce's Early Work* (Urbana: U of Illinois P, 1971) 150.

30. This duplicity of language has been explored by Clive Hart, "The Language of *Exiles*," *Coping with Joyce: Essays from the Copenhagen Symposium*, ed. Morris Beja and Shari Benstock (Columbus: Ohio State UP, 1989) 123–36.

31. Cf. Vicki Mahaffey, *Reauthorizing Joyce* 150.

32. I do not agree with Suzette Henke's conclusive interpretation of Bertha's role in her book on *James Joyce and the Politics of Desire* (London: Routledge, 1990). Henke eliminates the doubt that Bertha represents throughout the play by ascribing to her the stereotypical function of "the bride faithful in exile" (104) who confronts Richard with "the perdurance of female desire" thereby teaching her "wayward son" (99) to love her

again. In contrast, I believe that Bertha's final plea for love "'O, my strange wild lover, come back to me again!'" precisely to the extent that it does not receive a response, sounds as one more unanswered question, in reply to which a whole tradition of baffled Joyce critics has generated multiple and contradictory interpretations.

33. In *Reading the Book of Himself: Narrative Strategies in the Works of James Joyce* (Columbus: Ohio State UP, 1989), Michael Gillespie has noted that Bertha hovers between the consciousnesses of the two men, but he has failed to see the subversive function of this position. In his view, the woman begins to play a role only when the struggle over her body ceases; this is in the final act. I would argue, however, that Joyce's definition of Bertha's personality as the effect of an interaction between two oppositional views on women prefigures his experiment in *Ulysses*: for in that novel, as Gillespie also notices, Joyce's concern is with the action of the individual rooted as it is in the indeterminacy of human interaction and in the pattern of multiple perspectives.

34. This goes against Ruth Bauerle's interpretation of Bertha's "natural acquiescence" in "Bertha's Role in *Exiles*," *Women in Joyce*, ed. Suzette Henke and Elaine Unkeless (Brighton: Harvester, 1982) 108–31. Bauerle recognizes that Bertha functions as an object-victim in the hands of Richard and Robert, but she sees this as the effect of the woman's natural passivity. By thus "naturalizing" what she had earlier traced back to mythology, Bauerle ends up with a stereotypical analysis of Bertha's role in terms of tenderness, nurturing, and integrity.

Chapter 8

The chapter title is quoted from *Ulysses* 419.2401–2.

1. For a discussion of Joycean comedy in the light of Aristotle's and Aquinas's philosophies, see William T. Noon, *Joyce and Aquinas*, Yale Studies in English 133 (New Haven: Yale UP, 1957).

2. *Critical Writings* 39.

3. Francis MacDonald Cornford, *The Origin of Attic Comedy*, ed. with foreword and notes by Theodor H. Gaster (1914; New York: Anchor, 1961).

4. *Comedy: "An Essay on Comedy," George Meredith; "Laughter," Henri Bergson*, ed. Wylie Sypher (Baltimore: Johns Hopkins UP, 1980) 218.

5. Friedrich Nietzsche, *The Birth of Tragedy and The Case of Wagner*, translation and commentary by Walter Kaufmann (New York: Vintage Books, 1967).

6. *Critical Writings* 144.

7. Immanuel Kant, *Critique of Judgment*, trans. J. H. Bernard (New York: Macmillan, 1951) 181.

8. Sigmund Freud, *Jokes and Their Relation to the Unconscious*, trans. James Strachey (London: Routledge, 1966).

9. Charles Baudelaire, "On the Essence of Laughter and, in General, on the Comic in the Plastic Arts," *The Painter of Modern Life and Other Essays*, trans. Jonathan Mayne (London: Phaidon, 1964) 147–65.

10. G. W. F. Hegel, *Aesthetics: Lectures on Fine Art*, trans. T. M. Knox, vol. 2 (Oxford: Clarendon, 1975) 1199–1200, 1220–21, 1233–34.

11. *Critical Writings* 45.

12. *Exiles* 151.

13. *Ulysses* 87.677–81

14. *Ulysses* 469.4054–470.4059.

15. *Ulysses* 470.4061–64.

16. *Ulysses* 471.4091–92.

17. *Ulysses* 472.4132.

18. *Ulysses* 475.4241–45.

19. *Ulysses* 497.4940–49.

20. See, for instance, Zack Bowen, Ulysses *as a Comic Novel* (Syracuse: Syracuse UP, 1989).

21. *Ulysses* 55.472–79.

22. *Ulysses* 56.506–9.

Chapter 9

1. Julia Kristeva, *Revolution in Poetic Language*, trans. Margaret Waller, introd. Leon S. Roudiez (New York: Columbia UP, 1984).

2. Julia Kristeva, *Powers of Horror: An Essay on Abjection*, trans. Leon S. Roudiez (New York: Columbia UP, 1982).

3. Kristeva, *Powers of Horror* 15.

4. Kristeva, *Powers of Horror* 16.

5. Julia Kristeva, "Joyce 'the Gracehoper' or the Return of Orpheus," *James Joyce—The Augmented Ninth: Proceedings of the Ninth International James Joyce Symposium, Frankfurt 1984,* ed. Bernard Benstock (Syracuse: Syracuse UP, 1988) 167–80.

6. Kristeva, "Joyce 'the Gracehoper'" 174.

7. Kristeva, "Joyce 'the Gracehoper'" 174.

8. Kristeva, "Joyce 'the Gracehoper'" 180.

9. Kristeva, "Joyce 'the Gracehoper'" 178.

10. Kristeva "Joyce 'the Gracehoper'" 170 .

11. *Ulysses* 489.4691–93. Henceforth references to *Ulysses* in this chapter will be given as parenthetical citations in the text.

12. This focus on the grotesque, sublime, but impotent, style of the son-artist's work also characterizes Ewa Ziarek's fine essay on "Circe" referred to in chapter 7. A similar fascination with the carnivalesque pervades Lesley McDowell's "'A Pregnant Word': The Grotesque Mother in 'Oxen of the Sun,' *Ulysses*," read at the Easter workshop "The Maternal in Joyce," organized by the Zurich James Joyce Foundation, April 9–12, 1993.

13. Robert Janusko, *The Sources and Structures of James Joyce's "Oxen,"* Studies in Modern Literature 15 (Ann Arbor: UMI Research, 1983) 49.

14. For the role that medicine played in Joyce's life, see J. B. Lyons, *James Joyce & Medicine* (Dublin: Dolmen P, 1973).

15. As Stephen E. Soud has demonstrated, Joyce may also have been inspired by one of the numerous editions of the apocryphal *Aristotles [sic] Master-piece, or the Secrets of Generation Displayed in All Parts Thereof* (London: J. How, 1684), containing among other things a section on "The Midwife" and the "Midwife's Vademecum." "Blood-Red Wombs and Monstrous Births: *Aristotle's Masterpiece* and *Ulysses*," *James Joyce Quarterly* 32 (1995): 195–208.

16. This paradoxical attitude toward the female body—the fact that its absolute problematization depends upon its absolute valorization—is the focus of Catherine Gallagher's interesting essay "The Body versus the Social Body in the Works of Thomas Malthus and Henry Mayhew," *The Making of the Modern Body: Sexuality and Society in the Nineteenth Century*, ed. Catherine Gallagher and Thomas Laqueur (Berkeley: U of California P, 1987) 83–106.

17. Mary Lowe-Evans, *Crimes against Fecundity: Joyce and Population Control* (Syracuse: Syracuse UP, 1989): "as a result of the Famine, the

Irish began to take their economic plight more seriously than ever before and to respond to it at every level of activity. Underlying those responses was a perception, inculcated by the British, that the Famine was a Malthusian reproach . . ." (9).

18. Cf. Lowe-Evans 61–62, and Lesley McDowell's essay on "Oxen."

19. Mary Poovey, "'Scenes of an Indelicate Character': The Medical 'Treatment' of Victorian Women," *The Making of the Modern Body* 137–68. Paula A. Treichler, "Feminism, Medicine, and the Meaning of Childbirth," *Body/Politics: Women and the Discourses of Science*, ed. Mary Jacobus et al. (New York: Routledge, 1990) 113–38.

20. *A Portrait* 216.

21. Roderick E. McGrew, with the collaboration of Margaret P. McGrew, *Encyclopedia of Medical History* (London: Macmillan, 1985) 203–8.

22. See Monica Green, "Women's Medical Practice and Health Care in Medieval Europe," *Signs: Journal of Women in Culture and Society* 14 (1989): 434–73.

23. Patrick McGee, *Paperspace: Style as Ideology in Joyce's* Ulysses (Lincoln: U of Nebraska P, 1988) 19.

24. Don Gifford, with Robert J. Seidman, Ulysses *Annotated: Notes for James Joyce's* Ulysses, rev. ed. (1974; Berkeley: U of California P, 1988) 430.

25. Maud Ellmann, "The Ghosts of Ulysses," *James Joyce: The Artist and the Labyrinth*, ed. Augustine Martin (London: Ryan, 1990) 199.

26. Joyce as quoted by Budgen 179.

27. Karen Lawrence, *The Odyssey of Style in* Ulysses (Princeton: Princeton UP, 1981) 132.

28. In "Ambiviolences: Notes for Reading Joyce," Stephen Heath has identified Joyce's style as pastiche rather than parody, because of the suspension of meaning characteristic of the former. In contrast to parody, whose meaning lies in ridicule against the model imitated, pastiche is "a copying that fixes no point of irony between model and imitation, that rests, in this respect, in a hesitation of meaning . . . an initial meaning of pastiche (*pasticcio*) is, according to *O.E.D.*, 'a medley of various ingredients; a hotchpotch, farrago, jumble', the term being used of an opera composed in this way" (*Post-Structuralist Joyce: Essays from the French*, ed. Derek Attridge and Daniel Ferrer [Cambridge: Cambridge UP, 1984] 42).

29. Hugh Kenner, *Ulysses* (London: George Allen & Unwin, 1980) 108.

30. Cf. Caroline A. Van Eck et al., introduction, *The Question of Style in Philosophy and the Arts*, ed. Van Eck et al., Cambridge Studies in Philosophy and the Arts (Cambridge: Cambridge UP, 1995) 3.

31. *Critical Writings* 28.

32. *Critical Writings* 28.

33. That Joyce's philological approach to science may have been influenced by Vico's *New Science*, in which the history of language is viewed as the record of the history of civilization, is argued by Domenico Pietropaolo, "Vico and Literary History in the Early Joyce," *Vico and Joyce*, ed. Donald Phillip Verene (Albany: State U of New York P, 1987) 100–109.

Chapter 10

1. Terry Eagleton, *The Ideology of the Aesthetic* (Oxford: Blackwell, 1990).

2. Eagleton 20.

3. Eagleton 28.

4. Eagleton 91.

5. Eagleton 376.

6. Norris 22. I have also argued this point in my article "Joyce's 'Gentle Art of Advertisement': From Modernism to Mass Culture," *BELL: Belgian Essays on Language and Literature*, ed. Pierre Michel and Andrew Norris (Liège: Université de Liège, 1994) 136–42.

7. James Joyce, *Finnegans Wake* (London: Faber, 1982) 302.18. Henceforth parenthetical citations of page and line number will appear in the text.

8. Mark Osteen, *The Economy of* Ulysses: *Making Both Ends Meet* (Syracuse: Syracuse UP, 1995).

9. *Ulysses* 28.359.

10. *Ulysses* 25.251.

11. Osteen 29.

12. Jean-Michel Rabaté, "A Portrait of the Author as a Bogeyman," *James Joyce: Authorized Reader* (Baltimore: Johns Hopkins UP, 1991) 153.

13. For a marvelous discussion of Joyce's invention of his sigla, to prevent himself from becoming mad during the writing of the *Wake*, see

Jean-Michel Rabaté, *Joyce upon the Void: The Genesis of Doubt* (London: Macmillan, 1991) 69–111.

14. *Letters of James Joyce* 1: 250.

15. *Letters of James Joyce* 1: 216.

16. *Letters of James Joyce* 1: 220.

17. *Letters of James Joyce* 1: 249.

18. Joyce as quoted in Richard Ellmann, *James Joyce*, rev. ed. (1959; Oxford: Oxford UP, 1983) 546. Emphasis added.

19. For Joyce's condensation of his fictive characters to linguistic characters or signs, see Derek Attridge, "Joyce and the Ideology of Character," *James Joyce—The Augmented Ninth* 152–57. Roland McHugh has described the crucial function of Joyce's sigla in this process of personality condensation: *The Sigla of* Finnegans Wake (London: Edward Arnold, 1976).

20. This basic structure of language expanding in different directions, thereby questioning "the oppositional structures of the literary tradition," is what Derek Attridge associates with the function of the portmanteau word: "the portmanteau can be nothing other than a defining feature of language itself, because the portmanteau derives from the fact that the same segments (letters, phonemes, syllables) can be combined in different ways to encode different meanings. A language in which portmanteau formations were impossible would be a language in which every signified was matched with a unique and unanalyzable signifier—that is, not a language at all" ("The Peculiar Language of *Finnegans Wake*," *Critical Essays on James Joyce's* Finnegans Wake, ed. Patrick A. McCarthy [New York: Hall; Toronto: Maxwell Macmillan, 1992] 75).

21. Klaus Reichert, "Towards the Sublime," *The Languages of Joyce: Selected Papers from the 11th International James Joyce Symposium, Venice, 12–18 June 1988*, ed. R. M. Bollettieri Bosinelli, C. Marengo Vaglio, and Chr. van Boheemen (Philadelphia: Benjamins, 1992) 223–28.

22. That Joyce was familiar with Einstein's four-dimensional space-time continuum has been argued in Rabaté, *Joyce upon the Void* 2–4. See also Alan J. Friedman and Carol C. Donley, *Einstein as Myth and Muse* (Cambridge: Cambridge UP, 1985); Andrzej Duszenko, "The Relativity Theory in *Finnegans Wake*," *James Joyce Quarterly* 32 (1994): 61–70.

23. For a good discussion of Wyndham Lewis's critique of *Ulysses* as a time-book, see Udaya Kumar, *The Joycean Labyrinth: Repetition, Time, and Tradition in* Ulysses (Oxford: Clarendon, 1991) 54–63. See also Scott W. Klein, *The Fictions of James Joyce and Wyndham Lewis: Monsters of Nature and Design* (Cambridge: Cambridge UP, 1994).

24. *Letters of James Joyce* 1: 216.

25. In *Reading Voices: Literature and the Phonotext* (Berkeley: U of California P, 1990), Garret Stewart has brilliantly re-interpreted the Derridian *différance* of writing in a variety of authors (among whom Joyce) in terms of the drifting of the voice, what he calls the "transegmental drift": the crossing of boundaries between lexical elements (as in "I scream for ice cream") that marks the acoustic materiality of language and that cannot be noted unless pronounced. For a less complex reading of the sense of sound in the *Wake*, see Peter Myers, *The Sound of* Finnegans Wake (London: Macmillan, 1992). John Cage has tried to capture the *Wake*'s audible chaos on several occasions: *Roaratorio: Ein irischer Circus über* Finnegans Wake. *An Irish Circus on* Finnegans Wake, ed. Klaus Schöningh, 2nd ed. (Königstein: Athenäum, 1985). See (or hear) also Cage's "Writing for the Second Time through *Finnegans Wake*" and his musical setting "The Wonderful Widow of Eighteen Springs," *Light Rays: James Joyce and Modernism*, ed. Heyward Ehrlich (New York: New Horizon, 1984) 172–84.

26. In *Joyce's Book of the Dark:* Finnegans Wake (Madison: U of Wisconsin P, 1986), John Bishop compares the reader's sound-reception to the state of Joyce's sleeping hero, quoting Joyce's famous words: "in sleep our senses are dormant, except the sense of hearing, which is always awake, since you can't close your ears. So any sound that comes to our ears is turned into a dream" (273). Accordingly, Earwicker, the Ever-Waker, is the watchman sorting out the sounds of the world in the shape of a dream.

27. Karen Lawrence associates ALP's tea-stain with the ink-stain on Cyril Sargent's cheek in the "Nestor" episode of *Ulysses*. "Yet someone had loved him," Stephen muses at the sight of this pathetic student. This maternal stain, a birthmark perhaps, comes before the signature of the father and is the mark of *amor matris*, the only true thing "in this stinking dunghill of a world" ("Paternity, the Legal Fiction," *Joyce's* Ulysses: *The Larger Perspective*, ed. Robert D. Newman and Weldon Thornton [Newark: U of Delaware P, 1987] 89–97).

28. Budgen 136.

29. Shari Benstock has read the circulation of letters in the *Wake* as the feminine flux of repressed desires "displacing" the traditional concepts of writing and dreaming: "Nightletters: Woman's Writing in the *Wake*," *Critical Essays on James Joyce*, ed. Bernard Benstock (Boston: Hall, 1985) 221–33. See also the early version of the essay: "The Letter of the Law: *La Carte Postale* in *Finnegans Wake*," *Philological Quarterly* 63.2 (1984): 163–85. David Hayman's *The "Wake" in Transit* (Ithaca: Cornell UP, 1990) is very interesting in its reconstruction of the *Wake*'s "letter plot." According to Hayman, chapter 1.5 was first conceived as a short introduction to

ALP's epistolary defense of HCE, to be followed by the letter itself (now *Wake* 617–19) and its delivery by Shaun. As the *Wake* was being written, Joyce felt the need for supplementary information concerning the letter's composition and transcription, Shem and Shaun's personalities, and so on. All these transitional passages caused the actual letter to be delayed until the final book, so that the whole of the *Wake* can be regarded as the trajectory—the permanent parabasis—of ALP's epistolary document.

30. For a discussion of the symbolic function of the cross, see Clive Hart, *Structure and Motif in* Finnegans Wake (Evanston: Northwestern UP, 1962) 129–44.

31. Consider Derrida's "Ulysses Gramophone," in which he compares *Ulysses* to "an immense postcard" as follows: "Any public piece of writing, any open text, is also offered like the exhibited surface, in no way private, of an open letter, and therefore of a postcard with its address incorporated in the message and hereafter open to doubt, and with its coded and at the same time stereotyped language, trivialized by the very code and number. Conversely, any postcard is a public document, deprived of all privacy and, moreover, in this way laying itself open to the law" (*James Joyce—The Augmented Ninth* 30).

32. In "Deconstruction after Joyce," Christine van Boheemen describes Joyce's "preemptive inclusion and anticipation of all discourses" as an act of digestion: "Everything read, heard, thought, or dreamed of is preincluded, swallowed, and 'decomposed' in a process of digestion" (Scott, *New Alliances in Joyce Studies* 30).

33. I thank the members of the Buffalo *Wake* Reading Group for the congenial atmosphere in which I was offered the opportunity to develop my ideas and finally present the first draft of this chapter. For some stimulating reflections on the dynamics in *Finnegans Wake* Reading Groups see Fritz Senn, "Vexations of Group Reading: 'Transluding from the Otherman,'" *Finnegans Wake: Fifty Years*, ed. Geert Lernout, European Joyce Studies 2 (Amsterdam: Rodopi, 1990) 61–78. See also David Borodin's study of the performative aspects of such reading groups: "'Group Drinkards Maaks Grope Thinkards or How Reads Rotary' (*FW* 312.31): *Finnegans Wake* and the Group Reading Experience," *James Joyce's* Finnegans Wake: *A Casebook*, ed. John Harty, III (New York: Garland, 1991) 151–64.

34. Jacques Derrida, "Signature Event Context," *Margins of Philosophy*, trans. Alan Bass (Chicago: U of Chicago P, 1982) 328.

35. Patrick A. McCarthy has interestingly read the recovery of the letter in terms of the *Wake*'s ubiquitous references to the Irish Revival: "Reading the Letter: Interpreting the *Wake*," in Scott, *New Alliances in Joyce Studies* 238–42.

36. This stands in contrast to Clive Hart's claim that the color patterns in the *Wake* are of "very minor importance" (Hart, *Structure and Motif* 152). In contrast, Barbara DiBernard has written an interesting introduction to Joyce's symbolic use of colors: "Colors and Forgery," *Alchemy and* Finnegans Wake (Albany: State U of New York P, 1980) 85–107.

37. The manuscript dates from 800. It was stolen in 1006 and stripped of its gold binding, but it was recovered from sods of turf a few months later. It is now housed in Trinity College Dublin. For a reproduction of the "Tunc" page, see Danis Rose and John O'Hanlon, *Understanding* Finnegans Wake: *A Guide to the Narrative of James Joyce's Masterpiece* (New York: Garland, 1982) 85.

38. Cf. James S. Atherton, *The Books at the Wake: A Study of Literary Allusions in James Joyce's* Finnegans Wake (London: Faber, 1959) 64–67. See also Margaret C. Solomon, *Eternal Geomater: The Sexual Universe of* Finnegans Wake (Carbondale: Southern Illinois UP, 1969) 62–64. The book is also interesting for its analysis of the sexual connotations of the T-shaped letter.

39. Joseph Campbell and Henry Morton Robinson, *A Skeleton Key to* Finnegans Wake (New York: Harcourt, 1944) 103.

40. For a discussion of the similarities between the craft of illumination in the *Book of Kells* and Joyce's technique in the *Wake*, see Beryl Schlossman, *Joyce's Catholic Comedy of Language* (Madison: U of Wisconsin P, 1985).

41. Schlegel as cited in Lacoue-Labarthe and Nancy, *The Literary Absolute* 121.

Conclusion

1. Cf. Kari Elise Lokke, "The Role of Sublimity in the Development of Modernist Aesthetics," *Journal of Aesthetics and Art Criticism* 42 (1982): 421–29.

2. Jean-François Lyotard, "After the Sublime: The State of Aesthetics," *The States of "Theory": History, Art, and Critical Discourse*, ed. David Carroll (Stanford: Stanford UP, 1994) 297–304.

3. Jean-François Lyotard, *The Differend: Phrases in Dispute*, trans. Georges Van Den Abbeele, Theory and History of Literature 46 (Minneapolis: U of Minnesota P, 1988). Lyotard has often been criticized for his neo-Kantian idealism, see for instance Timothy H. Engström, "The Postmodern Sublime? Philosophical Rehabilitations and Pragmatic Evasions," *Boundary 2: An International Journal of Literature and Culture* 20.2 (1993): 190–204.

List of Works Cited

Works by James Joyce

The Critical Writings of James Joyce. Ed. Ellsworth Mason and Richard Ellmann. London: Viking, 1959.

Epiphanies. Ed. O. A. Silverman. Buffalo: Lockwood Memorial Library, U of Buffalo, 1956.

Exiles: A Play in Three Acts. Introd. Padraic Colum. Harmondsworth: Penguin, 1973.

Finnegans Wake. London: Faber, 1982.

Letters of James Joyce. Ed. Stuart Gilbert. Vol. 1. New York: Viking, 1966.

A Portrait of the Artist as a Young Man. Definitive text by Chester G. Anderson and reviewed by Richard Ellmann. New York: Viking, 1964.

Stephen Hero. Ed. Theodore Spencer. New York: New Directions, 1944.

Ulysses. Ed. Hans Walter Gabler et al. New York: Random House, 1986.

Works by Friedrich Schlegel, and Translations

Kritische Friedrich-Schlegel-Ausgabe. Ed. Ernst Behler, Jean-Jacques Anstett, Hans Eichner, et al. 35 vols. to date. München: Ferdinand Schöningh; Zürich: Thomas, 1958–.

Athenäum Fragmente. Charakteristiken und Kritiken I (1796–1801). Ed. Hans Eichner. Vol. 2 of *Kritische Friedrich-Schlegel-Ausgabe.* München: Ferdinand Schöningh; Zürich: Thomas, 1967. 165–255.

Dialogue on Poetry and Literary Aphorisms. Trans. Ernst Behler and Roman Struc. University Park: Pennsylvania State UP, 1968.

Friedrich Schlegel's Lucinde *and the Fragments.* Trans. Peter Firchow. Minneapolis: U of Minnesota P, 1971.

Geschichte der europäischen Literatur. Wissenschaft der europäischen Literatur: Vorlesungen, Aufsätze und Fragmente aus der Zeit von 1795–1804. Ed. Ernst Behler. Vol. 11 of *Kritische Friedrich-Schlegel-Ausgabe.* München: Ferdinand Schöningh; Zürich: Thomas, 1958.

Gespräch über die Poesie. Charakteristiken und Kritiken I (1796–1801). Ed. Hans Eichner. Vol. 2 of *Kritische Friedrich-Schlegel-Ausgabe.* München: Ferdinand Schöningh; Zürich: Thomas, 1967. 284–362.

Ideen. Charakteristiken und Kritiken I (1796–1801). Ed. Hans Eichner. Vol. 2 of *Kritische Friedrich-Schlegel-Ausgabe.* München: Ferdinand Schöningh; Zürich: Thomas, 1967. 256–72.

Kritische Fragmente. Charakteristiken und Kritiken I (1796–1801). Ed. Hans Eichner. Vol. 2 of *Kritische Friedrich-Schlegel-Ausgabe.* München: Ferdinand Schöningh; Zürich: Thomas, 1967. 147–63.

Literarische Notizen 1797–1801, Literary Notebooks. Ed. Hans Eichner. Frankfurt: Ullstein Materialien, 1980.

Lucinde. Dichtungen. Ed. Hans Eichner. Vol. 5 of *Kritische Friedrich-Schlegel-Ausgabe.* München: Ferdinand Schöningh; Zürich: Thomas, 1962. 3–82.

Philosophical Fragments. Trans. Peter Firchow. Minneapolis: U of Minnesota P, 1991.

Theorie der Weiblichkeit. Ed. Winfried Menninghaus. Frankfurt am Main: Insel, 1983.

Über das Studium der griechischen Poesie. Studien des klassischen Altertums. Ed. Ernst Behler. Vol. 1 of *Kritische Friedrich-Schlegel-Ausgabe.* München: Ferdinand Schöningh; Zürich: Thomas, 1979. 217–367.

"Über die Diotima." *Studien des klassischen Altertums.* Ed. Ernst Behler. Vol. 1 of *Kritische Friedrich-Schlegel-Ausgabe.* München: Ferdinand Schöningh; Zürich: Thomas, 1979. 70–115.

"Über die Philosophie: An Dorothea." *Studien zur Philosophie und Theologie.* Ed. Ernst Behler and Ursula Struc-Oppenberg. Vol. 8 of *Kritische*

Friedrich-Schlegel-Ausgabe. München: Ferdinand Schöningh; Zürich: Thomas, 1975. 41–62.

"Über die weiblichen Charaktere in den griechischen Dichtern." *Studien des klassischen Altertums.* Ed. Ernst Behler. Vol. 1 of *Kritische Friedrich-Schlegel-Ausgabe.* München: Ferdinand Schöningh; Zürich: Thomas, 1979. 45–69.

"Vom ästhetischen Werte der griechischen Komödie." *Studien des klassischen Altertums.* Ed. Ernst Behler. Vol. 1 of *Kritische Friedrich-Schlegel-Ausgabe.* München: Ferdinand Schöningh; Zürich: Thomas, 1979. 19–33.

Other Works

Alford, Steven E. *Irony and the Logic of the Romantic Imagination.* American University Studies, Comparative Literature 13. New York: Peter Lang, 1984.

Alleman, Beda. *Ironie und Dichtung: F. Schlegel, Novalis, Solger, Kierkegaard, Thomas Mann, Musil.* Pfullingen: Neske, 1956.

Atherton, James S. *The Books at the Wake: A Study of Literary Allusions in James Joyce's* Finnegans Wake. London: Faber, 1959.

Attridge, Derek, ed. *The Cambridge Companion to James Joyce.* Cambridge: Cambridge UP, 1990.

———. "Joyce and the Ideology of Character." *James Joyce—The Augmented Ninth: Proceedings of the Ninth International James Joyce Symposium, Frankfurt 1984.* Ed. Bernard Benstock. Syracuse: Syracuse UP, 1988. 152–57.

———. "The Peculiar Language of *Finnegans Wake.*" *Critical Essays on James Joyce's* Finnegans Wake. Ed. Patrick A. McCarthy. New York: Hall; Toronto: Maxwell Macmillan, 1992. 73–84.

Attridge, Derek, and Daniel Ferrer, eds. *Post-Structuralist Joyce: Essays from the French.* Cambridge: Cambridge UP, 1984.

Aubert, Jacques. *The Aesthetics of James Joyce.* Rev. ed. Baltimore: Johns Hopkins UP, 1992.

Bakhtin, M. M. *The Dialogic Imagination: Four Essays.* Ed. Michael Holquist. Trans. Caryl Emerson and Michael Holquist. University of Texas Press Slavic Series 1. Austin: U of Texas P, 1981.

Barthelme, Donald. *City Life.* New York: Farrar, 1968.

Barthes, Roland. *The Pleasure of the Text*. Trans. Richard Miller. New York: Hill and Wang, 1975.

Baudelaire, Charles. *The Painter of Modern Life and Other Essays*. Trans. Jonathan Mayne. London: Phaidon, 1964.

Bauerle, Ruth. "Bertha's Role in *Exiles*." *Women in Joyce*. Ed. Suzette Henke and Elaine Unkeless. Brighton: Harvester, 1982. 108–31.

Beck, Herbert, Peter C. Bol, and Eva Maek-Gérard, eds. *Ideal und Wirklichkeit der bildenden Kunst im späten 18. Jahrhundert*. Frankfurter Forschungen zur Kunst 11. Berlin: Mann, 1984.

Behler, Ernst. "Friedrich Schlegel: *Lucinde* (1799)." *Romane und Erzählungen der deutschen Romantik: Neue Interpretationen*. Ed. Paul Michael Lützeler. Stuttgart: Philipp Reclam jun., 1981. 98–124.

———. "Friedrich Schlegels Theorie der Universalpoesie." *Friedrich Schlegel und die Kunsttheorie seiner Zeit*. Ed. Helmut Schanze. Darmstadt: Wissenschaftliche Buchgesellschaft, 1985. 228–33.

———. "Friedrich Schlegels Theorie des Verstehens: Hermeneutik oder Dekonstruktion?" *Die Aktualität der Frühromantik*. Ed. Ernst Behler and Jochen Hörisch. Paderborn: Ferdinand Schöningh, 1987. 141–60.

———. "Friedrich Schlegel und Hegel." *Hegel-Studien*. Ed. Friedhelm Nicolin and Otto Pöggeler. Vol 2. Bonn: Bouvier, 1963. 203–50.

———. *German Romantic Literary Theory*. Cambridge: Cambridge UP, 1993.

Behler, Ernst, and Jochen Hörisch, eds. *Die Aktualität der Frühromantik*. Paderborn: Ferdinand Schöningh, 1987.

Beja, Morris, and Shari Benstock, eds. *Coping with Joyce: Essays from the Copenhagen Symposium*. Columbus: Ohio State UP, 1989.

Benjamin, Walter. *Der Begriff der Kunstkritik in der deutschen Romantik*. Vol 1.1 of *Gesammelte Schriften*. Ed. Rolf Tiedemann and Hermann Schweppenhäuser. Frankfurt am Main: Suhrkamp, 1974.

———. *Illuminations*. Ed. Hannah Arendt. Trans. Harry Zohn. 1968. New York: Schocken Books, 1969.

———. *The Origin of German Tragic Drama*. Trans. John Osborne. London: NLB, 1977.

Benstock, Bernard, ed. *Critical Essays on James Joyce*. Boston: Hall, 1985.

———, ed. *James Joyce—The Augmented Ninth: Proceedings of the Ninth International James Joyce Symposium, Frankfurt 1984.* Syracuse: Syracuse UP, 1988.

Benstock, Shari. "The Letter of the Law: *La Carte Postale* in *Finnegans Wake.*" *Philological Quarterly* 63.2 (1984): 163–85.

———. "Nightletters: Woman's Writing in the *Wake.*" *Critical Essays on James Joyce.* Ed. Bernard Benstock. Boston: Hall, 1985. 221–33.

Bishop, John. *Joyce's Book of the Dark:* Finnegans Wake. Madison: U of Wisconsin P, 1986.

Black, Joel. "The Aesthetics of Gender: Zeuxis Maidens and the Hermaphroditic Ideal." *New York Literary Forum* 8 & 9 (1981). *Fragments: Incompletion & Discontinuity.* Ed. Lawrence D. Kritzman: 189–209.

Blanchot, Maurice. "The Athenäum." Trans. Deborah Esch and Ian Balfour. *Studies in Romanticism* 23 (1984): 163–72.

———. *The Writing of the Disaster. L'écriture du désastre.* Trans. Ann Smock. Lincoln: U of Nebraska P, 1986.

Borodin, David. "'Group Drinkards Maaks Grope Thinkards or How Reads Rotary' (*FW* 312.31): *Finnegans Wake* and the Group Reading Experience." *James Joyce's* Finnegans Wake: *A Casebook.* Ed. John Harty, III. New York: Garland, 1991. 151–64.

Bosanquet, Bernard. *A History of Aesthetic.* London: Swann Sonnenschein; New York: Macmillan, 1892.

Bosinelli, R. M. Bollettieri, C. Marengo Vaglio, and Chr. van Boheemen, eds. *The Languages of Joyce: Selected Papers from the 11th International James Joyce Symposium, Venice, 12–18 June 1988.* Philadelphia: Benjamins, 1992.

Bowen, Zack. Ulysses *as a Comic Novel.* Syracuse: Syracuse UP, 1989.

Bowen, Zack, and James F. Carens, eds. *A Companion to Joyce Studies.* Westport, CT: Greenwood P, 1984.

Bowra, Cecil Maurice. "Dithyramb." *The Oxford Classical Dictionary.* 2nd ed.

Brandabur, Edward. *A Scrupulous Meanness: A Study of Joyce's Early Work.* Urbana: U of Illinois P, 1971.

Budgen, Frank. *James Joyce and the Making of* Ulysses. Bloomington: Indiana UP, 1960.

Bullock, Marcus. *Romanticism and Marxism: The Philosophical Development of Literary Theory and Literary History in Walter Benjamin and Friedrich Schlegel*. American University Studies, Germanic Languages and Literature 51. New York: Peter Lang, 1987.

Bürger, Peter. *Theory of the Avant-Garde*. Trans. Michael Shaw. Theory and History of Literature 4. Minneapolis: U of Minnesota P, 1984.

Cage, John. *Roaratorio: Ein irischer Circus über* Finnegans Wake. *An Irish Circus on* Finnegans Wake. Ed. Klaus Schöningh. 2nd ed. Königstein: Athenäum, 1985.

———. "Writing for the Second Time through *Finnegans Wake*" and "The Wonderful Widow of Eighteen Springs." *Light Rays: James Joyce and Modernism*. Ed. Heyward Ehrlich. New York: New Horizon, 1984. 172–84.

Campbell, Joseph, and Henry Morton Robinson. *A Skeleton Key to* Finnegans Wake. New York: Harcourt, 1944.

Carroll, David, ed. *The States of "Theory": History, Art, and Critical Discourse*. Stanford: Stanford UP, 1994.

Cheng, Vincent J., and Timothy Martin, eds. *Joyce in Context*. Cambridge: Cambridge UP, 1992.

Cixous, Hélène. *The Exile of James Joyce*. Trans. Sally A. J. Purcell. New York: David Lewis, 1972.

Comedy: "An Essay on Comedy," George Meredith; "Laughter," Henri Bergson. Ed. Wylie Sypher. Baltimore: Johns Hopkins UP, 1980.

Connolly, Thomas, ed. *Joyce's* Portrait: *Criticisms and Critiques*. London: Peter Owen, 1962.

Cornford, Francis MacDonald. *The Origin of Attic Comedy*. Ed. with foreword and notes by Theodor H. Gaster. 1914. New York: Anchor, 1961.

Crump, Ian. "Refining Himself out of Existence: The Evolution of Joyce's Aesthetic Theory and the Drafts of *A Portrait*." *Joyce in Context*. Ed. Vincent J. Cheng and Timothy Martin. Cambridge: Cambridge UP, 1992. 223–40.

Culler, Jonathan. *The Pursuit of Signs: Semiotics, Literature, Deconstruction*. Ithaca: Cornell UP, 1981.

Dällenbach, Lucien, and Christiaan L. Hart Nibbrig, eds. *Fragment und Totalität*. Frankfurt am Main: Suhrkamp, 1984.

De Man, Paul. *Allegories of Reading: Figural Language in Rousseau, Nietzsche, Rilke, and Proust*. New Haven: Yale UP, 1979.

———. *The Rhetoric of Romanticism.* New York: Columbia UP, 1984.

———. "The Rhetoric of Temporality." *Interpretation: Theory and Practice.* Ed. Charles S. Singleton. Baltimore: Johns Hopkins UP, 1969. 173–209.

Derrida, Jacques. "La loi du genre/The Law of Genre." *Glyph: Textual Studies* 7 (1980). *The Strasbourg Colloquium: Genre. A Selection of Papers.* Ed. Samuel Weber: 176–232.

———. *Margins of Philosophy.* Trans. Alan Bass. Chicago: U of Chicago P, 1982.

———. "Ulysses Gramophone." *James Joyce—The Augmented Ninth: Proceedings of the Ninth International James Joyce Symposium, Frankfurt 1984.* Ed. Bernard Benstock. Syracuse: Syracuse UP, 1988. 27–75.

DiBernard, Barbara. *Alchemy and* Finnegans Wake. Albany: State U of New York P, 1980.

Dierkes, Hans. "Friedrich Schlegels *Lucinde,* Schleiermacher und Kierkegaard." *Deutsche Vierteljahrsschrift für Literaturwissenschaft und Geistesgeschichte* 57.3 (1983): 431–49.

Dischner, Gisela. *Friedrich Schlegels* Lucinde *und Materialien zu einer Theorie des Müßiggangs.* Hildesheim: Gerstenberg, 1980.

Dunleavy, Janet Egleson, ed. *Re-Viewing Classics of Joyce Criticism.* Urbana: U of Illinois P, 1991.

Duszenko, Andrzej. "The Relativity Theory in *Finnegans Wake.*" *James Joyce Quarterly* 32 (1994): 61–70.

Eagleton, Terry. *The Ideology of the Aesthetic.* Oxford: Blackwell, 1990.

Edelman, Lee. "At Risk in the Sublime: The Politics of Gender and Theory." *Gender and Theory: Dialogues on Feminist Criticism.* Ed. Linda Kauffman. Oxford: Blackwell, 1989. 213–24.

Ehrlich, Heyward, ed. *Light Rays: James Joyce and Modernism.* New York: New Horizon, 1984.

Eichner, Hans. *Friedrich Schlegel.* Twayne's World Authors Ser. 98. New York: Twayne, 1970.

———. "Friedrich Schlegel's Theory of Romantic Poetry." *PMLA* 71 (1956): 1018–41.

Ellmann, Maud. "Disremembering Dedalus: *A Portrait of the Artist as a Young Man.*" *Untying the Text: A Post-Structuralist Reader.* Ed. Robert Young. Boston: Routledge, 1981. 189–206.

———. "The Ghosts of Ulysses." *James Joyce: The Artist and the Labyrinth*. Ed. Augustine Martin. London: Ryan, 1990. 193–227.

Ellmann, Richard. *James Joyce*. Rev. ed. 1959. Oxford: Oxford UP, 1983.

Engström, Timothy H. "The Postmodern Sublime? Philosophical Rehabilitations and Pragmatic Evasions." *Boundary 2: An International Journal of Literature and Culture* 20 (1993): 190–204.

Flavell, M. Kay. "Women and Individualism: A Re-examination of Schlegel's *Lucinde* and Gutzkow's *Wally die Zweiflerin*." *Modern Language Review* 70 (1975): 550–66.

Frank, Manfred. "The Infinite Text." *Glyph: Textual Studies* 7 (1980). *The Strasbourg Colloquium: Genre. A Selection of Papers*. Ed. Samuel Weber: 70–101.

———. "Intellektuale Anschauung: Drei Stellungnahmen zu einem Deutungsversuch von Selbstbewußtsein: Kant, Fichte, Hölderlin/Novalis." *Die Aktualität der Frühromantik*. Ed. Ernst Behler and Jochen Hörisch. Paderborn: Ferdinand Schöningh, 1987. 96–126.

Freud, Sigmund. *Jokes and Their Relation to the Unconscious*. Trans. James Strachey. London: Routledge, 1966.

Friedman, Alan J., and Carol C. Donley. *Einstein as Myth and Muse*. Cambridge: Cambridge UP, 1985.

Friedrichsmeyer, Sara. *The Androgyne in Early German Romanticism: Friedrich Schlegel, Novalis and the Metaphysics of Love*. Stanford German Studies 18. New York: Peter Lang, 1983.

Gadamer, Hans-Georg. "Frühromantik, Hermeneutik, Dekonstruktivismus." *Die Aktualität der Frühromantik*. Ed. Ernst Behler and Jochen Hörisch. Paderborn: Ferdinand Schöningh, 1987. 251–60.

———. "Hermeneutics and Logocentrism." *Dialogue and Deconstruction: The Gadamer-Derrida Encounter*. Ed. Diane P. Michelfelder and Richard E. Palmer. Albany: State U of New York P, 1989. 114–25.

Gallagher, Catherine. "The Body versus the Social Body in the Works of Thomas Malthus and Henry Mayhew." *The Making of the Modern Body: Sexuality and Society in the Nineteenth Century*. Ed. Catherine Gallagher and Thomas Laqueur. Berkeley: U of California P, 1987. 83–106.

Gallagher, Catherine, and Thomas Laqueur, eds. *The Making of the Modern Body: Sexuality and Society in the Nineteenth Century*. Berkeley: U of California P, 1987.

Gasché, Rodolphe. "Ideality in Fragmentation." *Philosophical Fragments*. By Friedrich Schlegel. Trans. Peter Firchow. Minneapolis: U of Minnesota P, 1991. vii–xxxii.

Gifford, Don, with Robert J. Seidman. Ulysses *Annotated: Notes for James Joyce's* Ulysses. Rev. ed. 1974. Berkeley: U of California P, 1988.

Gilbert, Stuart. *James Joyce's* Ulysses: *A Study*. Rev. ed. 1930. New York: Vintage Books, 1952.

Gillespie, Michael. *Reading the Book of Himself: Narrative Strategies in the Works of James Joyce*. Columbus: Ohio State UP, 1989.

Givens, Seon, ed. *James Joyce: Two Decades of Criticism*. New ed. 1948. New York: Vanguard P, 1963.

Gram, Moltke S. "Intellectual Intuition: The Continuity Thesis." *Journal of the History of Ideas* 42 (1981): 287–304.

Grathoff, Dirk, ed. *Studien zur Ästhetik und Literaturgeschichte der Kunstperiode*. Gießener Arbeiten zur neueren deutschen Literatur und Literaturwissenschaft 1. Frankfurt am Main: Peter Lang, 1985.

Green, Monica. "Women's Medical Practice and Health Care in Medieval Europe." *Signs: Journal of Women in Culture and Society* 14 (1989): 434–73.

Guerlac, Suzanne. "The Sublime in Theory." *MLN* 106 (1991): 895–909.

Hamacher, Werner. "Der Satz der Gattung: Friedrich Schlegels poetologische Umsetzung von Fichtes unbedingten Grundsatz." *MLN* 95 (1980): 1155–80.

Handwerk, Gary J. *Irony and Ethics in Narrative: From Schlegel to Lacan*. New Haven: Yale UP, 1985.

Hart, Clive. "The Language of *Exiles*." *Coping with Joyce: Essays from the Copenhagen Symposium*. Ed. Morris Beja and Shari Benstock. Columbus: Ohio State UP, 1989. 123–36.

———. *Structure and Motif in* Finnegans Wake. Evanston: Northwestern UP, 1962.

Harty, John, III, ed. *James Joyce's* Finnegans Wake: *A Casebook*. New York: Garland, 1991.

Hayman, David. "Language of/as Gesture in Joyce." *James Joyce: A Collection of Critical Essays*. Ed. Mary T. Reynolds. Englewood Cliffs: Prentice Hall, 1993. 37–47.

———. *The "Wake" in Transit*. Ithaca: Cornell UP, 1990.

Heath, Stephen. "Ambiviolences: Notes for Reading Joyce." *Post-Structuralist Joyce: Essays from the French*. Ed. Derek Attridge and Daniel Ferrer. Cambridge: Cambridge UP, 1984. 31–68.

Hegel, G. W. F. *Aesthetics: Lectures on Fine Art*. Trans. T. M. Knox. Vol. 2. Oxford: Clarendon, 1975.

———. *Introductory Lectures on Aesthetics*. Trans. Bernard Bosanquet. Ed. and introd. Michael Inwood. 1886. Harmondsworth: Penguin, 1993.

———. *Vorlesungen über Rechtsphilosophie: 1818–1831*. Ed. Karl-Heinz Ilting. Vol. 4. Stuttgart: Frommann-Holzboog, 1974.

Hendry, Irene. "Joyce's Epiphanies." *James Joyce: Two Decades of Criticism*. Ed. Seon Givens. New ed. 1948. New York: Vanguard P, 1963. 27–46.

Henke, Suzette. *James Joyce and the Politics of Desire*. London: Routledge, 1990.

Henke, Suzette, and Elaine Unkeless, eds. *Women in Joyce*. Brighton: Harvester, 1982.

Hertz, Neil. *The End of the Line: Essays on Psychoanalysis and the Sublime*. New York: Columbia UP, 1985.

Hotz-Steinmeyer, Cornelia. *Friedrich Schlegels* Lucinde *als "neue Mythologie": Geschichtsphilosophischer Versuch einer Rückgewinnung gesellschaftlicher Totalität durch das Individuum*. Frankfurt am Main: Peter Lang, 1981.

Huyssen, Andreas. *After the Great Divide: Modernism, Mass Culture, Postmodernism*. Bloomington: Indiana UP, 1986.

Immerwahr, Raymond. "The Subjectivity or Objectivity of Friedrich Schlegel's Poetic Irony." *The Germanic Review* 26 (1951): 173–91.

———. "Die symbolische Form des 'Briefes über den Roman.'" *Zeitschrift für deutsche Philologie* 88 (1969): 41–60.

Jacobus, Mary, et al., eds. *Body/Politics: Women and the Discourses of Science*. New York: Routledge, 1990.

Janusko, Robert. *The Sources and Structures of James Joyce's "Oxen."* Studies in Modern Literature 15. Ann Arbor: UMI Research P, 1983.

Jardine, Alice. *Gynesis: Configurations of Women and Modernity*. Ithaca: Cornell UP, 1985.

Johnson, Barbara. "Apostrophe, Animation, and Abortion." *Diacritics* 16 (1986): 29–39.

Jones, Ellen Carol, ed. *Modern Fiction Studies* 35 (1989): *Feminist Readings of Joyce.*

Kant, Immanuel. *Critique of Judgment.* Trans. J. H. Bernard. New York: Macmillan, 1951.

Kauffman, Linda, ed. *Gender and Theory: Dialogues on Feminist Criticism.* Oxford: Blackwell, 1989.

Kenner, Hugh. *Joyce's Voices.* Berkeley: U of California P, 1978.

———. "The *Portrait* in Perspective." *Joyce's* Portrait: *Criticisms and Critiques.* Ed. Thomas Connolly. London: Peter Owen, 1962. 25–60.

———. *Ulysses.* London: George Allen & Unwin, 1980.

Kierkegaard, Søren. *The Concept of Irony with Constant Reference to Socrates.* Trans. Lee M. Capel. Bloomington: Indiana UP, 1965.

Klein, Scott W. *The Fictions of James Joyce and Wyndham Lewis: Monsters of Nature and Design.* Cambridge: Cambridge UP, 1994.

Kluckhohn, Paul. *Die Auffassung der Liebe in der Literatur des 18. Jahrhunderts und in der deutschen Romantik.* Tübingen: Max Niemeyer, 1966.

Körner, Josef. "Neues vom Dichter der *Lucinde*: Mitteilungen aus Friedrich Schlegels jüngst entdecktem handschriftlichen Nachlaß." *Friedrich Schlegel und die Kunsttheorie seiner Zeit.* Ed. Helmut Schanze. Darmstadt: Wissenschaftliche Buchgesellschaft, 1985. 7–33.

Kristeva, Julia. "Joyce 'the Gracehoper' or the Return of Orpheus." *James Joyce—The Augmented Ninth: Proceedings of the Ninth International James Joyce Symposium, Frankfurt 1984.* Ed. Bernard Benstock. Syracuse: Syracuse UP, 1988. 167–80.

———. *Powers of Horror: An Essay on Abjection.* Trans. Leon S. Roudiez. New York: Columbia UP, 1982.

———. *Revolution in Poetic Language.* Trans. Margaret Waller, introd. Leon S. Roudiez. New York: Columbia UP, 1984.

Kühn, Renate. "Der Leser—die Frauen: Resultate einer pragmatischen Lektüre von Friedrich Schlegels *Gespräch über die Poesie.*" *Jahrbuch der deutschen Schillergesellschaft* 30 (1986): 306–38.

Kumar, Udaya. *The Joycean Labyrinth: Repetition, Time, and Tradition in* Ulysses. Oxford: Clarendon, 1991.

Lacoue-Labarthe, Philippe. "L'imprésentable." *Poétique* 21 (1975): 53–95.

Lacoue-Labarthe, Philippe, and Jean-Luc Nancy. "Le dialogue des genres: Textes de Shaftesbury, Hemsterhuis, Schelling." *Poétique* 21 (1975): 148–75.

———. *The Literary Absolute: The Theory of Literature in German Romanticism.* Trans. Philip Barnard and Cheryl Lester. Intersections: Philosophy and Critical Theory. Albany: State U of New York P, 1988.

Lange, Sigrid. "Zum Beispiel: *Lucinde.* Das 'Ewigweibliche' im Horizont der bürgerlichen Emanzipation." *Weimarer Beiträge* 33.4 (1987): 616–31.

Lawrence, Karen. *The Odyssey of Style in* Ulysses. Princeton: Princeton UP, 1981.

———. "Paternity, the Legal Fiction." *Joyce's* Ulysses: *The Larger Perspective.* Ed. Robert D. Newman and Weldon Thornton. Newark: U of Delaware P, 1987. 89–97.

Lernout, Geert. *The French Joyce.* Ann Arbor: U of Michigan P, 1990.

Lokke, Kari Elise. "The Role of Sublimity in the Development of Modernist Aesthetics." *Journal of Aesthetics and Art Criticism* 42 (1982): 421–29.

Lowe-Evans, Mary. *Crimes against Fecundity: Joyce and Population Control.* Syracuse: Syracuse UP, 1989.

Lühti, Kurt. *Feminismus und Romantik: Sprache, Gesellschaft, Symbole, Religion.* Wien: Hermann Böhlaus, 1985.

Lützeler, Paul Michael, ed. *Romane und Erzählungen der deutschen Romantik: Neue Interpretationen.* Stuttgart: Philipp Reclam jun., 1981.

Lyons, J. B. *James Joyce & Medicine.* Dublin: Dolmen P, 1973.

Lyotard, Jean-François. "After the Sublime: The State of Aesthetics." *The States of "Theory": History, Art, and Critical Discourse.* Ed. David Carroll. Stanford: Stanford UP, 1994. 297–304.

———. *The Differend: Phrases in Dispute.* Trans. Georges Van Den Abbeele. Theory and History of Literature 46. Minneapolis: U of Minnesota P, 1988.

MacNicholas, John. "The Stage History of *Exiles.*" *James Joyce Quarterly* 19 (1981): 9–26.

Mahaffey, Vicki. *Reauthorizing Joyce.* Cambridge: Cambridge UP, 1988.

Martin, Augustine, ed. *James Joyce: The Artist and the Labyrinth.* London: Ryan, 1990.

Mathy, Dietrich. "Zur frühromantischen Selbstaufhebung des Erhabenen im Schönen." *Das Erhabene: Zwischen Grenzerfahrung und Größenwahn.* Ed. Christine Pries. Weinheim: VCH, Acta Humaniora, 1989. 143–60.

McCarthy, Patrick A., ed. *Critical Essays on James Joyce's* Finnegans Wake. New York: Hall; Toronto: Maxwell Macmillan, 1992.

———. "Reading the Letter: Interpreting the *Wake.*" *New Alliances in Joyce Studies: "When It's Aped to Foul a Delfian."* Ed. Bonnie Kime Scott. Newark: U of Delaware P; London: Associated UP, 1988. 238–42.

McCormick, Kathleen. "Reproducing Molly Bloom: A Revisionist History of the Reception of 'Penelope,' 1922–1970." *Molly Blooms: A Polylogue on "Penelope" and Cultural Studies.* Ed. Richard Pearce. Madison: U of Wisconsin P, 1994. 17–36.

McGee, Patrick. *Paperspace: Style as Ideology in Joyce's* Ulysses. Lincoln: U of Nebraska P, 1988.

McGrath, F. C. "Laughing in His Sleeve: The Sources of Stephen's Aesthetics." *James Joyce Quarterly* 23 (1986): 259–75.

McGrew, Roderick E., with the collaboration of Margaret P. McGrew. *Encyclopedia of Medical History.* London: Macmillan, 1985.

McHugh, Roland. *The Sigla of* Finnegans Wake. London: Edward Arnold, 1976.

Mellor, Anne K. *English Romantic Irony.* Cambridge: Harvard UP, 1980.

———. "On Romantic Irony, Symbolism and Allegory." *Criticism* 21 (1979): 217–29.

———. *Romanticism & Gender.* New York: Routledge, 1993.

Mennemeier, Franz Norbert. "Unendliche Fortschreitung und absolutes Gesetz: Das Schöne und das Häßliche in der Kunstauffassung des jungen F. Schlegel." *Friedrich Schlegel und die Kunsttheorie seiner Zeit.* Ed. Helmut Schanze. Darmstadt: Wissenschaftliche Buchgesellschaft, 1985. 342–69.

Menninghaus, Winfried. *Unendliche Verdopplung: Die frühromantische Grundlegung der Kunsttheorie im Begriff absoluter Selbstreflexion.* Frankfurt am Main: Suhrkamp, 1987.

Michel, Pierre, and Andrew Norris, eds. *BELL: Belgian Essays on Language and Literature.* Liège: Université de Liège, 1994.

Michelfelder, Diane P., and Richard E. Palmer, eds. *Dialogue and Deconstruction: The Gadamer-Derrida Encounter.* Albany: State U of New York P, 1989.

Morgan, Bayard Quincy, and A. R. Hohlfeld, eds. *German Literature in British Magazines 1750–1860.* Madison: U of Wisconsin P, 1949.

Myers, Peter. *The Sound of* Finnegans Wake. London: Macmillan, 1992.

Neubauer, John. "Intellektuelle, intellektuale und ästhetische Anschauung: Zur Entstehung der romantischen Kunstauffassung." *Deutsche Vierteljahrsschrift für Literaturwissenschaft und Geistesgeschichte* 46 (1972): 294–319.

Newman, Robert D., and Weldon Thornton, eds. *Joyce's* Ulysses: *The Larger Perspective.* Newark: U of Delaware P, 1987.

Nietzsche, Friedrich. *The Birth of Tragedy and The Case of Wagner.* Translation and commentary by Walter Kaufmann. New York: Vintage Books, 1967.

Noon, William T. *Joyce and Aquinas.* Yale Studies in English 133. New Haven: Yale UP, 1957.

Norris, Margot. *Joyce's Web: The Social Unraveling of Modernism.* Literary Modernism Series. Austin: U of Texas P, 1992.

Oesterle, Günter. "Arabeske und Roman: Eine poetikgeschichtliche Rekonstruktion von Friedrich Schlegels 'Brief uber den Roman.'" *Studien zur Ästhetik und Literaturgeschichte der Kunstperiode.* Ed. Dirk Grathoff. Gießener Arbeiten zur neueren deutschen Literatur und Literaturwissenschaft 1. Frankfurt am Main: Peter Lang, 1985. 233–92.

———. "Friedrich Schlegels Entwurf einer Theorie des ästhetisch Häßlichen: Ein Reflexions- und Veränderungsversuch moderner Kunst." *Friedrich Schlegel und die Kunsttheorie seiner Zeit.* Ed. Helmut Schanze. Darmstadt: Wissenschaftliche Buchgesellschaft, 1985. 397–451.

———. "'Vorbegriffe zu einer Theorie der Ornamente': Kontroverse Formprobleme zwischen Aufklärung, Klassizismus und Romantik am Beispiel der Arabeske." *Ideal und Wirklichkeit der bildenden Kunst im späten 18. Jahrhundert.* Ed. Herbert Beck, Peter C. Bol, and Eva Maek-Gérard. Frankfurter Forschungen zur Kunst 11. Berlin: Mann, 1984. 119–39.

Osteen, Mark. *The Economy of* Ulysses: *Making Both Ends Meet.* Syracuse: Syracuse UP, 1995.

Pearce, Richard, ed. *Molly Blooms: A Polylogue on "Penelope" and Cultural Studies.* Madison: U of Wisconsin P, 1994.

Pietropaolo, Domenico. "Vico and Literary History in the Early Joyce." *Vico and Joyce*. Ed. Donald Phillip Verene. Albany: State U of New York P, 1987. 100–109.

Pinkert, Ernst-Ullrich. "Hegels *Lucinde*-Kritik—und ihre Aktualisierung in der Auseinandersetzung der Junghegelianer mit Romantik und Jungem Deutschland." *Text & Kontext* 9 (1981): 343–80.

Polheim, Karl Konrad. *Die Arabeske: Ansichten und Ideen aus Friedrich Schlegels Poetik*. München: Ferdinand Schöningh, 1966.

Poovey, Mary. "'Scenes of an Indelicate Character': The Medical 'Treatment' of Victorian Women." *The Making of the Modern Body: Sexuality and Society in the Nineteenth Century*. Ed. Catherine Gallagher and Thomas Laqueur. Berkeley: U of California P, 1987. 137–68.

Power, Arthur. *Conversations with James Joyce*. Ed. Clive Hart. London: Millington, 1974.

Pries, Christine, ed. *Das Erhabene: Zwischen Grenzerfahrung und Größenwahn*. Weinheim: VCH, Acta Humaniora, 1989.

Rabaté, Jean-Michel. *James Joyce: Authorized Reader*. Baltimore: Johns Hopkins UP, 1991.

———. *Joyce upon the Void: The Genesis of Doubt*. London: Macmillan, 1991.

Reichert, Klaus. "Fragment and Totality." *New Alliances in Joyce Studies: "When It's Aped to Foul a Delfian."* Ed. Bonnie Kime Scott. Newark: U of Delaware P; London: Associated UP, 1988. 86–90.

———. "Towards the Sublime." *The Languages of Joyce: Selected Papers from the 11th International James Joyce Symposium, Venice, 12–18 June 1988*. Ed. R. M. Bollettieri Bosinelli, C. Marengo Vaglio, and Chr. van Boheemen. Philadelphia: Benjamins, 1992. 223–28.

———. "Von den Rändern her oder Sortes Wakeianae." *Fragment und Totalität*. Ed. Lucien Dällenbach and Christiaan L. Hart Nibbrig. Frankfurt am Main: Suhrkamp, 1984. 294–307.

Reynolds, Mary T., ed. *James Joyce: A Collection of Critical Essays*. Englewood Cliffs: Prentice Hall, 1993.

Riffaterre, Michael. "Prosopopeia." *Yale French Studies* 69 (1985): 107–23.

Riquelme, John Paul. "*Stephen Hero, Dubliners*, and *A Portrait of the Artist as a Young Man*: Styles of Realism and Fantasy." *The Cambridge Companion to James Joyce*. Ed. Derek Attridge. Cambridge: Cambridge UP, 1990. 103–30.

———. *Teller and Tale in Joyce's Fiction: Oscillating Perspectives.* Baltimore: Johns Hopkins UP, 1983.

Rose, Danis, and John O'Hanlon. *Understanding* Finnegans Wake: *A Guide to the Narrative of James Joyce's Masterpiece.* New York: Garland, 1982.

Roughley, Alan. *James Joyce and Critical Theory: An Introduction.* New York: Harvester Wheatsheaf, 1991.

Ryf, Robert S. F. *A New Approach to Joyce: The* Portrait of the Artist *as a Guidebook.* Berkeley: U of California P, 1966.

Sanna, Simonetta. "Schlegels *Lucinde* oder der ästhetische Roman." *Deutsche Vierteljahrsschrift für Literaturwissenschaft und Geistesgeschichte* 61.3 (1987): 457–79.

Schanze, Helmut, ed. *Friedrich Schlegel und die Kunsttheorie seiner Zeit.* Darmstadt: Wissenschaftliche Buchgesellschaft, 1985.

———. *Romantik und Aufklärung: Untersuchungen zu Friedrich Schlegel und Novalis.* Erlanger Beiträge zur Sprach-und Kunstwissenschaft 27. Nürnberg: Hans Carl, 1966.

Schlossman, Beryl. *Joyce's Catholic Comedy of Language.* Madison: U of Wisconsin P, 1985.

Scholes, Robert. "In Search of James Joyce." *James Joyce Quarterly* 11 (1973): 5–16.

Scholes, Robert, and Marlena G. Corcoran. "The Aesthetic Theory and the Critical Writings." *A Companion to Joyce Studies.* Ed. Zack Bowen and James F. Carens. Westport, CT: Greenwood P, 1984. 689–705.

Scott, Bonnie Kime. *James Joyce.* Brighton: Harvester, 1987.

———. *Joyce and Feminism.* Bloomington: Indiana UP; Brighton: Harvester, 1984.

———, ed. *New Alliances in Joyce Studies: "When It's Aped to Foul a Delfian."* Newark: U of Delaware P; London: Associated UP, 1988.

Senn, Fritz. "Vexations of Group Reading: 'Transluding from the Otherman.'" *Finnegans Wake: Fifty Years.* Ed. Geert Lernout. European Joyce Studies 2. Amsterdam: Rodopi, 1990. 61–78.

Silverman, Hugh J., and Gary E. Aylesworth, eds. *The Textual Sublime: Deconstruction and Its Differences.* Contemporary Studies in Philosophy and Literature 1. Albany: State U of New York P, 1990.

Singleton, Charles S., ed. *Interpretation: Theory and Practice.* Baltimore: Johns Hopkins UP, 1969.

Solomon, Margaret C. *Eternal Geomater: The Sexual Universe of* Finnegans Wake. Carbondale: Southern Illinois UP, 1969.

Soud, Stephen E. "Blood-Red Wombs and Monstrous Births: *Aristotle's Masterpiece* and *Ulysses.*" *James Joyce Quarterly* 32 (1995): 195–208.

Spoo, Robert. *James Joyce and the Language of History: Dedalus's Nightmare.* Oxford: Oxford UP, 1994.

Stanley, Patricia. "Hoffmann's *Phantasiestücke in Callots Manier* in Light of Friedrich Schlegel's Theory of the Arabesque." *German Studies Review* 8.3 (1985): 399–419.

Stewart, Garret. *Reading Voices: Literature and the Phonotext.* Berkeley: U of California P, 1990.

Strohschneider-Kohrs, Ingrid. *Die romantische Ironie in Theorie und Gestaltung.* Tübingen: Max Niemeyer, 1977.

Szondi, Peter. *On Textual Understanding and Other Essays.* Trans. Harvey Mendelsohn. Foreword Michael Hays. Theory and History of Literature 15. Minneapolis: U of Minnesota P, 1986.

Treichler, Paula A. "Feminism, Medicine, and the Meaning of Childbirth." *Body/Politics: Women and the Discourses of Science.* Ed. Mary Jacobus et al. New York: Routledge, 1990. 113–38.

Van Boheemen, Christine. "Deconstruction after Joyce." *New Alliances in Joyce Studies: "When It's Aped to Foul a Delfian."* Ed. Bonnie Kime Scott. Newark: U of Delaware P; London: Associated UP, 1988. 29–36.

Van de Vall, Renée. *Een subliem gevoel van plaats: Een filosofische interpretatie van het werk van Barnett Newman.* Groningen: Historische Uitgeverij, 1994.

Van Eck, Caroline A., et al., eds. *The Question of Style in Philosophy and the Arts.* Cambridge Studies in Philosophy and the Arts. Cambridge: Cambridge UP, 1995.

Die verborgene Frau: Sechs Beiträge zu einer feministischen Literaturwissenschaft. With contributions by Inge Stephan and Sigrid Weigel. Literatur im historischen Prozeß 6. Berlin: Argument, 1983.

Verene, Donald Phillip, ed. *Vico and Joyce.* Albany: State U of New York P, 1987.

Verstraete, Ginette. "Friedrich Schlegel's Practice of Literary Theory." *The Germanic Review* 69 (1994): 28–35.

———. "Joyce's 'Gentle Art of Advertisement': From Modernism to Mass Culture." *BELL: Belgian Essays on Language and Literature.* Ed.

Pierre Michel and Andrew Norris. Liège: Université de Liège, 1994. 136–42.

Waith, Eugene M. "The Calling of Stephen Dedalus." *Joyce's* Portrait: *Criticisms and Critiques*. Ed. Thomas Connolly. London: Peter Owen, 1962. 114–23.

Weigel, Sigrid. "Wider die romantische Mode: Zur ästhetischen Funktion des Weiblichen in Friedrich Schlegels *Lucinde*." *Die verborgene Frau: Sechs Beiträge zu einer feministischen Literaturwissenschaft*. With contributions by Inge Stephan and Sigrid Weigel. Literatur im historischen Prozeß 6. Berlin: Argument, 1983. 67–82.

Weiskel, Thomas. *The Romantic Sublime: Studies in the Structure and Psychology of Transcendence*. Baltimore: Johns Hopkins UP, 1976.

Wellbery, David E. "Rhetorik und Literatur: Anmerkungen zur poetologischen Begriffsbildung bei Friedrich Schlegel." *Die Aktualität der Frühromantik*. Ed. Ernst Behler and Jochen Hörisch. Paderborn: Ferdinand Schöningh, 1987. 161–73.

Wilson, Rob. *American Sublime: The Genealogy of a Poetic Genre*. Madison: U of Wisconsin P, 1991.

Yaeger, Patricia. "Toward a Female Sublime." *Gender and Theory: Dialogues on Feminist Criticism*. Ed. Linda Kauffman. Oxford: Blackwell, 1989. 191–212.

Young, Robert, ed. *Untying the Text: A Post-Structuralist Reader*. Boston: Routledge, 1981.

Ziarek, Ewa. "'Circe': Joyce's *Argumentum ad Feminam*." *James Joyce Quarterly* 30 (1992): 51–68.

INDEX

A

B

C

D

E

F

G

H

L

M

N

O

P

Q

R

S

T